Madison's Managers

Johns Hopkins Studies in Governance and Public Management

Kenneth J. Meier and Laurence J. O'Toole Jr., Series Editors

Madison's Managers

Public Administration and the Constitution

ANTHONY M. BERTELLI AND
LAURENCE E. LYNN JR.

The Johns Hopkins University Press
Baltimore

*This book has been brought to publication with the generous
assistance of the Robert L. Warren Endowment.*

2 4 6 8 9 7 5 3 1

The Johns Hopkins University Press
2715 North Charles Street
Baltimore, Maryland 21218-4363
www.press.jhu.edu

Library of Congress Cataloging-in-Publication Data
Bertelli, Anthony Michael.
Madison's managers : public administration and the Constitution /
Anthony M. Bertelli and Laurence E. Lynn Jr.
p.   cm. — (Johns Hopkins studies in governance and public management)
Includes bibliographical references and index.
ISBN 0-8018-8262-1 (hardcover : alk. paper)
ISBN 0-8018-8319-9 (pbk. : alk. paper)
1. Public administration—United States. 2. Separation of powers—United States.
3. Constitutional history—United States. 4. Madison, James, 1731–1836—Influence.
I. Lynn, Laurence E., 1937– II. Title. III. Series.
JK421.B385 2006
351.73—dc22
2005013357

A catalog record for this book is available from the British Library.

Contents

Series Editors' Foreword

The Johns Hopkins Studies in Governance and Public Management seeks to publish the best empirically oriented work at the junction of public policy and public management. The goal is to build knowledge that can make a difference in how we understand public policies and that can make their operation more effective. The Johns Hopkins Studies in Governance and Public Management takes a special interest in the problems of governance and performance, including managerial issues linked to institutional arrangements, policy instruments, human resources, and finance. The series reflects the increased interest in these subjects not only in the United States but also in other developed democracies. The Studies are distinguished by the use of diverse, sophisticated, and innovative methods; and they are expected to make important and enduring theoretical contributions.

This study, by Anthony M. Bertelli and Laurence E. Lynn Jr., fits centrally amidst these emphases. The authors tackle one of the big questions: how to justify the managerial function, given the inevitability of managerial discretion over crucial public tasks. The focus is on U.S. national government, but their reach is exceedingly broad and deep. In their general orientation and intent, Bertelli and Lynn write in the spirit of many earlier theorists of and for the cause—those ranging from proponents of a democratic administration to enthusiasts of the New Public Management. Their goal is nothing less than the explication and justification of a "precept of managerial responsibility" to reconcile managerial actions with Madisonian constitutional design.

The argument proffered by Bertelli and Lynn is distinctive in at least three respects. First, it is fundamentally grounded in American constitutional thought and experience. The authors render vividly a connection that has been conspicuous by its absence in the American-based scholarship on governance and public management: the link between the rule of law, and the separation-of-powers principle and administrative law in particular, and support for the nitty-gritty functions of public management. Bertelli and Lynn offer crucial insights as to the centrality of the administrative law–based debates and decisions for the operations of public agencies and their management.

Second, and equally unusually, these authors treat the early, classic works in public administration with detailed and sympathetic attention. Perhaps not since the early scholarship of Dwight Waldo—which, not incidentally and very provocatively, they regard as mistaken at its core—have researchers plumbed the details of the beginnings of self-aware U.S. public administration with the care and nuance shown by Bertelli and Lynn. The result is a forward-looking analysis that is nonetheless steeped in the insights of history. They argue with conviction and not a little evidence that most of us harbor only a caricatured view of the best of the traditional thinking; it is time, they suggest, to let the scales fall from our eyes.

Third, and most distinctively of all, the volume is neither legalistic nor exclusively historicist. The analysis put forward by the authors is fully insinuated into some of the most sophisticated of the recent social scientific work based in formal theory—in particular, the economics of contracts and social choice theory—to derive a theoretical answer to the framers' challenge of ensuring that managerial action will reflect the popular will. Perhaps unexpectedly, this formal analysis leads to a conclusion that the public personnel function lies at the core of the challenge. Bertelli and Lynn use this line of theoretical exegesis to derive a set of injunctions regarding the practical details of personnel policy that, they argue, can help to solve the core governance challenge that they seek to address.

In its careful scholarship, its ambitious intent, and particularly its unprecedented synthesis of historical, theoretical, legal, and formal forms of analysis, *Madison's Managers* offers a contribution nonpareil—one designed to reshape the field in fundamental ways. The most recently developed tools of social science are mobilized to divine a route back to the basics. Bertelli and Lynn formalize the intuitions of the framers and channel the results toward the core issues of governance and public management. They provide a fundamental contribution to the field and a weighty challenge in equal measure to its defenders and critics.

Kenneth J. Meier and Laurence J. O'Toole Jr.

Preface

The seeds that have grown into *Madison's Managers* (the title is Bertelli's inspiration) were sown several years ago when Lynn agreed to be an expert witness for New York City's Administration for Children's Services in a class-action lawsuit alleging that agency mismanagement was causing systematic violations of the statutory and constitutional rights of the children in its care. Lynn's report to the federal district court having jurisdiction over the case argued that, whatever the agency's past failings, the current administration was capable of meeting its statutory and constitutional responsibilities and that active intervention by the court was unwarranted (a view substantially upheld by the court in its ruling).

Shortly after Lynn had completed his analysis, Bertelli began his Ph.D program at the University of Chicago. A *Juris Doctor* with experience in the Pennsylvania Office of Attorney General, Bertelli was familiar with the legal issues raised by this type of lawsuit, which the legal literature named "institutional reform litigation." We began a conversation on what to Lynn was something of an epiphany: competent public management in America's scheme of governance is, to a significant extent, what judges and lawyers specializing in administrative law say it is. In other (more academic) words, American public administration is *endogenous* to, and legitimized by, the constitutionally prescribed separation of powers. Refreshed by this insight, Lynn was able to convince Bertelli that he had indeed learned at least one thing in law school.

We began to explore this proposition in depth in a series of co-authored papers (Bertelli and Lynn 2001, 2003, forthcoming) as well as in single-authored works concerned, in Lynn's case, with ideas of administrative responsibility in the field's traditional literature (Lynn 2001) and, in Bertelli's case, with the ramifications of institutional reform litigation for administrative performance and collective justice (Bertelli 2004). At some point, we became convinced that the concept of managerial responsibility within the constitutional separation of powers deserved book-length development. The result, we believe, is an argument that is considerably more than the sum of the parts just cited.

Madison's Managers proposes a constitutional theory of public administration in the United States. Combining insights from traditional thought and practice and from contemporary analyses of American political institutions, we show how managerial responsibility depends, in a constitutional sense, on official respect for the separation of powers and commitment to specific public service values: judgment, balance, rationality, and accountability. Focusing on these axiomatic values rehabilitates the theoretical and practical importance of two long-neglected aspects of public administration: the personnel function, responsible for ensuring constitutionally qualified public servants, and administrative law, a collection of rules regarding administrative practice within the separation of powers. By engendering the trust of the political branches, this approach to managerial responsibility overcomes a common failing of well-known prescriptions—such as emphasis on equity, democracy, performance, or best practices—which are typically invoked without meaningful reference to the constitutional separation of powers.

With public administration now on the defensive before advocates for privatized government, the profession needs a persuasive constitutional theory of its own legitimacy. To situate public administration as a constitutional institution, *Madison's Managers* employs a unique analytic strategy, which combines two intellectual traditions often regarded as antagonistic. Modern political economics has gained analytical leverage in American politics with theories that recognize public administration as an entity to be controlled in the bargaining among the separate powers and organized interests within the polity. Traditional public administration also appreciates the dynamics of public administration as managing public policies established by the political branches of government—legislatures and elected executives—while maintaining respect for procedural and substantive rights ensured through litigation in the courts. It is in their respect for how the separation of powers affects administration, we argue, that these literatures mutually reinforce one another. *Madison's Managers* challenges the profession to recognize, once again, that the legitimacy of public administration depends on its constitutional foundations and, moreover, that responsible administrative practice must be defined in terms of precepts that are derived from, rather than capriciously asserted on behalf of, constitutional principles.

Our intellectual and personal debts are numerous. David H. Rosenbloom, J. Patrick Dobel, Norma M. Riccucci, and James H. Svara provided valuable published comments on Lynn's initial effort to revise the conventional interpretation of the field's traditional literature; H. George Frederickson, Laurence J. O'Toole Jr., John Rohr, and Gary L. Wamsley provided critical comment and encouragement. Melissa Forbes provided invaluable research assistance. Bertelli's work has benefited from the insights of numerous individuals, including John Brehm, Randall Calvert, Phillip

Cooper, Colin Diver, Christian Grose, Thomas Hammond, John Mark Hansen, Hank Jenkins-Smith, Christopher Kam, J. Edward Kellough, George Krause, Gary Miller, Hervé Moulin, Hal Rainey, Lilliard E. Richardson Jr., Paul Van Riper, Richard Waterman, and William West over the years during which this project was conceived. Bertelli owes a special debt of gratitude to Sven Feldmann, a patient scholar and co-author who encouraged him to pursue the implications of formal theory into such a project as this. Series editors Kenneth J. Meier and Laurence J. O'Toole Jr. encouraged us to pursue this project and provided useful commentary on the entire manuscript. We are especially grateful for the superbly detailed and constructive critique of the manuscript by an anonymous reviewer for Johns Hopkins University Press.

Finally, Bertelli would like to thank his father, Felice Bertelli, Nora L. Danilov, and Erin J. Ray for tremendous personal encouragement throughout the process of writing this book, and Laurence E. Lynn Jr. for guiding him around the curves on the path to scholarship. Lynn owes his usual debt of gratitude to his wife, Pat, for her understanding of what writing a book requires.

Madison's Managers

CHAPTER ONE

Separated We Stand

The goal to be sought combines adequate recognition of personal rights as declared in the constitution with effective achievement of great social programs.
—*Leonard D. White*

The welfare of all Americans depends upon effective public management. The security of the nation, the assurance of civil and criminal justice, the stability and fairness of the economy, equitable access to the resources necessary for individual and collective growth and well-being, and the achievement of the multifarious public policy goals approved by voters and legislatures at all levels of government depend upon the ability of public managers to "get the job done." But these officials must both fulfill policy goals and, in the minds of citizens and their representatives, fulfill them in ways that are legitimate, that is, that are rightfully exercised (Rourke 1987).[1] Public management is as important to social welfare as any other institution in government.

At the same time, Americans are all too ready to express their dissatisfaction with the main form of administrative action and the most common setting for the public management on which they depend: public bureaucracy. When public management becomes newsworthy, it is usually because of mistakes by the large, visible public agencies that provide the services and protections on which citizens depend: the Internal Revenue Service, the Federal Bureau of Investigation, the Central Intelligence Agency, agencies that regulate safety and health, urban police departments, child welfare agencies, public school systems, mental health departments, and the like. When the quality of these agencies' management is noticed or acknowledged by citizens, it is usually because they have been harmed or inconvenienced by what they perceive to be impersonal, incompetent public officials mired in red tape and poorly led.[2] Aggrieved or simply angry citizens can and do take their complaints to their elected representatives, to groups representing their interests, or, individually and collectively, to court, with consequences—new regulations, injunctions, and other forms of micromanagement—which rarely include visibly better public management and heightened trust in government.

Following official or unofficial investigation, blame for conspicuous managerial failures may be assigned to particular officials, to failures of oversight, to poor policy designs, to inadequate resources, to dysfunctional organizational cultures, or to any of a number of familiar causes.[3] Those who engage in the professional study of this ongoing drama of dependence, resentment, frustration, and blame can, however, usually identify its fundamental causes: complications associated with the very way that American democracy is organized. To ensure that the power of central government would never become unduly concentrated, the framers of the Constitution created three separate branches, each with authority to check the ambitions of the other two. In so doing, the Founders gave birth to the central problem of American politics: ensuring that the capacity to govern is sufficient to satisfy the aspirations of citizens and their representatives while remaining well within their control.

Public management's fundamental problem is not hard to deduce. While citizens and their representatives expect public managers to "get the job done," significant aspects of "the job" that public managers are supposed to accomplish are often ambiguous. These unelected officials must decide what the law, circumstances, and common sense require of them in given situations. Once they have exercised their best judgment, it is all too common for these same citizens and their representatives —and often judges to whom they have appealed for a redress of their grievances— to say to an offending public manager, "No, that's not the job we wanted you to do. That's not lawful, not constitutional," or, most frustrating of all, "not what we meant."

Although, as argued in *The Federalist, No. 10*, these expressions of dissatisfaction are not in themselves unhealthy, the typical response of legislators to this sort of political unhappiness (stemming as it does from what political scientists call "bureaucratic drift") is to impose controls, either ex ante "police patrols" or ex post "fire alarms," on public managers to preclude their wandering off the path and to catch them when they do. But the element of judgment is almost never thereby expunged from the public manager's job description; the intentional or unintentional delegation to public managers of the authority to decide matters within their purview is inevitable. Nor would legislatures necessarily wish to stultify their administrative agents' ability to make choices; these agents, after all, are chosen for having expertise that citizens and legislators lack.

Despite repeated efforts by legislatures and courts to clarify matters, therefore, the fundamental question remains: how can public managers be relied upon to exercise their judgment—that is, use their delegated authority—in ways that will be viewed as legitimate, not to mention effective, by those who hold sovereignty over them? We argue that this is a matter not only of inducing a given manager consistently (in probabilistic terms) to make good judgments in particular cases but also of ensuring, through the personnel function of public administration, that the right sorts of individuals, those whom legislators, elected executives, and citizens can trust to make "good" judgments, come to populate the public service.

Specifically, we argue, there is a mechanism within the personnel function of public administration for would-be public managers to provide to their political environments information about their reliability, such that constitutional institutions, despite the separation of powers, tend toward producing outcomes that are both socially just and legitimate. We term that mechanism a *precept of managerial responsibility* and show that it comprises four desiderata, or axioms: judgment, balance, rationality, and accountability.

CIVILIZATION, ADMINISTRATION, AND RESPONSIBILITY

What we know of the history of organized administration across millennia and civilizations suggests that common forms of self-awareness and bodies of codified knowledge concerning the structures, practices, and values of public administration and management accompanied the emergence of organized societies (Lynn forthcoming; Lepawsky 1949; Waldo 1984). Broadly construed, problems with delegating authority to administrators have been associated with the earliest quests for order, security, wealth, and civilization. From the sixteenth through the nineteenth centuries in continental Europe, two remarkable institutions—public bureaucracy and *Rechtsstaat* (the rule of law as the foundation for public administration)—gradually became the primary instruments for protecting and effecting the interests of the state and its citizens.

Public administration found its home in public bureaucracies. These organizations were transformed into institutions of governance ranking in significance with legislatures and courts, premiers and presidents. In the authoritarian states that arose following the Peace of Westphalia in the mid-seventeenth century, the practice of so-called administrative sciences achieved this transformation. In the aftermath of the

French and nineteenth-century popular revolutions in Europe, however, public bureaucracy—the bulwark of state sovereignty in the authoritarian era—came under increasing criticism. A primary solution to these popular, potentially dangerous, discontents was *Rechtsstaat*, rule by a formal system of civil law, which promised that a strong, capable bureaucracy constrained by that law could be reconciled with popular democracy and with individual and social liberty and security. By the end of the nineteenth century, the field of public administration and management, once thought to be "scientific," had become preoccupied instead with the de facto separation of powers, that is, with "the tensions between an institution, bureaucracy, that exhibited imperialistic proclivities and the revolutionary idea of popular sovereignty, with its expectation of democratic accountability" (Lynn 2005).[4] Administrative law, not administrative science, came to be regarded as the ultimate protection for the democratic ideal (Bertelli forthcoming; Lynn forthcoming).

Organized democracy in England, its commonwealth, and its former colony, the United States of America, was founded on a system of common law that, in contrast to Continental experience, preceded and governed the development of public bureaucracies. Despite Anglo-American similarities, however, the field of public administration evolved differently in Great Britain and the United States due in the main to differences in their political institutions. Great Britain is a parliamentary democracy with virtually no separation of powers and a far more direct relationship between citizens and public servants (Bertelli forthcoming). Public administration and management in the United States, by contrast, is governed by the constitutionally formalized, if imprecise, separation of powers between the executive, legislative, and judicial branches of government. The intellectual and practical challenge of conceptualizing managerial responsibility under circumstances in which the formal distance between citizens and their public servants is much greater than in Great Britain has proven to be formidable.[5] This book is our attempt to address that challenge.

The significance of these differences between Great Britain and the United States did not become apparent, however, until the dramatic rise in delegation and the development of the American bureaucratic state beginning in the late nineteenth and early twentieth centuries and accelerating during the New Deal. To be sure, delegation and public administration played a role in American governance before that period, but in one of the earliest attempts to define the field of public administration and management, Leonard White (1935, 418) observed: "So long as American administrative systems remained decentralized, disintegrated, and self-governmental and discharged only a minimum of responsibilities, the necessity of highly developed machinery for its control was unknown. Administration was weak and threatened no civil liberties; it was unorganized and possessed no power of resistance; it was elective and quickly responsive to the color and tone of local feeling." The problems of delegation, control, and accountability that now preoccupy the field were not acute in prebureaucratic America.

By the late nineteenth century, satisfying popular aspirations in a rapidly growing and nationalizing society seemed to require large public bureaucracies staffed by officials chosen for their competence and protected against arbitrary political reprisals and the allegedly corrupting effects of spoils system politics (Wiebe 1967; Skowronek 1982; Carpenter 2001). The emergence of a "permanent government" (Friedrich 1940; Mosher 1968) staffed by professional civil servants in the trappings of bureaucracy—appointments based on qualifications, specialized functions, and in time, tenure in office—raised a fundamental issue among those instinctively suspicious of "Prussian bureaucracy": how might citizens, legislators, judges, and administrators themselves be assured that this unelected administrative corps would reflect the popular will or the public interest?

As the reach and power of the administrative state grew through the Progressive Era, the New Deal, and the Great Society, interbranch competition ensued in government over the authority to superintend or control what John Gaus as early as the 1920s termed "the new administration." Some even believed that civil servants, chosen for their technical competence, constituted a "fourth branch of government" that, within the framework of formal public law, should be largely self-governing, or in the opposing view, "headless."[6] The question of bureaucratic control began to absorb the attention of scholars in the emergent field of public administration as well as in administrative law: How can we ensure that the administration of public affairs is always and continuously responsible to the American people?

The doctrine of managerial responsibility became a shining thread in the literature of public administration and management (Bertelli and Lynn 2003).[7] Assaying both literature and practice, Frederick Mosher (1968, 7; 1992, 201) believed that "responsibility may well be the most important word in all the vocabulary of administration, public and private . . . the first requisite of a democratic state." The idea of responsible government is even older than the administrative state, however. The centrality of the idea was well recognized by the Founders. In *The Federalist*, No. 70 (reiterated in No. 77), Hamilton contrasted the need for "energy in the Executive" with an equal need for "safety." In Hamilton's view, "The ingredients which constitute safety in a republican sense are, first, a due dependence on the people, secondly, a due responsibility."

Woodrow Wilson (1887, 213) was the first scholar associated with modern public administration to observe that "there is no danger in power, if only it be not irresponsible." In an essay that revealed his scholar's grasp of European administrative traditions, Wilson argued that Americans need not fear that the professional administration of public affairs will lead inevitably to overbearing, European-style bureaucratic government so roundly denounced by, among others, John Stuart Mill. The bulwark against such a bureaucracy was not *Rechtsstaat*, however, but conduct by administrators that is responsible to the polity.

Responsibility may thus be defined, with Hamilton, as "due dependence on the people in a republican sense." The argument in this book is based on the concept of responsibility so defined. As we argue in chapter 6, responsibility is the most important unifying idea in the traditional literature of public administration. Notwithstanding its preeminent status in administrative history, however, the theoretical significance and practical meaning of managerial responsibility remain underdeveloped. Furthering this development is our principal task in the pages that follow.

THE ARGUMENT IN BRIEF

Our project is both theoretical and philosophical. We wish to clarify the concept of managerial responsibility under the separation of powers and define its implications for the principled performance of public managerial roles. Our political philosophy, moreover, is Madisonian, that is, concerned with perfecting institutions that control faction and power. But any philosophy grounded in the Constitution is necessarily Madisonian. As William Riker (1995) has shown, the remarkable internal consistency of American constitutional principles is due to Madison's pervasive influence, both through his various letters to Jefferson, Randolph, and Washington and, thus, through his inspiration for the Virginia Plan, on which the original constitution scheme was based.[8]

We are hardly unique in putting forth a normative ideal of responsible public management, even one that appeals to constitutional principles. As we argue in chapter 6, scholars—including Carl Friedrich, Reinhard Bendix, those associated with the so-called New Public Administration and the Blacksburg Manifesto, David Osborne and Ted Gaebler, John Rohr, Robert Denhardt, H. George Frederickson, and postmodernists of various orientations (for the sake of brevity we omit mention of numerous others)—have produced idealizations of public service values, ranging from equity to individual rights to representation to constitutional trusteeship, that they proclaim to be relevant to resolving the dilemmas arising from the separation of powers. Our argument is different in an important respect, however.

Deus or Derivation?

A common failing of the well-known prescriptions for public managers' performance of their duties is that they are invoked in the manner of a deus ex machina rather than derived from consideration of constitutional (or, to be precise, Madisonian) principles. This tendency to resort to extraconstitutional values reflects widespread, although not universal, dissatisfaction with the tenor and content of the traditional literature of public administration and even with the political institutions of the Constitution.

Beginning in the late 1930s and 1940s, traditional ideas and scholarship came under sharp attack from a variety of perspectives. The most prominent and damaging of these attacks was that of Dwight Waldo, who, in *The Administrative State* (1948), asserted that traditional thinking had congealed almost from the outset into an "orthodoxy" (now often labeled a bureaucratic paradigm) that offered "shallow and spurious" solutions to the problems of democratic administration. From that time on, Waldo's characterization—we hold it to be a caricature—of traditional thinking has itself become an orthodoxy that is only infrequently questioned by contemporary scholars, in large part because, as Laurence O'Toole (1984, 141) notes, "few have inspected that body of ideas in its original form." With little of value to be found in the traditional literature, preoccupied as it was with responsible administration within the separation of powers, a deepening crisis of professional identity ensued that shadows the literature to this day. This sense of crisis inspires, at least in part, the tendency to neglect the separation of powers and the significance of administrative law and to find extraconstitutional solutions to public managerial dilemmas.

Depending on one's values, it may be that public management *should* emphasize the rights of individuals, *should* give voice to all oppressed or marginalized groups, *should* develop an independent view as to what the Constitution requires, *should* allow all publics to participate in or to decide matters affecting them, and so on over a wide range of principles. But *why* should such values be embraced? Further, are such values the only alternatives? Why not a theocracy, or a *Rechtsstaat*, or a dictatorship of the proletariat, or classical liberalism, or anarchy? We are with Hamilton in holding that the answer is clear in a republican sense. As Colin Diver (1982, 404) put it: "Public managers are, after all, public servants. Their acts must derive their legitimacy from the consent of the governed, *as expressed through the Constitution and laws*, not from any personal system of values, no matter how noble" (emphasis added).

What sets our argument apart from other normative arguments is our claim that our theory is *required as a practical matter* by the evolving doctrines and modes of thinking in administrative law. We argue that it is the theoretical encapsulation of the pragmatic intellectual project of the early history of public administration. As John Millett (1956, 181) observed half a century ago, "One of the great gaps in our knowledge about administration is an adequate and accurate theory of constitutional status."[9] Though we have much that is critical to say about the contributions of Dwight Waldo in chapter 3, we agree with him (1984, xxxiii) that serious political theory "is not likely to result from isolation from government with a conscious intent to theorize or 'be philosophical' about it. . . . 'Consequential' political theory, that is, political theory recognized contemporaneously or subsequently as related importantly to political reality and capable of generating belief and action, is characteristically produced (1) by a person not directly engaged in government but close enough to it for first-hand knowledge, and (2) [by] a person not by intention 'theorizing' but rather seeking solutions to problems judged to be important and urgent." We argue throughout this book that the most important and urgent problems of public management are created by the Constitution's separation of powers.

Separate Intellectual Traditions, Sharing Power

A key feature of our approach to theorizing—in the face of the practical necessity to which the separation of powers gives rise—is our drawing upon two scholarly traditions of public administration that are often thought to be incompatible: the classical tradition of public administration and the contemporary analysis of political economics. Despite important differences of motivation and methods, both approaches are fundamentally concerned with establishing a rationale for legislative delegation of authority to officials of the executive branch and independent agencies while holding them responsible through our constitutional system of checks and balances. There is every reason, therefore, to investigate synergies between these two intellectual traditions.

In addressing the problem of delegation and responsibility, traditional authors tended to be normative and intuitive, their ideas and ideals grounded in reform politics, in the personal experiences of scholar-activists, in a systematic observation of governments and departments, and in efforts to understand and interpret pragmatically what democratic values require. The informal, experiential qualities of the traditional literature are its strengths. That literature often exhibits the kind of insight and sapience, motivated by the urgent tasks of state building, all too rare in contemporary, often self-referential public administration literature.

Invoking the traditional literature as authority for public management theory is fully consistent with our common law traditions, which emphasize the authority of precedents. "To achieve legitimacy in American society," Daniel Feldman (1993, 239) argues, "policy makers do well to try to match the value mix that has come down to us (evolving all the way) through the American constitutional tradition. Certainly, those values reflect our peculiar national history and experience, and the interests of the dominant forces in our society. How could they not?" Adds J. Donald Kingsley (1945, 89), "If . . . administration is a branch of politics, it follows that our approach to the discovery of administrative principles must be historical" or else we shall misunderstand political ideas because they are divorced from their contexts (compare Nash 1969; Gladden 1972).

Yet those who would heed such advice lack the analytic tools to adapt traditional insights—particularly the idea of responsibility—to the variegated problems and circumstances of contemporary public management.

Fortunately, such analytic tools are readily at hand. While the largely formal literature upon which we rely necessarily lacks the verisimilitude that comes from an intuitive and existential grasp of government in practice, it offers insightful analytic models of how legislative policy choices and agency policy making might be aligned both ex ante, through the terms of delegation of authority, and ex post, through legislative oversight and judicial review. Models of any kind are just that; they abstract from a complex reality to assist our limited minds in explaining it. We intend to show (in chapter 5) that powerful theoretical tools, such as game theory and social choice theory, can be used to address the problem of managing in a separation-of-powers regime in a way that is both formally and intuitively accurate.

Invoking rational choice assumptions to study political phenomena is not without its critics in political science, public administration, and administrative law. Surely, many argue, the world of managerial practice is too complex for such abstract models, with their often unacknowledged biases and blind spots. We have chosen this framework because it is a plausible basis for modeling activities whose objective is to effect the goals of society in an efficient manner, albeit subject to constraints that express higher-order values. Public management is necessarily instrumental—not a "fourth branch of government" but a means for the purposeful achievement of collective purposes.

That this is true is not simply our own view. As we argue more fully in chapter 4, the instrumental view of public management is fully institutionalized in the perspectives of courts and legislatures at all levels of government. Small wonder, then, that rational choice modeling has proven to be a useful strategy for reducing the formidable detail of political life to a manageable number of essential and revealing interactions (see for example Miller 1992; Knott and Miller 1987; Epstein and O'Halloran 1999; Huber and McCarty 2004; Brehm and Gates 1997). These models, and the analytic narratives and statistical analyses inspired by them, guide the most insightful thinking into the complex dynamics of the separation of powers available in the literature and can be used to address its most pressing practical problems.[10]

The complementary nature of these two disparate intellectual traditions becomes apparent in the equivalence of Frank Goodnow's problem of "securing harmony between the expression and the execution of the will of the state" (1900, 98) with the mechanism design problem: discovering social institutions that enable the maximization of total welfare by disparate actors who are assumed to act rationally (Mas-Colell, Whinston, and Green 1999, 857). Both the traditional thinkers exemplified by Goodnow and mechanism designers have the tools to address the problem of securing a welfare-maximizing proportion between discretionary administration and institutionalized checks and balances.

There is yet another tradition and intellectual community, however, that not only shares these concerns but also wields formidable political influence over public management: administrative law.

Bringing the Law Back In

Though David Rosenbloom (2003, 23) argues that "the separation of powers . . . goes directly to the matter of what public administration should be," his view is given infrequent attention by public administration scholars. Indeed, administrative law is often regarded as something of a nuisance, as a procedural obstacle to effective management. The role of courts can go entirely unacknowledged in contemporary literature, with possibly a passing reference to the distractions of institutional reform lawsuits. On the other hand, though separation-of-powers games are common in the political economics literature, those scholars pay little attention to the implications of their results for managerial practice that is constitutionally sufficient.

The field of administrative law is also concerned with the separation of powers— but with a decisive difference. The field includes those with the power to put into actual practice their views concerning the implications of that separation for public administration. As David Epstein and Sharyn O'Halloran (1999, 21) note, "many of the procedural innovations imposed by courts on agencies . . . began as suggestions in the scholarly community." By contrast, ideas concerning managerial responsibility originating in the precincts of public administration or political economics have little long-term practical impact in part (and ironically) because such ideas are seldom shown to be compatible with prevailing doctrines and precepts of administrative law. Public administration is reluctant to concede that among the many sources of legitimacy for managerial practice, one has superordinate power: administrative law, with its abiding concern for preserving and adjusting the separation of powers. Argues Kenneth Warren (1993, 250), "The administrative state is legitimate because the law says it is."

We embrace the premise, therefore, that a theory of public management must be grounded in administrative law and, therefore, be framed by the separation of powers and its implications for the appropriate scope of administrative discretion. In doing so, however, we immediately encounter well-known difficulties.

Individual and Collective Justice

While administrative law has been more responsive to the political environment since the advent of the civil rights era in the 1960s, it is nonetheless founded on reasoning that is distinctly different from the kind of reasoning characteristic of the other, more political literatures. Legal reasoning tends to be more scientific, deriving principles from precedent that, once identified in particular cases, are applied to the facts to reach a "principled" decision. Political reasoning, by contrast, concerns compromise intended to achieve the greatest good inherent in a given situation. A usually localized balance of competing interests is then incorporated in various concrete expressions of public policy: authorizing statutes, appropriations and their accompanying language, regulations and guidelines, organizational and administrative structures, and eventually, institutionalized norms of practice.

The essential nature of a social optimum on which the legitimacy of the political process depends can be expressed as the achievement of an appropriate balance between individual justice and collective justice. Traditional authors understood that the goal of responsible administration is a balancing of collective justice, defined by legislatures and the Bentleyan (1908) "parallelogram" of interest group forces (Bertelli and Lynn 2005), and individual justice, to which individual citizens are entitled under the Constitution and common law.

The Aristotelian distinction between collective and individual justice is recognized in both administrative law and traditional public administration. In administrative law, we find a differentiation of the administration of justice from the administration of government, or "the execution, in non-judicial matters, of the law or will of the state as expressed by the competent authority" (Goodnow 1905, 14). "The rules of law governing the organization of the administration must be quite different from the rules of law governing the relations of individuals, since the whole purpose of such rules is the public rather than the individual welfare" (Goodnow 1902, 9). Somewhat later, Ernst Freund (1915) similarly distinguished between powers directly affecting private rights and the administrative powers in the management and operation of public services.[11]

This concept of balance has implications for the conduct of public administration and management. "If . . . we . . . imply that the main purpose of the technical agency is to adjudicate according to rules," argued John Dickinson (1927, 156), "will we not have abandoned the characteristic and special advantage of a system of administrative justice, which consists in a union of legislative, executive, and judicial functions in the same body to secure promptness of action, and the freedom to arrive at decisions based on policy?"[12] He continued: "The argument is plausible that a régime of law is not adapted to fields of human relationships which involve significant questions in issue between competing social forces" (218). Among traditional public administration scholars, Leonard White put the matter succinctly: "The goal to be sought combines adequate recognition of personal rights as declared in the constitution with effective achievement of great social programs" (1935, 455).

PLAN OF THE BOOK

Our central claim is that a mechanism of governance ensuring the optimal performance of our separation-of-powers regime is *a precept of managerial responsibility*. This precept incorporates four axioms derived from our analysis of the literatures that inform this book: *judgment, balance, rationality*, and *accountability*. Far from arbitrary, these four axioms are shown to fully comport with constitutional requirements for the exercise of the managerial discretion that is inevitable in a separation-of-powers state. The precept enjoins the conduct of public management and, if consistently adhered to, ensures the optimal performance of government and is both theoretically sound and demonstrably legitimate within our constitutional scheme. This is true *because the precept is derived from that scheme*. It compels the personnel function to select those potential civil servants best suited to uphold it.

Our argument is developed as we explore the issue of managerial responsibility under the separation of powers from the three intellectual perspectives sketched in the preceding section. In chapters 2 and 3, we reexamine the traditional literature and revisit the controversies associated with its interpretation. In chapter 2, "That Old-Time Religion," we review, albeit selectively, the main contributions to traditional thinking, the contexts that inspired them, and the main ideas and "habits of thought" to be found there. We find substantive convergence on ideas and ideals that are essentially Madisonian. In chapter 3, "Orthodoxy and Its Discontents," we reevaluate the claim that traditional thinking constituted a rigid, antidemocratic dogma. We argue instead that there is, ironically, far more concern for democratic responsibility in traditional literature than can be found in most contemporary approaches to public management reform. It is doubly ironic that the resort by these scholars to such democratic habits of thought earned the opprobrium of Dwight Waldo, Robert Dahl, and other critics of earlier ideas who were ostensibly dedicated to democratic values.

While traditional public administration evolved in what has been characterized as "an anti-legal temper," administrative law was itself evolving from an earlier skepticism toward any delegations of authority to the executive department into a source of justifications for just such delegations. These intellectual and legal developments are discussed in chapter 4, "Raising the Bar: Law and the Administrative Process," where we conclude that, by neglecting its foundations in administrative law, public administration has isolated itself from a vital source of ideas and doctrines that legitimize the administrative state in both theory and practice.

How shall the precept of managerial responsibility be institutionalized? In chapter 5, "A Theory of Politically Responsive Bureaucrats," we provide a formal, though nonmathematical, argument that a precept of managerial responsibility located in the personnel function of public administration is a principled and practical solution to the coordination problems associated with the separation of powers. That this argument reinforces the more intuitive and experiential insights of the traditional literature contributes to an important goal: providing an analytic framework within which traditional insights, while lacking formal coherence, can be shown to be a coherent guide to managerial practice toward the goal of securing its legitimacy.

The mechanism that is at the center of our argument is explored more fully in chapter 6, "Managerial Responsibility: A Precept." We review the literature on managerial responsibility from The Federalist to more recent contributions, showing how deeply the idea penetrated into the foundations of the field. There we argue that judgment is the sine qua non of responsible administration, necessitated by delegation. Its content consists of balance—acceptance of responsibility for identifying and equilibrating the inevitable conflicts among interests, mandates, and desires—and rationality—habitual resort to reason to ensure transparent justifications for managerial actions. Balanced and rational judgments sum to accountability: an institutionalized acceptance of the authority of the separation of powers in a Madisonian sense.

In chapter 7, "Public Management: The Madisonian Solution," we contrast our perspective on public management with other perspectives on administrative behavior, including the best-practices-oriented views that have been popular in recent decades. We argue for the sufficiency of the precept of managerial responsibility in a republican sense and, therefore, for its inherent superiority to perspectives based on extrinsic values and over the expedient "principles" associated with best-practices perspectives. We show how the precept, incorporated in the personnel function of government, constitutes a foundation for public management reforms that are constitutionally and practically superior to reforms of recent years.

CHAPTER TWO

That Old-Time Religion

The acceptability of public administration principles is dependent upon
their consistency with and contribution to those democratic values
which the community is determined to preserve at all costs.

—*Marshall Dimock*

As the field of public administration has outgrown its youth, generation gaps have
opened and widened. The field's seminal figures and ideas have increasingly been
regarded as rustic and naïve, even deluded, rather than insightful and prescient
when confronting the enduring challenges of constitutional governance. Though
there are exceptions (see for example O'Toole 1984; Moe and Gilmour 1995; Rohr
1986; Svara 1999; Wamsley and Wolf 1996), contemporary commentors have been
variously patronizing, contemptuous, or indifferent toward their progenitors.

Public administration's rejection of its past is puzzling. One explanation is the
tendency in most critiques of the older credos is to evaluate them as divorced from
their historical and institutional context, as if their originators' reasons for responding
as they did to the administrative problems of their day are of no intrinsic intellectual
or practical interest. Denuded of context, these older ideas may appear sterile, even
foolish, from a contemporary perspective.

A more specific explanation is that dismissive attitudes toward the field's founding
contributors appear to reflect the influence of the publication in 1948 of Dwight
Waldo's *The Administrative State*. Waldo condemned traditional public administration as a collection of outdated credos, an "old-time religion" (also see Peters 1996,

3). The implication of such condemnation is clear: Why study ideas that have been authoritatively held to be both inconsequential and wrong?

We argue in this book that traditional thinking in public administration is of vital importance to understanding contemporary problems of public management. Our intention is not to cavil over the meaning of auld texts, however. As we note in chapter 1, our main purpose in writing this book is theoretical, even philosophical, not historical. But theorizing in public administration needs historical perspective: ideas and arguments in their cultural, intellectual, and institutional contexts.[1] Such perspective enables us to comprehend the fundamental dynamics of American state building, the better to evaluate contemporary prospects for further reform of the administrative state. In this sense, our approach is similar in spirit to that of American political development scholars (see for example Skowronek 1982; Carpenter 2001). Accordingly, in this chapter we exhume and reconsider public administration's traditional thinking. Our objective is to lay foundations for our argument, elaborated in chapters 5 and 6 and summarized in chapter 7, concerning how to achieve constitutionally responsible public administration and management.

In this chapter, through its intellectual history, we review the emergence of the American administrative state and the concomitant rise of a nascent professional field of public administration. We review the first generation of ideals and ideas that constitute the bedrock of what we now know as traditional public administration. We also review the emergence beginning in the 1930s of a maturing academic discourse on governance in America's rapidly evolving administrative state. We conclude by summarizing the habits of professional reasoning or, in popular parlance, the paradigm that had evolved by the end of the 1930s.

In a nutshell, we argue that traditional public administration, as expressed in the ideas and agendas of activist reformers, in the practices of public managers, and in the reflections and conceptualizations of scholars, was, contrary to most contemporary accounts, profound *in a republican sense*. That is, these ideas were concerned with creating a legitimate role for public administration and management *within our constitutional scheme*. Early thinking, moreover, converged on ideas and ideals that are essentially Madisonian: concerned with perfecting institutions that control faction and power on behalf of a "public interest." What better source for insights on public management under the separation of powers than the early literature of traditional public administration?

"A STEADY AND QUIET DEVELOPMENT"

Because later generations of public administration scholars have been, with few exceptions, innocent of active political engagement, they may lack an adequate appreciation of the extent to which their field originated in the reform movements that first took hold in the nation's large cities and spread within a generation to state and national governments.[2] So-called orthodox ideas—"scientific" management, separation of politics and administration, neutral competence, unity of command— far from being products of abstract theorizing, were elements of reform agendas intended to empower government to meet the challenges of a growing, industrializing, urbanizing, and diversifying society. Early public administration was a reform movement reflecting "a fundamental optimism that mankind could direct and control its environment and destiny for the better" (Mosher 1975, 3).

University scholars had only modest influence on the accumulating body of ideas and common knowledge concerning public administration and management, at least until there were a sufficient number of academics self-identified with public administration to conduct a scholarly discourse. What is most striking about the intellectual history of public administration is its genesis in practical discourse. Central to its development were civic organizations, public commissions, and independent training and research institutes whose surveys, reports, activities, and leaders defined the essential content of the emergent field.[3] These organizations addressed the Jamesian question, "What, in short, is the truth's cash-value in experiential terms?" Their failure was a failure, as Kant observed, of too little theory but certainly not of too little knowledge. We take up their theoretical project in chapter 5 and show that their ideas were quite closely related to constitutional incentives.

Ideas now (incorrectly) regarded as rigid credos were in their time pragmatic responses to problems of governance devised by men and women of affairs, advocates of administrative reform, and public officials, together with the reform-minded organizations they founded, led, or consulted. American intellectuals and activists of the early period, argues Laurence O'Toole (following Morton White 1949), rejected European formalism (which used abstractions, deductive systems of logic, and formal coherence as initial principles) in favor of pragmatism, institutionalism, behaviorism, legal realism, economic determinism and historicism.[4] "Our administrative tradition," O'Toole claims, "was developed by individuals who were hostile to doctrine, who have banked on experience, who have exaggerated the defects of previously proposed solutions and the probable beneficial consequences of the currently fashionable ones, and who were simultaneously held in thrall by the imperatives of technique and the goal of democracy" (1984, 149). Contemporary criticism of traditional thinking, then, is criticism not of academic doctrines but of the pragmatic and strategic judgments of those actively engaged in shaping the emerging administrative state into a coherent, transparent instrument of governance.

By the beginning of the 1930s, a vigorous academic discourse on issues of the emerging administrative state, now writ large in the unprecedented challenges created by the Great Depression, was under way. We begin to see for the first time a divergence between public administration as a reform movement and public administration as a field of scholarship, a divergence that would have profound consequences for the contemporary study of public administration. This divergence was to culminate in the scholarly critiques of Herbert Simon, Robert Dahl, and Dwight Waldo of the ideas-in-action of quintessential activist-reformers such as W. F. Willoughby, Luther Gulick, Charles Merriam, and Louis Brownlow. Issues and ideas began to compete with, and even nudge aside, concern for reforms themselves.

"What E'er Is Best Administer'd Is Best"

The point of departure for the emergence of modern public administration was the nineteenth-century "clerkship" state, "the old, informally-coordinated system of legislatively dominated administration" (Stillman 1990, 62).[5] As a legal and practical matter, writes Daniel Carpenter (2001, 43), "federal agencies existed only to carry out with a minimum of forethought the laws that Congress had passed and that the courts had legitimized and interpreted. . . .The patronage system so thoroughly yoked national officers to state and local party machines as to render the national state invisible in community life." Governance by parties, legislatures, and courts was even more evident in state and local government. According to John Mathews (1917, 20), state administration was "decentralized and disintegrated" in part because the functions they perform "have hitherto been of relatively slight magnitude or complexity . . . a high degree of state efficiency has not been found necessary to state life." But all was hardly benign. Charles Merriam (1940, 305) referred pointedly to the pathologies of "corruption, ignorance, indolence, incompetence, favoritism, oppression."

The serious study and practice of public administration originated in the efforts of educated, bourgeois reformers to replace administration that was, as Frederick Cleveland (1913, 129) put it, no better than "a convenient tool of the spoilsman," with something more professional and, from the reformers' perspective, more democratic —that is, responsive to rapidly growing business, commercial, and charitable interests. In this sense, Cleveland's orientation was similar to that of the New Deal reforms such as the National Industrial Recovery Act (discussed in its constitutional context in chapter 4), which placed business interests squarely at the table in setting regulatory policy. The goal was to substitute "knowledge for indignation, to deliver [politics] from vague sentimentalities. But efficiency was to be measured not only with respect to established frameworks and goals but also with respect to those community needs that were not yet satisfied" (Haber 1964, 111). Citizens were to be armed with facts so that they could be efficient in monitoring their representatives. Of course such high-minded pronouncements obscured the underlying struggle for power in public affairs by the new industrial, urban, and philanthropic elites, but that struggle underscores the point that early reform ideas were favored to the extent that they promised the sought-after political result.

The groundwork for change had been laid at the federal level by the civil service reform movement, which produced a major victory in the Pendleton Act of 1883. It seems clear, however, that, as Frederick Mosher (1975, 8) puts it, "the real origins of public administration lay in the cities, especially the big ones, not" he adds as if to underscore the nonacademic origins of the profession "in theories of sovereignty or the state or the separation of powers." Growing from seeds sewn in rocky terrain at the federal level by Presidents Theodore Roosevelt and William Howard Taft, administrative reform first took firm root in the more fertile soil of state government. Administrative reform finally reached the federal level with the Budget and Accounting Act of 1921 and, later, with Franklin Roosevelt's New Deal reforms.

Although congruent in many respects—Leonard White (1926, vii) felt confident that administration was "a single process" that did not justify separate municipal, state, and national analyses—each of these three streams of reformist thought and action had a distinctive emphasis (or, rather, various ideas had different salience at each level of government). At the municipal level, reform was oriented toward the efficiency and impartiality of the rapidly expanding administrative operations essential to business development and social stabilization. At the state level, the dominant theme was reorganization: of independent boards and commissions into a more coherent departmental format subject to rational oversight by elected officials. At the federal level, the theme came to be the strong executive, a theme that was to culminate in the concept of the president as chief administrative officer which inspired the work of President Roosevelt's Committee on Administrative Management (the Brownlow committee) and, after World War II, of the Commission on the Organization of the Executive Branch of Government (the first Hoover commission).

We briefly consider each of these streams in order to illuminate some important facts about traditional public administration. First, we note the seminal contributions to the evolving field by "collectivities" (Van Riper 1997)—that is, organized entities engaged in administrative reform. Second, it will become evident that the field's core ideas were not the product of a sustained, self-aware intellectual process, originating with Woodrow Wilson's 1887 essay, "The Study of Administration," but rather were constituted from experiential learning, reflection, and diffusion of ideas associated with widely dispersed but ultimately convergent efforts to create a public administration that was both capable and constitutional.[6]

Reforming "Ramshackle Governments"

Public administration as a field of systematic study and practice originated in America's cities with the ideas and ideologies first of Mugwump and then of Progressive reformers seeking to rescue local governments from the excesses of the spoils system (Pfiffner 1935; Mosher 1975; Van Riper 1997).[7] In the latter decades of the nineteenth century, independent-minded Republicans committed to public service and government reform began advocating the procedural separation of politics from administration, nonpartisanship, and a strong executive (Haber 1964; Hirschorn 1997). The National Municipal League, formed in 1895, embraced these themes, first incorporating into its model city charters the Galveston–Des Moines, or commission, plan and, when the plurality of commission government was recognized as a weakness, the soon-to-be-popular council-manager plan.[8]

Supporters of council-manager government were hardly unanimous in their thinking, however. In the view of Richard Childs, a Mugwump who was the plan's founding spirit, the city manager should have only delegated authority; he was merely to execute. The National Municipal League and the early leaders of the City Managers' Association had a different idea: to avoid bossism, they wanted the city manager to exercise certain definite duties and powers without political interference, and this idea was increasingly written into city charters (Stone, Price, and Stone 1940).

Reflecting the triumph of an idea (or an ideology) in the service of a political agenda, the City Managers' Association, whose focus was public management explicitly modeled on business administration, was founded in 1914, and a professional identity for these officials began to emerge. The Association produced two significant milestones: the publication of its journal *The City Managers' Bulletin* beginning in 1917 (renamed *Public Management* in 1927) and the adoption in 1924 of public administration's first code of ethics.[9] "By then," argues Martin Schiesl (1977, 188), "most managers had altered their 'politics is business' approach to government and were viewing city hall as the place where representatives of interest groups meet to resolve their conflicts."[10]

Arguably the most influential of the reform organizations in shaping the new profession of public administration was the New York Bureau of Municipal Research, incorporated on May 3, 1907. Organized on January 1, 1906, as the Bureau of City Betterment and composed of engineers, accountants, experienced administrators, and social workers, it began its work in 1907 with Henry Bruère, a social worker, as its first director (Allen 1908). The bureau's objective, according to Bruère, was "applying the test of fact to the analysis of municipal problems and the application of scientific method to governmental procedure" (quoted in Dahlberg 1966, 16). Overarching themes of these reform efforts included more business in government (Stone, Price, and Stone 1940), control of government by enlightened elites (Nelson 1982), and administration by experts.[11] New York, Boston, Chicago, and other cities began overhauling the lines of authority and functional competence of municipal government in accordance with the corporate model.

Contrary to contemporary interpretations, the intention of these elite reformers was not antidemocratic. Their goal was to make transparent that which had been obscured by boss rule. The public was to be armed with facts so citizens could be efficient in performing their role of providing consent (Dahlberg 1966; Stillman 1974), and increasing numbers of Americans were granted suffrage and given new avenues to express or withhold their consent.[12] It is nevertheless true that the importance of the expertise necessary to producing relevant facts was gaining prominence. Said an early president of the National Municipal League: "It is not the politicians not even the people at large who have initiated the great modern improvements in city governments, but experts, sanitary and civil engineers, architects and landscape gardeners, bacteriologists, physicians, educators, and philanthropists" (quoted in Schiesl 1977, 128).

Of particular significance to the emergence of the profession was the bureau's reliance on a type of study termed the "survey." Surveys "constituted a new kind of literature about public administration," argue Stone and Stone (1975, 21). "They developed facts about the functioning of governments, the advantages and disadvantages of alternative policies, administrative arrangements, and procedures. Principles, doctrine, and requisites of good organization were delineated." With the establishment of this new form of research, "comparison and exchange of information became a major purpose of the Governmental Research Association," which was founded in 1915 (22). "*The establishment of public administration as a field of study and professional practice could not have taken place without this empirical experience*" (21, emphasis added).

The influence of the bureau's approach to municipal research and its model of governance spread, perhaps especially as the popularity of "scientific management" became a unifying theme of bureau work following publication in 1911 of Frederick Taylor's extraordinarily influential book, *The Principles of Scientific Management*. Bureaus of municipal research were created in a number of other American cities. In 1915, the bureau founded the Government Research Association, the annual meetings of which became a forum for the exchange of information among bureau directors (Pugh 1988; Stone and Stone 1975).[13] By 1921 (the year of the federal Budget and Accounting Act's enactment), the bureau recognized the national and even international implications of public administration as a field of study and, in a significant transition, changed its name to the National Institute of Public Administration (Dahlberg 1966).

Professionalized public management required trained administrators. Recognizing this emerging fact, the bureau in 1911 started its own Training School for Public Service, implementing the belief that public administration as a process was generic, similar on all governmental levels. The Society for the Promotion of Training for the Public Service, a forerunner of the American Society for Public Administration, held conferences in 1914, 1915, and 1916, and a journal, *The Public Servant*, was begun in February 1916 (Caldwell 1968). A number of leading academic institutions provided professional education for city managers, prominently including Texas A&M University, the University of Michigan, and Syracuse University. Few practicing city managers became professionally trained, however, as they tended to be skeptical of the reformers' theories (Stillman 1974).

During its first generation, therefore, the field of public administration established a definite identity and firm footing at the municipal level of government.

Laboratories of Democracy

The Civil War dealt a vicious blow to states' rights as a fundamental principle of American governance, contributing to the ambiguous role the states began to assume in the American federal system (Hart 1925).[14] As the nineteenth century wore on, state legislatures declined in public esteem, their honesty suspect, criticized by the public and academicians alike (Graves 1938). Under pressure from various constituencies, legislators turned increasingly to putatively more objective and expert boards and commissions to oversee state services. In the resulting "unconscious and consequently haphazard" (Mathews 1917, 499) process, a new set of problems emerged. Administration came to consist of "a complicated mass of separate and disjointed authorities, operating with little reference to each other or to any central control" (Mathews 1917, 499).[15]

A movement for state reorganization began around 1910, stimulated by President Taft's Commission on Economy and Efficiency, which finally reported to Congress in 1912.[16] In 1917, following the recommendation of its own economy and efficiency commission, the state of Illinois enacted the "first comprehensive plan of administrative reorganization" (Buck 1938, 7). State-level reorganization in Illinois—and subsequently in many other states—usually involved the consolidation of the various offices, boards, commissions, and agencies that administered the state's affairs into a few orderly departments, set up along general functional lines. Such efforts were impeded, however, by the difficulty of amending state constitutions, for example, to adopt the short ballot in order to reduce the number of elected commissioners. Moreover, an "educated public opinion" supporting increased administrative efficiency often did not exist (Mathews 1917).

Though the state reorganization movement was never as successful as municipal reform, its proponents identified standards that "are no longer theoretical, but are based upon experience and supported in whole or in part by actual practice in a number of states" (Buck 1938, 14). These standards were "concentration of authority and responsibility; departmentalization, or functional integration; undesirability of boards for purely administrative work; coordination of the staff services of administration; provision for an independent audit; [and] recognition of a governor's cabinet." James Hart (1925, 270–271) proclaimed: "The people of the several States and of the nation have hit upon a really fruitful means of adjusting the representative system of the nineteenth century to the economic needs of the twentieth: . . . the exaltation of the Executive, first as a sort of tribune of the people and leader of the legislature in the effectuation of popular mandates, and then as an organ suited to work out by detailed regulations or individual decisions the specifics of policy which the legislature is not fitted to provide."

Thus the states provided laboratories, if not many successful models, for the emergence of another version of executive-centered government. Leslie Lipson (1939) noted dramatic growth in the power of the governor during the twentieth century, encompassing reorganization (abolishing boards and commissions in favor of consolidated departments), the executive budget, the short ballot, and powers of appointment and removal, albeit unevenly across the states. John Mabry Mathews (1917, 397, echoing Wilson's 1887 essay, which he cites) argues: "There is no great danger in conferring on the governor increased power if it is accompanied with commensurate responsibility. This responsibility will be enforced in part through the simplified machinery and the greater publicity in which the work of the administration will be conducted under the reorganized system."

"Executives Vigorous and Safe"

Though the foundation for the modernization of American government was the Pendleton Act of 1883, it was the Budget and Accounting Act of 1921 that began to institutionalize executive government at the federal level.[17] During the intervening years, a number of developments laid the groundwork for that important legislation: Theodore Roosevelt's Commission on Departmental Methods; William Howard Taft's Commission on Economy and Efficiency; the congressionally initiated Bureau of Efficiency; Woodrow Wilson's Central Bureau of Planning and Statistics; and the wartime Overman Act, which, though unused, formally authorized the president to reorganize executive agencies.

The Commission on Departmental Methods, better known as the Keep Commission after its chairman, operated from 1905 to 1909 to advance President Theodore Roosevelt's public management agenda.[18] It represented "the assertion for the first time of presidential responsibility for administration" (Kraines 1970, 53), thus initiating the erosion of the tendency of Congress to retain full legislative authority over public agencies. In investigating scandals and specific problems as well as a wide range of generic management issues, "one of its major accomplishments was to change the connotation of the word 'administration' from its long-held simple meaning of the personnel of the executive departments to the art of managing the public business" (52).

Whereas the Keep Commission was a presidential management tool, President Taft's Commission on Economy and Efficiency, chaired by Frederick Cleveland (and with Frank Goodnow as a member), has been termed the first coherent national-level reform initiative (Haber 1964). Thinking that he was avoiding Roosevelt's mistake, Taft secured formal congressional authorization for his commission, in the process eliciting legislative recognition of the principle that such an undertaking was an executive, not a congressional, responsibility (Kraines 1970). Though Congress rejected the commission's principal recommendation, creation of an executive budget to replace the Department of the Treasury's "Book of Estimates," momentum for its eventual adoption gradually gained strength.

In a seldom remembered but notable development, Congress established the Bureau of Efficiency in 1916 as an independent unit with a broad general power to survey organization and methods, investigate duplication of activities, and make recommendations to the president. Although it served primarily as a staff agency to Congress, its relations with the Bureau of the Budget were never clarified, and in 1933 it was abolished. "During its two decades of existence, however, as the first federal agency of over-all administrative reforms it had an impact on the spirit of self-improvement within the executive establishment that continued to be felt long after its demise" (Emmerich 1950, 21–22).[19]

An important legacy of the Taft Commission was the creation in 1916 of the Institute for Government Research (IGR) with the support of Robert Brookings and other leaders in public affairs. William F. Willoughby, then at Princeton but an experienced public administrator, became its director. Intending to replicate at the national level the contributions of the New York Bureau of Municipal Research, he hired experienced officials and researchers, built a constituency for his nonpartisan, collaborative approach to government reform, and initiated an active publication program extending beyond the work of the research bureaus and the economy and efficiency commissions. Said Willoughby (1918, 49), "Its establishment represents the conviction on the part of its founders that the work of administration is, if not a science, a subject to the study of which the scientific method *should be rigidly applied*" (emphasis added).[20]

With the active involvement of Willoughby and the IGR and the support of President Warren Harding, Congress passed the Budget and Accounting Act of 1921, which authorized the Bureau of the Budget in the Department of the Treasury and the General Accounting Office affiliated with Congress with the power to conduct preaudits of proposed federal outlays.[21] Henceforth, the institution of the president was "a responsible executive leader," assisted by the Bureau of the Budget, his new staff agency (White 1933, 174). In the same year, the Business Organization of the United States, comprising 2000 responsible representatives of the business organization of the federal government, was first convened. Subsequently scores of local coordinating bodies, termed *federal business associations*, were created. "The President," said Leonard White (1933, 174), "is now in effective control of administrative policy and operation. . . . The departments have lost their independent and uncoordinated position."[22] As we note in chapter 4, the question of which branch has the greatest control over the bureaucracy was the principal theme of the pulling and hauling that defines the history of American administrative law.

Brookings continued his institution-building role. He obtained a large grant from the Carnegie Foundation to found the Institute of Economics in 1922, and its assistance was immediately in demand by official Washington (Saunders 1966). In 1924, Brookings established the Graduate School of Economics and Government in Washington (independent of his former affiliation with Washington University of St. Louis), its doctoral program taking advantage of its access to official Washington. Brookings's purpose in founding the Graduate School was "to teach the art of handling problems rather than to impart accumulated knowledge; and its end is to turn out craftsmen who can make contributions to an intelligent direction of social change" (Saunders 1966, 36). Charles A. Beard, Roscoe Pound, Felix Frankfurter, and Harold Laski participated in its intellectual life. It foundered, however, owing in part to the inclination of its faculty toward wholly academic pursuits, and in 1928 it and the two institutes were incorporated into a new Brookings Institution, with Harold Moulton as its first president and Frank Goodnow on its boards.

"The New Administration"

The cumulative result of these various transformations at local, state, and federal levels of government was dramatic, wrote Harold Laski in the new British *Journal of Public Administration* in 1923. "A state built upon *laissez-faire* has been transformed into a positive state. Vast areas of social life are now definitely within the ambit of legislation; and a corresponding increase in the power of the executive has been the inevitable result" (92). In the same year, John Gaus, in an article that drew heavily on examples from state-level administration and adjudication, stated with prescience and conceptual coherence that "the new administration includes a wide share of policy formulation; it requires a large measure of discretion on the part of the civil servant; it claims wide exemption from judicial review of its findings of fact; in brief, we are seeing a development somewhat akin to the rise of the administration in the days when the Tudors and the great monarchs were welding together the modern national state" (220).

What must be emphasized, however, is how experimental this transformation was. "The administrative state began in an ad hoc fashion, more haphazardly, much less auspiciously—some might say ignominiously—beginning roughly in the 1880s with its own peculiar lines of institutional and intellectual development that were separate, distinctive, and often quite elusive" (Stillman 1990, 56). It would be decades before the potential of a merit system would be realized at the federal level, much longer than that at state and local levels. Writing in 1933, Leonard White notes the persistence of the spoils system in the larger cities and "the almost unqualified adherence to the practice of popular election of a very large number of officials, most with administrative duties" (7).[23] Throughout its first half century, developments in public administration thought and practice continued to be fueled by the urge to complete the modernization of the administrative state and of all levels and functions of government, together with the associated shifts of political power. The goal, both implicit and explicit in the emerging literature, was to strengthen administrative capacity and to broaden the bases of its legitimacy through responsible management.

IDEALS AND IDEAS: THE FIRST GENERATION

Richard Stillman (1990, 14) notes that "the growth of the American state that began roughly a century after the formation of the American Republic and the growth of the subject of public administration *as ideals and ideas* were intimately connected." Public administration's seminal contributors were closely associated with institutionalized reform movements and organizations. Ideals and ideas became influential as they shaped reform agendas, were put into practice by governments, and were codified into practice models.

The ideas of Frank Goodnow, Richard Childs, Frederick Cleveland, William F. Willoughby, Charles G. Dawes, Charles A. Beard, Luther Gulick, Louis Brownlow, and a host of others became influential through their leadership of the commissions, organizations, and agencies that were shaping the emerging administrative state.[24] Childs persuaded Goodnow, Charles Merriam, A. Lawrence Lowell, and others prominent in the academy to support his council-manager plan (Stillman 1974). Goodnow, the first president of the American Political Science Association (APSA), published extensively on municipal reform and became a ubiquitous presence in reform activities.[25] Dawes, the first director of the Bureau of the Budget, "had a remarkable impact on administration and budgeting" (Stone and Stone 1975, 15). In the founding period, thought and action were in a very real sense seamless.

The ideals and ideas associated with early modern administrative practice, as John Gaus was perhaps the first to recognize, constitute a distinctive domain of thought and practice. Scholars in growing numbers began to be attracted to this emerging new subfield of political science (Van Riper 1990).[26] Many public administration historians tend to view this period as a series of *movements* (for example, scientific management, economy and efficiency [Waldo 1984],[27] principles,[28] training[29]), of themes (for example, a Wilsonian-Hamiltonian fusion[30]), of *values* (for example, representativeness, neutral competence, executive leadership [Kaufman 1956]), and of *doctrines* (such as the politics-administration dichotomy, neutral competence, or the bureaucratic paradigm).[31]

Such interpretive lenses can distort and obscure as much as they clarify the character of the period's intellectual developments, however, especially insofar as they suppress the narrative of pragmatic government that lies at the heart of the nascent field. This narrative is described succinctly by Luther Gulick (1990, 601): "Public administration . . . as a field of knowledge [developed] through research and case study, and as a collection of operational technologies designed to overcome inefficiencies, to reduce corruption, and to help humankind on its way to survival and advancement in a changing and competitive world."

The Intellectual Context

Although early literature claimed that public administration was unique compared to business administration and to politics (Goodnow 1900; White 1926), the field's intellectual growth was unquestionably influenced in significant ways by intellectual currents in business administration as well as in political science and other fields and disciplines.[32]

Concurrent with the emergence of "the new administration," a contemporaneous "management movement" (Person 1926) was gathering strength in the industrial sector, reflecting the thinking primarily of engineers like Henry R. Towne, Henry Metcalfe, and Frederick W. Taylor (George 1972).[33] From concerns with efficient use of labor and wage-cost systems there arose a concern for organization and coordination, that is, for management. Under the banner of "scientific management," the idea of "management" (Church 1914) was to gain a following in public administration.[34]

Interest in scientific management accelerated in public administration, and especially among municipal reformers, beginning in 1911 owing mainly to the Eastern Rate Case hearings, the publication of Taylor's influential book, and America's entry into World War I.[35] Seminal publications such as A. Hamilton Church's *Science and the Practice of Management* (1914), Leon Marshall's *Business Administration* (1921), and Oliver Sheldon's *The Philosophy of Management* (1924) amplified the theme, simply stated by Sheldon (49): "The management of a generation ago . . . relied on chance or on initiative. . . . Initiative without knowledge is too risky."[36]

Meanwhile the discipline of political science, under the influence of Progressive ideas, was engaged in defining the meaning of "science" in political science (Somit and Tannenhaus 1967). Departing from German historical traditions, Woodrow Wilson's *Congressional Government* (1885), James Bryce's *The American Commonwealth* (1888), Arthur Bentley's *The Process of Government* (1908), and the works of Charles Merriam are empirical and process oriented. Charles Beard argues for scientific methods that separate the study of politics from theology, ethics, and patriotism. The APSA presidential addresses by A. Lawrence Lowell in 1908 and Woodrow Wilson in 1910 endorse statistics, functionalism, and the development of public policy. National conferences on the science of politics were held in 1923, 1924, and 1925. These conferences gave the stamp of professional respectability to the movement for a "new science of politics" (Somit and Tannenhaus 1967).[37]

For the most part, the very early academic study of politics reflected a descriptive orientation toward its formal structures and processes rather than analysis of the dynamics of its operations and consequences. Scientism in political science was controversial, however, and public administration adapted to it slowly.[38] "In intellectual terms, [public administration] was picked up by a scattering of scholars in the late nineteenth and early twentieth centuries—Wilson, Goodnow, Mathews, and others—and they drew on European literature and examples" (Mosher 1975, 8).[39] Traditions of empirical social science research were in their infancy, and the idea of specialized training for public administration had not attracted much of a following in the academy.

With these developments influencing the intellectual ambience of public management reform, much of the early public administration literature consists of reform tracts and a variety of surveys and studies by good government groups such as the New York Bureau of Municipal Research and the National Municipal League and commission reports by such groups as the Keep and Taft commissions (Stillman 1974; Garvey 1995). Dwight Waldo (1948, 35) notes that "the movement to reorganize state governments . . . has produced a characteristic and distinct literature," citing, for example, the *Appraisal* of the New York State constitution and government by the New York Bureau of Municipal Research as establishing a framework for American political science and public administration. The Columbia University professor and former New York Bureau staff expert A. E. Buck wrote an authoritative treatise on administrative consolidation, which was published by the National Municipal League (Buck 1928).

Along with these official or quasi-official reports, a series of seminal publications was, to varying degrees, describing, interpreting, reflecting on, and codifying developments in public administration. These include Frank Goodnow's *Comparative Administrative Law* (1902) and *Politics and Administration* (1900), John Mabry Mathews's *Principles of American State Administration* (1917), Frederick Cleveland and Arthur Buck's *The Budget and Responsible Government* (1920), Everett Kimball's *State and Municipal Government in the United States* (1922), Leonard White's *Introduction to the Study of Public Administration* (1926), John Dickinson's *Administrative Justice and the Supremacy of Law in the United States* (1927), and W. F. Willoughby's *Principles of Public Administration* (1927).

To be sure, university professors and their publications contributed to informed opinion. State-level reform produced a bona fide academic-analytic literature, including John Burgess (1886), Simon Patten (1890), Henry Jones Ford (1900), Cleveland and Buck (1920), Mathews (1917, 1922), and Leonard White (1927).[40] "While the [Keep] commission members were experts on administration, they were influenced by the writings of Frank Goodnow, Ernst Freund, and William F. Willoughby, which were appearing on the administrative scene" (Kraines 1970, 49). William Willoughby (1930, 49) notes that the committees and commissions on economy and efficiency drew on faculties of political science of the universities and other specialists (these academics' "most important work," he opines) in moving the field of public administration forward.

The related development of education and training for public service is, as with the development of early ideas, "irrevocably linked" to "the struggle to overcome political patronage, malfeasance, disorder, special privilege, and waste in government" (Stone and Stone 1975, 13). University curricula, said Stone and Stone (1975, 29), "gave increasing attention to government, public issues, and public administration," but the studies were academic rather than practical. Not until the 1930s did the federal government deliberately search for administrative talent, promoting a significant advance "in establishing a connection between the newly emerging curriculum in public administration and certain career lines in government" (Waldo 1984, xx).[41]

Hardly a decade following the founding of the New York Bureau of Municipal Research, textbook-like treatments of the emergent field began to appear. Although Leonard White's 1926 *Introduction to the Study of Public Administration* is almost universally regarded as the field's first textbook and a touchstone of professional self-awareness, that claim is not easy to sustain. Herbert Storing (1965, 41) notes, for example, that "in every respect but one the main outlines of White's book follow those of Goodnow's [*Principles of the Administrative Law of the United States*], occasionally chapter by chapter and even section by section." John Mabry Mathews's 1917 book, *Principles of American State Administration*, is certainly a textbook. Everett Kimball's 1922 treatise, *State and Municipal Government in the United States*, is described by Harold Laski (1923) as "a complete vision of public administration in the United States."[42] Oliver Sheldon's 1924 *The Philosophy of Management* is arguably the first textbook on generic management.[43]

The Magisters

Some of the "ideals and ideas" in this emerging literature of practice and reflection are, as noted, closely associated with reform movements. The council-manager model of municipal government, for example, incorporates three distinct ideas: the use of a nonpartisan ballot and at-large elections to ensure capable, public-spirited representation; the delegation of administrative authority to a competent, trained, nonpartisan executive; and accountability to the voters through the representative council (Stone, Price, and Stone 1940). A. E. Buck (1928) identifies two essential principles of state reorganization: that administrative activities should be grouped by purpose; and that administrative functions should be placed under individual, rather than collective, responsibility. Leslie Lipson (1939, 66) summarizes the state reorganization movement in one sentence: "Recognize the governor's responsibility for directing all administrative activities of the state" through devices such as the executive budget, centralized functional administration, and the short ballot.

Many ideals and ideas are also closely associated with the seminal figures of the early era. Undoubtedly the most important of these figures is Frank J. Goodnow.[44] Goodnow is important for several reasons: his grasp of administrative law and of the separation of powers;[45] his articulation of the importance of administration in the overall scheme of governance; his practical interest in municipal reform; and his familiarity with European thought and practice. Before Goodnow, argue Charles Haines and Marshall Dimock (1935), the field of government was considered to comprise a recounting of constitutional powers and limitations. Goodnow first directed attention to the operations and techniques of the governmental mechanism, his administrative law course being substantially the same as a typical public administration course in the 1930s. His 1893 and 1905 books on administrative law represent the "first effort at a systematic delineation of the study of public administration" (Millett 1956, 173).

Some see Goodnow (following Wilson) as propagating a rigid doctrinal dichotomy between politics and administration (Waldo 1984; Stillman 1990). While Goodnow does argue that "the necessity for this separation of politics from administration is very marked in the case of municipal government" (1900, 84), his work and authoritative commentary on it suggest a much more subtle interpretation.[46] "The great complexity of political conditions," he argues, "makes it practically impossible for the same governmental organ to be intrusted in equal degree with the discharge of both [politics and administration]" (24), an arrangement that, incidentally, was found wanting under the Articles of Confederation.[47] Goodnow continues: "That administrative hierarchies have profound influence on the course of legislative policy is elementary" (146). In discussing exceptions to the theory of the separation of powers, Goodnow (1902) makes clear that the legislative and executive branches share each other's powers, and that is as it should be.[48]

Arguably, Goodnow's most sophisticated insight is that harmony between the expression and the execution of popular mandates requires the sacrifice of independence by the branches of government (Lynn 2001). This becomes clear in his noting that the "semi-scientific, quasi-judicial, and quasi-business or commercial" functions of administration might be relieved from the control of political bodies (Goodnow 1900, 85). In lieu of political control, officials charged with such functions are to be subject to the control of judicial authorities upon the application of aggrieved parties. In advancing this complex scheme, Goodnow (97–98) is prescient, perfectly expressing the dilemma of reconciling administrative capacity with political control:

> Detailed legislation and judicial control over its execution are not sufficient to produce harmony between the governmental body which expresses the will of the state, and the governmental authority which executes that will. . . . The executive officers may or may not enforce the law as it was intended by the legislature. Judicial officers, in exercising control over such executive officers, may or may not take the same view of the law as did the legislature. No provision is thus made in the governmental organization for securing harmony between the expression and the execution of the will of the state. The people, the ultimate sovereign in a popular government, must . . . have a control over the officers who execute their will, as well as over those who express it.

As demonstrated in subsequent chapters, harmonization is the crucial problem in defining the theoretical role of public administration under the separation of powers.

While Frederick A. Cleveland was a founder of the New York Bureau of Municipal Research and closely associated with its practice models, he is also the author of *The Growth of Democracy in the United States* (1898).[49] In that work, he advocates "studying political life as a continuous process" (vi) and enumerates the problems that reformed government should address: "incompetency in office . . . inequality in elections . . . the employment of the spoils system in appointments . . . the corruption of our legislatures . . . the subversion of municipal government in the interest of organized spoliation" (387). To Cleveland, the expansion of the civil service would lead to a government to which every citizen could, in principle, aspire, in contrast to the class-based fiefdoms of Germany and Great Britain.

In *Organized Democracy* (1913), Cleveland writes: "The picture drawn [in this book] is one of the continuing evolution of the means devised by organized citizenship for making its will effective; for determining what the government shall be, and what the government shall do; for making the qualified voter an efficient instrument through which the will of the people may be expressed; *for making officers both responsive and responsible* . . . government should exist for common welfare" (v, emphasis added). The contemporary problem, he argues, "is to provide the means whereby the acts of governmental agents may be made known to the people—to supply the link which is missing between government and citizenship" (454).

Cleveland was undoubtedly a technocrat but not the kind derided by contemporary critics. "Technically," he says, "the problem is to supply a procedure which will enable the people to obtain information about what is being planned and how plans are being executed—information needed to make the sovereign will an enlightened expression on subjects of welfare" (1913, 454–455). To him, "a budget, a balance sheet, an operation account, a detail individual efficiency record and report, a system of cost accounts, and a means for obtaining a detail statement of costs" are means by which government could be made transparent to citizens. His entire goal is "an enlightened people" and "an informed public conscience" (465), as well as a government that provides service to the people to counter "the threatened dominancy of a privileged class and of institutions inconsistent with the spirit of democracy" (26).

William F. Willoughby is associated primarily with the idea that the emerging practice of administration and management should be guided by universal, scientific principles.[50] The goal of his Institute for Government Research was, as noted above, scientific analysis to identify the principles that ought to govern in the interest of economy and efficiency of the national government (Willoughby 1918).[51] But Willoughby's contributions are broader. As John Millett (1956, 174) sees it, Willoughby attempts to provide a theoretical justification "for the years of practical endeavor," viewing the legislature as the board of directors and the chief executive as the general manager. "That the theory today strikes us as poor constitutional doctrine need not detract from an important contribution. At a minimum Willoughby sought to place the study of public administration in a carefully formulated conceptual framework" (174). There was, moreover, "no doubt in Willoughby's mind that the chief executive's position could be made into that of general manager only by legislative enactment" (182).

Willoughby was both intellectually and politically influential. "Almost everyone entitled to professional consideration who wrote on public administration from 1915 to 1936," says Charles Hyneman (1939, 64), "accepted the 'principles' which [Willoughby] announced; and most of them appeared as convinced of their incontestability as Mr. Willoughby himself." (Mathews's 1917 textbook, recall, is titled *Principles of American State Administration*.) In his first budget circular, Charles Dawes, director of the Bureau of the Budget, calls for basic principles to serve as concepts and rules of action that would never be questioned: impartial, impersonal, nonpolitical (Morstein Marx 1945).

Yet Willoughby is no advocate for Prussian-style bureaucracy or for a scientistic cameralism. Cameralism advocates meritocracy rather than noble birth, administrative science rather than feudal law, standardized principles rather than local particularity, and formalism and professionalism rather than traditionalism (Hood and Jackson 1991). He notes with reference to the German bureaucracy that "there are inherent in it certain disadvantages or dangers which go far toward justifying the deep-seated distrust that Americans have of it" (Willoughby 1919a, 153). He is critical of the aristocratic nature of the British civil service, noting that the American civil service is "radically different" (155) because selection of its members is clearly consistent with our democratic form of government. "Scientific principles" are, in his view not ends in themselves but, because their application guarantees transparency, are a bulwark against an arrogant, unresponsive, civil service. To Willoughby, the problem is to put all public institutions—political, social, and economic—"upon a democratic basis" (160). His intellectual influence is found in John Preston Comer (1927), who refers to "fickle popular bodies" and the "whim of popular opinion"; administrators work out "principles from numerous experiments in enforcement of policy" (16–17), and they bring expertise to bear on "the exercise of the great powers vested in Congress by the Constitution" (18).

It is important to note that the idea that there might be principles of administration is not always understood in the same way that Willoughby expresses it. For example:

- Goodnow, anticipating the Dahl and Simon critiques by over thirty-five years, argues that "the postulation of fundamental political principles of universal application [is] the statement of 'mere useless opprobrious theory'" (1911, 3–4, quoted in Waldo 1984).
- The most general principles of management distilled by A. Hamilton Church (1914) are steeped in common sense: the systematic accumulation and use of experience, the economic control (or regulation) of effort, and the promotion of personal effectiveness.
- Of principles, Ernst Freund (1915, 675) argues: "We have come to associate a due recognition of permanent principles with the administration of justice and its methods of procedure tending to emphasize the impartial and objective point of view. The judiciary has however by no means a monopoly in this regard. Similar results are likely to attend other official action, provided that it be sufficiently detached from the strife of interest and imbued with a sense of professionalism. It shares with judicial action *the respect of precedent and the respect of expert opinion, habits of mind which distinguish both from the irresponsible action of popular bodies*" (emphasis added).
- In his seminal business textbook, Leon Marshall (1921, 756) argues: "There has been quite a considerable volume of writing directed at the question, 'What are the fundamental "laws" or "principles" of administration?'" Let us arbitrarily... use the term administration to include (a) policy formation, (b) the planning and setting up of the organization, and (c) the running of the organization. . . . *Administration implies action* and it is more appropriate to speak of sound *rules of action* in the field of administration than it is to speak of principles or laws," an idea equally applicable to business, public, school, and other administration.

- Argues Oliver Sheldon (1924, 36), "There is a tendency, in the modern cult of efficiency, to imagine that, given a basis of scientific principles, the art of the manager consists only in applying those principles. This is far wide of experience. . . . But we have to recognize that such *scientific methods are as likely to fail as to succeed, unless there is more in the manager than the knowledge of a set of working principles which he tries to twist around to meet the situation*" (emphasis added). Sheldon believed that business and government were converging on similar principles of management.

Because it is so elastic, the appeal of the idea of principles has proven robust, its critics notwithstanding. The usefulness of principles and the methods for deriving them—are they syntheses of experience or scientific laws?—were vigorously debated well into the 1940s, providing a foil for the Simon and Dahl critiques. The notion of universalistic principles has, moreover, enjoyed a renaissance owing to the influence of the best-practices literature, which has been the primary format for prescriptive public management in the twenty-first century.

The first chapter of John Mabry Mathews's 1917 book is a synoptic analysis of the field of public administration. He notes on the first page that the work of government can be divided into the formulation and execution of public policy. But he chides Montesquieu for falling into the error of identifying functions with departments and echoes Goodnow: "There can scarcely be, in the nature of things, any exclusive assignment of one of the two primary functions of government to a single department, but the work of each department involves the exercise of a combination of such functions" (7), although a department may be predominantly concerned with one or the other. He identifies various means for controlling administration, but he emphasizes the need for administrative discretion to deal with conditions as they arise and for the integration and coordination of disparate activities.

Mathews (1917, 12), like Cleveland, advocates transparent government: "The representatives of the people in the law-making body should be in a position to criticize the administration and to prevent or remedy any abuses which may grow up in the conduct of the administration." But, he argues, the administration should not be relegated to being "a mere tool in the legislative hand" (13). "Statutes should not contain elaborate and detailed administrative provisions, but such details should rather be left to the discretion of the executive" (13) Legislators cannot anticipate all contingencies, they are not technically qualified to control complex functions, and they are not suited to continuous monitoring.

In what is virtually a consensus view in the emerging field, John M. Gaus (1923–1924) is highly critical of parties and legislatures, who love statutes "crammed with detail, with concessions to special interests but overriding many considerations of effective enforcement" (221). "Today our problems are hardly capable of solution by statute" as they were in simpler agrarian times (218). "Actually, the administrative agency itself makes a policy because of the sheer failure of preceding agencies—parties and legislatures—to perform their primary functions" (218). "And those administrative agencies must develop their own standards through their 'sense and experience,' pragmatically" (223). A similar argument applies to judicial interventions: "Despite reluctance to permit the final control to escape from the court, sheer necessity requires a large share of power being conferred upon administrative agencies by legislatures; and the kind of technical problem raised often makes it difficult for the court to review administration effectively" (224–225).

A RIPENING DISCOURSE

Articles by John Gaus (1931) and Marshall Dimock (1933) signal the maturing of a genuine professional discourse in public administration, a movement from description and prescription to reflection, conceptualization, inquiry, and debate.[52]

Gaus, having called attention to "the increasing role of the public servant in the determination of policy, through either the preparation of legislation or the making of rules under which general legislative policy is given meaning and application," argued nearly a decade later that it was time to reexamine the assumption that a "centralized and responsible executive" would supply political leadership (1931, 123). He called for more extended inquiry into the "relationship between representatives of 'pressure groups' . . . the political heads, legislative committees, and permanent civil servants or semi-judicial administrative commissions" (124).[53] Two years later, in a remarkable essay titled "What Is Public Administration?" Marshall Dimock argued that "any view should be discouraged which tends to regard public administration as a detached, self-sufficient entity. . . . Like other branches of government, it is concerned with human beings, attitudes, traditions, clashing interests, and widely different social situations. . . . Technical efficiency is sometimes not efficient at all when the wider implications of the problem are carefully examined" (261–262).

In effect, Gaus and Dimock were engaged in formulating a perspective on public management that today would be termed "governance," deliberately broadening the scope of the field to include its wider political and social significance. In modern parlance, governance is "nothing less than the steering of society by officials of what are organizationally the 'commanding heights' of society" (Goodin 1996, 13). In spite of the many changes in society and government, governance remains the planning function that Gaus and Dimock considered it to be.

We can see the ripening of the discourse, for example, in the continuing discussions of "principles of administration."[54] "Those who are engaged in professional [administrative] surveys," Dimock observes in his 1933 essay (261), "indicate a remarkable awareness that principles should be regarded as tentative, and that different political, social, and institutional settings necessarily condition the application of standards which have been found successful in other situations."

In the same year, Luther Gulick moderated a panel of practitioners, researchers, and scholars on the subject of principles. Herman Finer (in the spirit of William James) gave lengthy remarks on principles as cause-and-effect relations identified from bodies of fact using mother wit and logic.[55] Gulick (1933b, 276–277) asks: "Is there anyone who disagrees with the important elements of Dr. Finer's suggestion that the principles must be finite and that we cannot think of them as having a universal application?"[56] Subsequent discussion revealed serious confusion and lack of agreement on the definition and applicability of—and on the intellectual justification for—principles. How does a principle differ from a law? A policy? How far does a principle have to apply? That is, must it be universal? Leonard White agrees with Finer's formulation and says of his own 1926 textbook that he had "carelessly slipped" into using the term "principles" "here and there" (see Gulick 1933b, 285).[57] White continues: "I think most principles are usually statements of personal experience, many of which might turn out on the basis of further experience to be perfectly sound, but which hardly rise to the dignity of a principle until they have passed at least beyond the stage of individual experience."[58]

By the 1930s, then, awareness of a professional literature, of theory and method, and of active debate is evident. Interpretations, syntheses, critical analyses of first-generation scholars and ideas, efforts to place ideas and contributions in wider perspective, and deeper, more penetrating analyses of particular issues all enter the discourse. Up through the 1920s, contributions tended to be isolated from an overall sense of intellectual development; they were contextualized by reform goals and organizational agendas but not tested in intellectual crucibles. Beginning in the 1930s, under the influence of disciplinary and professional scholarship, ideas begin to coalesce, issues emerge, controversies sharpen, and a professional discourse sustained by academic trappings evolved.[59]

The New Magisters

A notable development in this ripening discourse is that intellectual agendas begin to differentiate themselves from administrative reform agendas. Now we meet, in addition to seasoned veterans, a younger, second generation of scholars and increased emphasis on published, individual scholarship. The growing number of landmark books are more theoretical, analytical, and differentiated than earlier treatises, and journal articles proliferate.[60]

Marshall Dimock (1933, 260) is perhaps the first to reflect at length on the field's founders. He interprets Wilson as saying that "the good administrator is the master of policy as well as the technician who coordinates the machinery through which laws are enforced." In his analysis of Wilson's 1887 essay, Dimock selectively quotes Wilson as follows: "The principles on which to base a science of administration for America must be principles which have democratic policy very much at heart." And "we should not like to have had Prussia's history for the sake of having Prussia's administrative skill. . . . It is better to be untrained and free than to be servile and systematic" (1937b, 28). "The ideal for us is a civil service cultured and self-sufficient enough to act with sense and vigor, and yet so intimately connected with the popular thought by means of elections and constant public counsel, as to find arbitrariness or class spirit quite out of the question" (40). Dimock's Wilson is rather more sophisticated than the Wilson who stood for a rigid dichotomy between politics and administration.[61]

Dimock (1933) offers similarly nuanced interpretations of other early contributors to the literature. "The doctrinal content of public administration was first clearly formulated in this country by Frank J. Goodnow . . . [who] emphasized the discretionary, legislative, and judicial characteristics of administrative officials; in other words, he did not attempt to put law-making and law-enforcement in water-tight compartments" (259–260). Of Willoughby (still, of course, very much in the picture), Dimock says: "His method is largely deductive and analytical. The legislature, the political executive, and the non-discretionary administrators are viewed as distinct departments. For that reason the feeling of relationship—administration as a going concern—is somewhat lost sight of. The ends of government are regarded as outside of the narrow competence of the skilled administrator" (260). White (Dimock's future co-author) comes off worse. His emphasis on scientific management, Dimock says, "is institutional and descriptive. The social and governmental problems with which administrators grapple are not emphasized, nor are the legislative and judicial aspects of administrative action tied in definitely with the broad process of law-making and law enforcement" (260).[62]

Of the general problem of governance, Pendleton Herring (1936, 20–21) argues: "The problem is twofold: (1) to keep the bureaucrat responsive and uncorrupted; (2) to join the citizen with the administrative process in order to utilize his particular expertness or to gain the sanction of his consent. Herein lies the meaning of modern democratic government. . . . If the democratic process is to continue, it must be guarded, not simply by exhorting the citizen to his duty, but *by making guardianship part of the duty of officials*. Opinion is like water. Administrators must dig for it" (emphasis added).

Herring favors close contact between citizens and "pressure groups," which are better acquainted with problems than are legislators. But although "the bureaucracy must be guarded from domination by economic groups or social classes . . . it must be kept free of the abuses of aloof, arbitrary, and irresponsible behavior to which public servants are so often prone. . . . In short, it must not develop a group interest within itself that will become its raison d'être" (384). Herring continues: "Consultation with the persons and groups most directly concerned must . . . become a regular feature of administration. This is the greatest safeguard against arbitrary or ill-considered action" (388).[63]

In 1936 a remarkable book appeared. *The Frontiers of Public Administration* is a trim volume of essays by University of Chicago colleagues John Gaus, Leonard White, and Marshall Dimock. Their scope is synoptic: the meaning and scope of public administration; the meaning of such contested "phrases and concepts" as principles and responsibility; the role of discretion; a theory of organizations; and public administration's role in American society. Gaus, for example, notes that "the relinquishment by electorate, legislature, and court, at so many points, of the power and the function of determining or defining policy" has created confusion as to the nature of administrative responsibility. "We find," he says, "that the problems of discretion and of responsibility are intermingled from the very beginnings of public administration in the modern national state" (Gaus 1936, 35). His solution is an "inner check" (39), "the attitude of the civil servant as an individual toward his work and his profession, as an integral part of the complex society gradually taking form before our eyes" (43), an attitude that will lead to active collaboration with groups of citizens, thus earning their trust.

Dimock's 1937 essay, "The Study of Administration," exemplifies how the ripening discourse was enriching the content of public administration. There are, Dimock argues in a "New York Bureau" manner, "universal rules to be uncovered. . . . Organization principles aim at a structure in which all authority is concentrated in the chief executive, lines of responsibility are hierarchical, staff officers clear through officials of the line, adequate attention is given to staff services, sufficient freedom is guaranteed to operating heads, and the entire organization is meshed at hierarchical levels and simply controlled at the top" (1937b, 35–36). Yet, he notes, "governmental administration is less responsive than business management because it is more accountable" (37). Thus "how to make administration flexible and responsive and at the same time legally accountable and constitutionally responsible . . . is one of the most difficult adjustments of democratic government" (37). "Effective administration," Dimock argues, "must be produced by those who can be trusted. The acceptability of public administration principles is dependent upon their consistency with and contribution to those democratic values which the community is determined to preserve at all costs" (40). Dimock continues: "We do not want efficiency for its own sake; we want it for the sake of our democratic form of government. . . . Public administration in a democracy cannot expect to be concerned solely with efficiency" (39).

Willoughby (1937, 41) remains rather rigidly schematic, arguing that "present unsatisfactory conditions with respect to the administration of public affairs" result from a failure to determine and apply scientific principles.[64] He notes that "in point of fact real administrative authority, and primary responsibility for the conduct of the administrative affairs of the government, reside, under our political system, in the so-called legislative, rather than in the executive branch of government," although he questions the desirability of this arrangement. He also notes, then questions, the clear distinction between executive and administrative responsibilities and the movement to make the executive the "administrator-in-chief." Finally, he distinguishes, as have others, between "overhead administration," the true province of "the science of administration," and "direct administration."[65]

"It is an arresting fact," observes Leonard White (1942, 213), "that the great improvements in government since 1910 have been designed to make the public service more effective in the management and direction of public affairs, not to keep it responsible or make it more amenable to control." He continues: "Responsibility of officialdom to legislature and to courts, sometimes to the electorate, is a matter of law; it is one of the essential elements of a democratic system long well established in this country. . . . *Responsiveness* of officialdom to enacted policies, to broad public purposes, to sentiments and preferences, and to individual needs is not a matter of law but of the spirit. Both are important to the proper administration of laws in a democracy. Neither is achieved with full satisfaction by the formal relationship of dependency of administration on popular assemblies; the full responsiveness of officialdom to citizenry requires other and supplementary institutions of a more intimate nature."

In addition to a literature betraying deepening insight and wisdom concerning administration in a republican sense, a tradition of empirical research was in an early stage. Herbert Simon's earliest work attempts to measure the output of public service agencies (Ridley and Simon 1938; Simon and others, 1941). In their study of the first twenty-five years of city manager government, Harold Stone, Don Price, and Kathryn Stone (1940) undertake a systematic study of fifty city manager municipalities using a retroactive before-and-after comparison, a control group of nonmanager cities having been rejected as infeasible. Their study produces some nuanced empirical insights: "A complete separation between politics and administration developed in the tradition of those cities that conducted their political campaigns entirely without reference to the city manager or the administration, electing councilmen solely for their own policies or personal characteristics" (248). They continue: "In other cities, the city council refused to assume total political responsibility for administration, and therefore the city manager was not regarded as neutral. . . . The success of the city manager plan depends upon the actions and attitudes of the council" (248).

Leslie Lipson's 1939 study of state government reorganizations (Lipson 1939), using field methods similar to those of Stone, Price, and Stone, produced similar contingent insights. In the states studied, reorganization made it easier to locate responsibility, diminished the extent of duplication, and improved coordination, although not uniformly, and administrative work of the state was better planned. Whether waste was reduced could not be determined.

The New Management

Mathews, White, and Willoughby had already produced comprehensive treatises on what Gaus in 1923–1924 calls "the new administration" (White's would go through four editions). In a series of new treatises, Leonard White (1933), John Pfiffner (1935), and Harvey Walker (1937) elaborate on what White now called "the new management" and Pfiffner terms "the new public administration."[66] In these works we find what is arguably the most definitive statements of the habits of professional reasoning that later generations were to label "orthodoxy."

In a monograph prepared for President Hoover's Research Committee on Social Trends, Leonard White (1933) refers to developments from 1900 to 1930 as the "new management." By this term, he means the emergence of "a contemporary philosophy of administration" favoring consolidation of the administrative powers of the elected chief executive and the city manager. Echoing earlier president-centric administrative philosophy at the subnational level, White cites a series of principles put forward by Governor William T. Gardner of Maine on January 21, 1931: consolidation and integration in departments of similar functions; fixed and definite assignments of administrative responsibility; proper coordination in the interests of harmony; executive responsibility centered in a single individual rather than a board" (1933, 144).[67] "The changes of the last three decades," argues White, "have been primarily dedicated to greater efficiency, toward improved methods, better and more extensive services and the elimination of waste and irresponsibility" (4). But he also notes what has *not* been of concern: "We have not been deeply concerned on the whole with more effective ways and means of citizen participation in administration . . . [or] with developing machinery for employee participation . . . [or] with the fundamental alteration of administrative relations between federal and state governments" (4–5).[68]

John Pfiffner (1935), an exemplar of orthodoxy,[69] nevertheless acknowledges that "there is a danger in permanent officials, which is best conveyed by the adverse connotation given to the term 'bureaucracy' by Anglo Saxons. A smug self-satisfaction is thought to breed aversion to change, resulting in a general level of mediocrity" (18). In contrast, "the new public administration is essentially democratic in spirit and practice. . . . [It] combines power with responsibility" (19) to political officers who are under popular control. Administration is "society working through government to solve the collective problems of a technological age" (20). As concerns scientific management, Pfiffner says that "the keynote of the new public administration is experimentation and research. . . . Administrative institutions and practices must bear up under the white light of exhaustive examination, observation, and inquiry on the part of trained and experienced observers" (9). He continues: "To secure the proper equilibrium between politics and administration it will be necessary to have a working arrangement between political officers and administrative officers" (11).[70]

Harvey Walker's *Public Administration in the United States* appeared in 1937. A professor of political science at Ohio State University, Walker had published *Law Making in the United States* in 1934, and he intended the two volumes to be based on the "functional distinction" between "politics" and "administration" (for which the quoted source is Goodnow 1895). "The case for the dual concept," Walker says, "rests upon a pragmatic basis. . . . The work which the government does to give effect to a law is called administration" (4–5). But Walker's ensuing discussion identifies most of the complexities and ambiguities in the administrative process with which we are now familiar: the two branches poaching on the spheres of the other and the courts falling on both sides depending on the issue and the decision.

Administrators engage in politics, says Walker. "Administrative officers may, by the promulgation of subordinate legislation, give meaning to an otherwise incomplete law, and fill in the interstices left blank by the lawmakers" (6). That they do so, though, is problematic in a democracy. "Public administrators cannot be permitted to construe laws in their own way. . . . If the laws are executed by administrators irresponsible to and even contemptuous of the public will and desires, democracy is only a name. . . . It is not bureaucracy . . . but lack of control over it that must be avoided" (99). In this respect, says Walker, there is more work to be done. "Many more intricate and ingenious devices must be constructed than are available today if popular control over administrative officers is to be asserted and maintained. The absence of such control permits the administration to degenerate into a bureaucracy" (9). In the last analysis, Walker says, "effective administrative control is a matter of common sense, competence, compromise, and division of labor" (133).

Traditional public administration as expressed in the synoptic works of these three scholars expose a professional reasoning process that explores the interrelationships among the values of democracy; the dangers of an uncontrolled, politically corrupted, or irresponsible bureaucracy; the corruptibility of legislative processes; the imprecision of popular control of administration; and judicial and executive institutions that can balance capacity with control in a constitutionally appropriate manner (Lynn 2001). The field could now identify itself with a literature evincing a subtle, pragmatic wisdom concerning administrative practice that is, at the same time, infused with democratic idealism and a keen awareness, if not a conceptual grasp, of the challenges created by America's separation of powers.

The next generation of public administration scholars, however, is to take a rather different view of their intellectual and practical accomplishments. Harvey Walker extends the logic of Frank Goodnow one step but does not discredit his intellectual forbears. A break in the intellectual history of the field is on the horizon. What came before is coherent, if pragmatic, and sensible. What follows is the development of a critical school, which will provide more questions for administration than answers.

CHAPTER THREE

Orthodoxy and Its Discontents

Perhaps the ideal of our profession is the faith of a priesthood rather
than the skepticism of a science; if so, it is no offense to dogmatize
assumptions and eschew inquiry. Perhaps a code of ethics is too clear a
luxury for a profession still driving hard to establish prestige; if so, who
shall condemn us if we indulge occasionally in cozenage or venture
close to barratry?   —*Charles Hyneman*

The tenets, ideas, and prescriptions of public administration's most prominent
pre–World War II contributors enjoyed a fair measure of prestige by the late 1930s.
Following Wallace Sayre (1958), traditional thinking is widely (although incorrectly)
held to have reached its apogee of influence with the 1937 report of the President's
Committee on Administrative Management (PCAM 1937, also known as the Brownlow report, after the committee's chair, Louis Brownlow) and its companion volume,
a compendium of background papers edited by Luther Gulick and Lyndall Urwick
and published concurrently as *Papers on the Science of Administration.*[1]

That "high noon" of prestige was short-lived. In *The Administrative State,* a
condensed version of his doctoral dissertation published in 1948, the young, undeniably well-read Dwight Waldo fixed a withering gaze on the prewar literature. His is
only one of a series of direct hits on what came to be regarded in the late 1940s as
traditional (or classical) thinking. Robert Dahl and Herbert Simon also published
widely read critiques of the kind of thinking that had been given heightened status by
the Brownlow report. But Waldo's broad and devastating indictment of early ideas

and his pejorative use of the term "orthodoxy" to characterize them have become the canonical view of the early literature.[2]

We argue in chapter 2 that traditional thinking exhibited sophistication and prescience. Early contributors helped to shape, to promote, and to sustain the creation—out of the ruins of the nineteenth-century spoils system—of responsible, stable, competent, and democratic administration at all levels of government.[3] This project is hardly inconsequential. Yet with too few exceptions, a view of this literature as lacking the rigor of the academy prevails to this day. This, we think, is inherently strange, for the field of public administration stands at once proud to embrace inductive learning from practice and dismissive of exactly such efforts at the most critical time in the development of the American administrative state.

In this chapter, we evaluate Waldo's critique, and those of many others, in the light both of the academic discourse that preceded publication of *The Administrative State* and of subsequent developments. We reach a paradoxical conclusion. Traditional thinkers, before and after Waldo's critique, have a great deal of temerity and an evident wish to "grasp the scheme of things entire." Meanwhile, antitraditionalists show a clear affinity for exactly the habits of thought that Waldo finds so shallow and spurious.

INDICTMENTS

The salvos launched against traditional thinking by Robert Dahl, Herbert Simon, and Dwight Waldo between 1946 and 1948 are neither the first nor the most intense criticisms of classical ideas. As we discuss below, a critical discourse was sufficiently well developed by then to call into question the very notion of a reigning orthodoxy. Nor are these three critics united in their discontents. That they pursue distinctively different intellectual agendas becomes clear as they begin engaging each other. Nonetheless, the combined impact of their critiques created a watershed in the intellectual history of public administration. The contributions of the founding generations were seldom taken seriously again except as a straw man for a succession of "new" schools of thought, which began to proliferate.

Did these three critics of classical ideas thereby leave the field stronger than they found it? A brief overview of their purposes and ideas will be helpful in forming a judgment.

"Shallow and Spurious Answers"

"Devastating" is not too strong a word for Waldo's critique of traditional thinking. "The indictment against public administration," he says, "can be only that, at the theoretical level, it has contributed little to the 'solution' or even the systematic statement of [problems posed by large-scale, technically advanced, democratic society]. . . . We have had a spate of shallow and spurious answers. And no one has had the temerity in his thinking to attempt to 'grasp the scheme of things entire' " (1984, 98, 99). Moreover, unlike Dahl and Simon, who moved on to new intellectual ground, Waldo persisted in his cause. In a later essay, Waldo (1961, 220) expresses himself as follows: "Since publication of the *Papers [on the Science of Administration]* in 1937, a generation of younger students have demolished the classical theory, again and again; they have uprooted it, threshed it, thrown most of it away. By and large, the criticisms of the new generation have been well-founded. In many ways the classical theory was crude, presumptuous, incomplete—wrong in some of its conclusions, naive in its scientific methodology, parochial in its outlook. In many ways it was the End of a Movement, not the foundation for a science."

Although some mellowing had apparently occurred when he reflects on the reissue of his book in 1984, Waldo continues to refer to "the unreality or inconsequentiality of a substantial part of the prewar literature" (1984, xii).[4] These intemperate judgments from a scholar widely regarded as accommodating beg for an explanation, and fortunately Waldo provides one, admitting to "a certain animus toward, even contempt for, the literature of Public Administration" (1965a, 6).[5] He attributes this animus in part to his feeling of superiority as a political theorist, but another reason is that "a former mentor and good friend . . . had viewed the literature of Public Administration as dull, pretentious nonsense."

Waldo summarizes the substance of his critique by noting that the early scholars' "claim to science was, with respect to substance, premature and, with respect to method, immature or erroneous. . . . The 'principles' which were the issue of the science were, at best, summary statements of common sense. . . . Economy and efficiency as goals or criteria were either too narrowly conceived or were misconceived. . . . The separation between politics and administration is arbitrary or false and must be abandoned or thought through on new terms" (1968, 5). In his view, which many see as his most important contribution, early public administration constituted a "new philosophy of government [that] sought the attainment of Jeffersonian ends by Hamiltonian means" (1955, 19).

Waldo's gravest charge, however, is that early public administration was "in an important and far-reaching sense false to the ideal of democracy" (1952b, 87). Reformers such as Wilson, Goodnow, and Beard, he argues, "laid the foundation for a pattern of thought according to which democracy was for a generation to be a political principle external to the field of professional interest in public administration. In fact, the later students [such as Gulick] not only came to see democracy as external to their field of professional interest, but frequently regarded it as hostile to their central principle, efficiency. They became ambivalent, schizoid, seeking ardently to advance democracy by denying its relevance to the administrative process" (85). The last sentence of this astonishing indictment contains an important clue not only to Waldo's substantive animosity toward classical ideas but also to his enduring popularity in the field.

Waldo's normative goal for democracy is pure in the sense that citizens exercise influence directly rather than indirectly through republican institutions founded on representation, delegation, and accountability. "To achieve democracy," Waldo argues, "citizen groups of all kinds must be brought into the administrative process and given the opportunity to state their interests and to help make and execute decisions affecting their lives" (1952b, 92). More or less following Mary Parker Follett, Waldo says that "the essence of democracy lies not in these mechanical counterfeits [parties, federalism, referenda, natural rights, popular voting], but in the development of common, shared purposes in organizations in which all participate" (95), admittedly a dream "in which education and general culture are consonant with a working world in which all participate both as 'leaders' and 'followers' according to 'rules of the game' known to all. Such a society would be post-bureaucratic" (103). Later he recants somewhat: "A democratic country must limit participation *because* it is committed to democracy" (1971, 262)—noting, characteristically, that "the issues involved are of all but mind-paralyzing complexity" (264). But, at heart, Waldo appears to distrust politics as much as any proponent of "the dichotomy," favoring the attainment of Jefferson's ends by Jeffersonian means.

Dwight Waldo is almost playful in his refusal to be intellectually pinned down. When Peter Drucker accuses him of equating democracy with participation, Waldo retorts: "What democracy in administration may mean precisely I confess I don't know. What I said was—let's find out" (1952a, 501). Although handing up blanket indictments of traditional thinking, he also offers perceptive, fair-minded, even admiring assessments of individual authors and contributions. While dense with insights and ideas, his works also feature inscrutable adages: "The way forward is forward"; "Neither centralization nor decentralization is right or wrong, but . . . both are right *and* wrong. . . . We need more centralization and more decentralization. We also need less of both" (1971, 260).

Waldo's admirers—legion and often fervent—suggest why he is so difficult to corner. Brack Brown and Richard Stillman (1986, 9) credit Waldo with "a pattern of thinking notable for its avoidance of the concrete, the immediate, the fashionable, one that is deliberately outside the flux of passing leaders, programs, policies, and political issues of the day." James Carroll (1997, 203) says that "if Waldo's thought stands for any conceptual and methodological proposition it is that for public admin-istration reductionism is the path to perdition." Frank Marini (1993) notes that Waldo characterized his own stance on social science methods as accommodating, catholic, ecumenical, pragmatic, and ambiguous.[6] Waldo himself says that "admin-istrative thought must establish a working relationship with every major province in the realm of human learning" (1984, 212).

What we, as political economists and Madisonians, see as Waldo's elusiveness may well account for his enduring influence within public administration. Many see his ideas as postbureaucratic—Waldo concedes as much—and postmodern, anti-positivist.[7] In retrospect, Marini notes, Waldo is a practitioner of hermeneutics. One might see in Waldo's persistent skepticism of institutions and in his self-confessed "humanist-literary bias" (Brown and Stillman 1986, 38) intimations of Derrida and deconstructionism. "The guiding insight of deconstruction," argues Mark C. Taylor (2004, A29), "is that every structure—be it literary, psychological, social, economic, political or religious—that organizes our experience is constituted and maintained through acts of exclusion. In the process of creating something else inevitably gets left out. These exclusive structures can become repressive—and that repression comes with consequences. . . . What is repressed does not disappear but always returns to unsettle every construction, no matter how secure it seems." While Waldo never puts the matter so clearly, this formulation may well sum up his worldview.

Proverbs and Problems

While Herbert Simon and Robert Dahl went on to establish themselves as among the finest social scientists of their generation, their influence on the ethos of public administration was at its apogee following the publication of their critiques of tradi-tional public administration in 1946 and 1947, respectively, in *Public Administration Review*. Waldo, however, not Simon or Dahl, epitomizes the field's intellectual values; it is Simon who was awarded the American Society for Public Administra-tion's Dwight Waldo Award, not vice versa.

Simon's critique of the field's approach to principles grew directly out of research with a colleague on public organizations and his realization that the principles are of no help in addressing practical problems of how to make decisions about organizing services to achieve effectiveness—that is, how to make correct decisions (Storing 1962). Simon's specific objective is to discredit the pretensions to scientific standing of the principles of administration associated with the Brownlow report and, specifically, with the essay by Luther Gulick in *Papers on the Science of Administration* (Gulick

1937). In particular, he aims at the concepts of specialization, unity of command, span of control, and organization by purpose, process, clientele, or place. Such principles are no more than proverbs, he insists. "For almost every principle one can find an equally plausible and acceptable contradictory principle" (1946, 53). Simon continues: "What is needed now is empirical research and experimentation to determine the relative desirability of alternative administrative arrangements" (66).[8]

This episode is notable in the field's intellectual history in two ways. A similarly devastating critique of the kind of thinking represented by the Brownlow report had been conducted by the Brookings Institution and was published in 1937 by the U.S. Senate Select Committee to Investigate the Executive Agencies of the Government; and a carefully reasoned book taking a similar view was published by Schuyler Wallace in 1941. Although these publications had virtually no impact when compared with Simon's article, Simon himself makes the point that a body of scholarship of unprecedented sophistication was establishing the conditional nature of principles of administration; critiques of the field's most popular ideas appeared to be having a cumulative effect. This fact combined with the sobering experience of actual wartime administration by many of the field's contributors and the advent of behaviorism in political science, public administration's parent discipline, meant that Simon's was a critique whose time had come.

On the other hand, the field continues to ignore fatal criticisms of how Simon characterizes Gulick's ideas. Herbert Storing (1962) points out that although Simon is right about the inadequacy of the principles he is wrong in attributing to Gulick the definitions of unity of command and efficiency that Simon provides.[9] Thomas Hammond elaborates on this critique (without, however, citing it) in a 1990 essay. Gulick's essay, says Hammond, "clearly exhibited by far the most sophisticated understanding of the problem of organizational design by any scholar up to that time. . . . It had an intellectual subtlety, coherence, and sophistication which Simon completely failed to recognize or acknowledge" (1990, 143, 145). Hammond goes on to argue that a very promising line of scholarship on the political aspects of hierarchies was thereby snuffed out in favor of the focus on decision making and its psychological and sociological foundations.[10]

Dahl, too, aims his criticism at principles of public administration purporting to have universal validity. In addition to Gulick, he cites W. F. Willoughby's 1927 book and the essay by Lyndall Urwick in *Papers on the Science of Administration* (Urwick 1937). He sees three problems in their approach. The problem of values, Dahl argues, cannot be suppressed. Problems of delegation, organization, and responsibility are in fact problems of values. Human behavior, moreover, cannot be assumed to be rational and amenable, as Urwick does. It is behavior that a science of public administration must understand. Finally, he argues, one cannot ignore the comparative aspects of settings and cultures.

Ironically, neither Simon nor Dahl argues for the abandonment of principles. Simon claims that principles must be contextualized and conditional, a result of the appropriate applications of scientific methods. Dahl argues rather expansively that we must build a body of comparative studies "from which it may be possible to discover principles and generalities that transcend national boundaries and peculiar historical experiences," but these, too, would result from empirical methods of hypothesis testing (1947a, 11).[11] Their animus is directed at principles that lacked empirical foundations in positive science.[12]

Both Simon and Dahl went on to produce distinguished bodies of scholarship. Simon's subsequent work, which includes two public administration classics, *Administrative Behavior* and *Public Administration* (the last co-authored with Victor A. Thompson and Donald W. Smithburg) developed into the body of contributions that earned him a Nobel Memorial Prize in Economic Science.

In an effort to promote "empirical research that would build a more veridical description of organizations and management," Simon (1995, 404) chooses to focus on decision making as the elemental unit of organizational analysis, viewing it as so constrained by contextual and psychological factors as to be properly characterized as bounded rationality guided by the criterion of efficiency. The task of administration, then, "is so to design [the organizational] environment that the individual will approach as close as practicable to rationality (judged in terms of the organization's goals) in his decisions" (Simon 1976, 241). The organization, in other words, is the context for restricting the domain of choice (Storing 1962). "The rational individual is, and must be, an organized and institutionalized individual" (Simon, Smithburg, and Thompson 1950, 102). Hal Rainey sums up Simon's importance for public administration well: "What Simon really said years ago was that we need to go out and observe decision-making and other administrative processes as they actually occur; we need to go and see what is there. In so doing, more and more of us can aspire to making a contribution half so fine and half so valuable as his" (Rainey 1989, 408).

Waldo finds little to admire in these contributions: "The conceptual apparatus of logical positivism proved in Professor Simon's hands to be a very effective instrument for reasserting and defending the doctrines of public administration which were pictured above as in full retreat" (1955, 44). Simon's formulation, says Waldo (1965a, 16), "was novel, even radical, but also very 'traditional' in some major lineaments. Its traditional features consisted in this: that a science is possible, that principles can be achieved, that our world is divisible indeed into two distinct realms, that efficiency is the proper criterion." For his part, Simon (1952, 494) sneers at "political theorists" and their unconvincing antipositivist and antiempiricist views, which are "decorated with assertion, invective, and metaphor" and at Waldo's failure to make the logic of his own criticism clear.[13]

A persistent aim of Dahl's thinking is "to find ways in which rank-and-file citizens can effectively participate, even when . . . they can exercise vanishingly little influence one by one as voters (or as participants in other ways)" (Bailey and Braybrooke 2003, 104). In this motivation, Dahl does not differ greatly from Waldo. The difference lies in the fact that Dahl produced an enduring idea: his theory of polyarchy. In this Dahl agrees with Madison that pluralism is an inevitable consequence of democracy on a large scale. But "pluralism diminishes the importance, and even the possibility, of discovering the common good and giving it effect" (Bailey and Braybrooke 2003, 104). Dahl argues, say Bailey and Braybrooke, that "pluralism is inevitable and demands a strategy of tensions, trade-offs, and second-best solutions."

Two Orthodoxies

For Waldo, the term "orthodoxy" is an expository, even a polemical, device, but others invested the idea with sociological importance. Orthodox tenets "gave a form and purpose, a self-confidence, to both the practice and the study of administration in the 1920s and early 1930s" with respect to all levels of government," says Englishman Andrew Dunsire (1973, 94). From Richard Stillman's perspective, orthodox ideas justify differentiating the study of administration from the study of politics and viewing issues of administration apart from issues of human purpose and values, thus enabling a boundary-defining self-consciousness to develop (Stillman 1990). Orthodoxy, in other words, is an identity that sufficiently differentiates public administration from law and politics to enable it to survive its birth and adolescence.

The view that the tenets of traditional public administration constitute an orthodoxy has itself become an orthodoxy, the received view of the field's first half century. Post-Waldonian scholars have produced ever more distilled characterizations of the ideas that Waldo was the first to condemn, thus reifying his view of traditional thought. According to later versions (Barzelay 1992; Osborne and Gaebler 1992), the original orthodoxy is a "bureaucratic paradigm" that embraces a dichotomy between politics and administration, scientific principles as the basis for administration, and therefore a politically neutral, insulated, technically oriented civil service organized into hierarchical, inertial bureaucracies that perform POSDCORB functions: planning, organizing, staffing, directing, coordinating, reporting, budgeting.[14] Though contemporary critics of orthodoxy do not say so, their clear implication is that there is little substantive difference between the American and the notorious Prussian models of bureaucratic administration.

When the field's wide-ranging traditional thinking is compressed into a "bureaucratic paradigm" (Barzelay 1992) that presupposes willful hostility to virtually all democratic values, any sense of the issues and controversies that riveted traditional scholarship is inevitably suppressed. The adumbrations, insights, ideas, arguments, philosophies, and wisdom described in chapter 2 go to the heart of American public administration's existential problem: to deduce a role for a growing corps of unelected officials that comports with constitutional values and institutions and is profoundly democratic in spirit. Bundled into an orthodoxy, however, in which all sense of the knowledge-creation process is suppressed, this intellectual capital is perceived as irrelevant to contemporary efforts to address the same problem.

This suppression seriously undermines the intellectual credibility of the profession. What is being suppressed is nothing less than the emergence of public administration as a forum for significant intellectual and practical discourse.

THE RIGIDITY OF THESE DOGMAS

In Dwight Waldo's 1952 account of the field's pre–World War II intellectual controversies, the rigidity of the dogmas that held the field in thrall began to break down after 1940.[15] But how rigid were these dogmas in the minds of the field's pre-1940 researchers, reformers, and scholars? Is it reasonable, or responsible, to view the field as in the grip of an orthodoxy, an old-time religion, a bureaucratic paradigm?

Certainly, as we discuss in chapter 2, there were advocates for patterned or principled solutions to the growing agenda of administrative issues and problems arising at federal, state, and local levels of government. Leonard White proclaimed that there is but one public administration; Frank Goodnow and White favored politically neutral administration of municipal affairs; and William Willoughby, A. E. Buck, Luther Gulick, and others synthesized into various principles the ideas that were shaping federal, state, and local institutions. In his memorable 1939 polemic, Charles Hyneman says that "with virtually all students of public administration 'efficiency in operation' was the end of government and integration through reorganization the only path to that goal" (64). Albert Lepawsky (1949, 45), whose *Administration* reveals a mastery of the literature rivaling Waldo's, notes that "Wilson's well-phrased though somewhat ambiguous demarcation [between politics and administration] continued to be the accepted formula among many political scientists and most specialists in public administration."[16] The dominant administrative values as of

1940, according to Wallace Sayre (1951), are concisely reflected in the Brownlow report and in *Papers on the Science of Administration*.

Yet with few exceptions, none of the so-called dogmas is put forward in nearly the simplistic, unqualified manner claimed by later commentators.[17] "Fortunately," observes William Siffin (1956, 366) in a British journal, "the emergence of public administration as a field of study in the United States has been both pragmatic and volant. . . . The result has been diffusion and diversity of thought and approach, both complicated and alleviated to an extent by a sometimes palliative search for 'principles,' or universalistic rules to serve as guides to diagnosis and even prognosis." James Svara (1999, 679) notes that orthodoxy's central tenet, a dichotomy between politics and administration, "emerged well after the initial founding period" and that during the "high noon" period of the 1920s and 1930s "there were many who presented an alternative view."[18] Of those who began using the term "dichotomy" beginning in the 1940s, not all used it so simply.

Within two generations, public administration's leading scholars and reformers developed a sophisticated and dynamic understanding of the constantly and rapidly evolving administrative state. Tensions began to emerge between those closely associated with the reform of practice and more academically inclined researchers. Explicit and implicit controversies were growing in intensity.

The founding of the American Society for Public Administration, preceded by disputes over the future of the Governmental Research Association, pitted the university and research-oriented "eggheads," such as those associated with the Social Science Research Council's Committee on Public Administration, against research bureau professionals and practitioners with affinities for the old bureau model of reform (Pugh 1988). Louis Brownlow, who brokered the creation of the Public Administration Clearing House, an association of public administration professional organizations, in 1931, was reluctant to support creation of a professional association owing to his association with the University of Chicago, where Charles Merriam and Leonard White were in residence. There, public administration was viewed as an instrument of human fulfillment, not an occupationally bound profession based on formal, "vocational," education (the view prevailing at Syracuse University's Maxwell School, where William Mosher was dean).

In addition to these internecine disagreements, professional controversies took the form of "great debates" over issues of considerable public importance. The developing sense of intellectual engagement was to emerge in full force in three controversies that took place between 1937 and the beginning of World War II: the dispute between the Brownlow committee and the Brookings Institution on executive branch reform, the debate between Carl Friedrich and Herman Finer on the sources of administrative responsibility, and the debate on the Walter-Logan Bill (discussed in chapter 4), which sought to impose extensive procedural restraints on federal administrative discretion.

Brownlow versus Brookings

The Brownlow report has been hailed (mistakenly) as the "high noon of orthodoxy" (Sayre 1958, 103).[19] Because of its iconic status within the profession of public administration, the Brownlow report is regarded as orthodox kitsch: to be celebrated but not read. More obscure is the intense controversy that arose over a competing report by the Brookings Institution.

In his message endorsing the Brownlow report, President Franklin Roosevelt insisted that democracy must be efficient or risk becoming a dream that "could not do the job" (PCAM 1937, iii). Increased efficiency could be achieved if the president were in a position "to coordinate and manage the departments and activities [of the government] in accordance with the laws enacted by the Congress" (iv), achievement of which would require an expanded White House staff; stronger management agencies; a strengthened and expanded civil service system; a subordination of independent agencies, administrations, authorities, boards, and commissions to major executive departments; and an independent postaudit of the fiscal transactions of an executive with complete responsibility for accounts and current transactions. "There is nothing [in this program]," Roosevelt insisted, "which is revolutionary, as every element is drawn from our own experience either in government or large-scale business" (iv).[20]

As Alasdair Roberts (1995) notes in his study of the Brownlow-Brookings controversy, the Brownlow recommendations produced intense controversy not only within Congress, which rejected them, but also in the academic community. Experts argued in particular over the proposal to modify the General Accounting Office's power to control spending within the executive branch in such a way as to weaken it. Both specialists like A. E. Buck and the New Dealers were opposed to the preaudit power of the comptroller general to block disbursements not properly authorized.

The Brookings study (U.S. Senate 1937), which was conducted at the request of the U.S. Senate Select Committee to Investigate the Executive Agencies of the Government (the so-call Byrd committee, after its chair), disputes the view that the executive had to be strengthened, arguing for giving the president instead better mechanisms to enable him more easily to perform his functions. Brookings experts preferred that the existing balance of power between Congress and the executive be maintained. "In their report to the Byrd committee in 1937," notes Charles Hyneman (1939, 65), "the Brookings group managed to challenge nearly every one of the tenets of orthodox administrative theory."[21] A particular bone of contention was the Brookings report's opposition to Brownlow's proposed changes in the status and functions of the General Accounting Office.[22]

But there was a hidden agenda behind the policy dispute. Brownlow himself was particularly concerned to avoid an open conflict over his committee's report, fearing that the impartiality of government research would be questioned and the public administration community destabilized. "All of the parties to this fight were preoccupied with larger concerns about the status of the new community of 'specialists in public administration'" (Roberts 1995, 337, n. 6), whose neutrality might be questioned if specialists disagreed over fundamental issues of governmental organization. The committee pressured Brookings not to issue its report, which infuriated the Brookings leadership (in particular Harold Moulton, director of the Institute for Governmental Research, of which William F. Willoughby, the author of the Budget and Accounting Act of 1921, was the first director). Brookings nevertheless issued its report to Congress, and hearings were held, at which Brownlow supporters tried to undermine the credibility of the Brookings study.

Brownlow claimed that his study (but not the Brookings study) was based on scientifically grounded principles of good administration (Roberts 1995, 334). But his claim is specious. The 1,229-page Brookings report, and especially its first chapter, "The Problem of Administrative Organization," is sophisticated, insightful, and deeply analytical. Therein lies another puzzle in the intellectual history of public administration. The Brookings material (along with Schuyler Wallace's 1941 study *Federal Departmentalization: A Critique of Theories of Organization*) could be profitably studied today by students of administrative organization. Even Waldo recognized their merits. Yet such works, and their keen insights, are literally forgotten. Thus deprived of its heritage, the profession lacks the temerity to address the organization of homeland security or intelligence activities.

Friedrich versus Finer

In a series of publications that began in the mid-1930s, Carl Friedrich and Herman Finer, two leading (and European-born) political scientists, the former at Harvard, the latter at the London School of Economics (and later at the University of Chicago), debate the guarantors of administrative responsibility.

Friedrich (1940, 6) argues that "public policy, to put it flatly, is a continuous process, the formation of which is inseparable from its execution. Public policy is being formed as it is being executed, and it is likewise being executed as it is being formed. Politics and administration play a continuous role in both formation and execution, *though there is probably more politics in the formation of policy, more administration in the execution of it*" (emphasis added).[23] He spells out the consequences of this view: "We have a right to call . . . a policy irresponsible if it can be shown that it was adopted without proper regard to the existing sum of human knowledge concerning the technical issues involved; we also have a right to call it irresponsible if it can be shown that it was adopted without proper regard for existing preferences in the community, and more particularly its prevailing majority. Consequently, the responsible administrator is one who is responsive to these two dominant factors: technical knowledge and popular sentiment. Any policy which violates either standard, or which fails to crystallize in spite of their urgent imperatives, renders the official responsible for it liable to the charge of irresponsible conduct" (12).[24]

In contrast, Finer (1941, 336) questions whether a subjective sense of responsibility "is sufficient to keep a civil service wholesome and zealous" or whether political responsibility must be imposed as the adamant monitor of the public service. "Are the servants of the public to decide their own course, or is their course of action to be decided by a body outside themselves? My answer is that the servants of the public are not to decide their own course; they are to be responsible to the elected representatives of the public, and these are to determine the course of action of the public servants *to the most minute degree that is technically feasible*" (emphasis added). "Who," asks Finer, "would define the public interest—who could define it? Only the public, I believe, or its deputies. . . . Moral responsibility is likely to operate in direct proportion to the strictness and efficiency of political responsibility, and to fall away into all sorts of perversions when the latter is weakly enforced" (347, 350).

While arguing for "the primacy of the people over officeholders," Finer emphasizes elections and the power to sanction. Popular "mastership needs institutions, and particularly the centrality of an elected organ, for its expression and the exertion of its authority" (337). Also crucial is "the authority and power to exercise an effect on the course which [officials] are to pursue, the power to exact obedience to orders" (337). Finer interprets Friedrich as holding that responsibility is "a sense . . . largely unsanctioned, except by deference or loyalty to professional standards" (335) or by the conscience of the official. To Friedrich, he says, official responsibility is moral, not political, disciplined by a sense of responsibility to the profession, enabled by a superior understanding of the issues; political responsibility is only a minor element in the mechanism of democratic government (342).[25]

As we discuss in the following chapter, the question of law versus discretion, another great debate, was the plot of a multi-institutional drama, with Congress, the president, and the courts grappling with the question from the 1930s to the present day.

So Who's Orthodox?

If the pro–New Deal side of each of these debates might be said to reflect an expedient orthodoxy in Waldo's sense, influential critics within public administration were present and accounted for. Perhaps it is New Deal Democrats, relatively unified in their support of Brownlow committee reforms and in their opposition to the Walter-Logan Act, and not the more fractious public administration profession (that is, its scholars and teachers), that are the truly orthodox in the sense that they continued to press forward with the reform agenda that originated in the Progressive Era.

Strictly academic controversies also sharpened before and during World War II. While implying that a certain unwavering point of view characterized the agendas of administrative reformers, participants in these controversies also suggest that yesterday, no less than today, seemingly entrenched views could expect a vigorous contest.

A. C. Millspaugh (1937, 70), for example, argues that "an evolutionary process produces administrative organizations that are unsightly, sprawling, and apparently haphazard. In reality, however, they reflect with a fair degree of accuracy the social conditions and social changes to which democracy must continually adapt itself."[26] This insight is echoed by contemporary political scientists through claims that administrative agencies are the outcomes of political decisions over their structure, a theme to which we shall turn in chapter 5. Therefore, argues Millspaugh, the "efficiency and economy" movement is theoretically unsound because it "largely disregarded American experience and the implications of popular government" (66). He continues: "It suffered from unimaginativeness, impractical theorizing, and, of course, inadequate factual support. Trapped by superficial analogies and misled by structural appearances, the administrative reorganizer momentarily forgot that democracy is a fundamental issue and a conditioning factor in all aspects of American government" (65).[27]

With the same targets in view, Charles Hyneman's 1939 critique of the state reorganization movement "orthodoxy" is sardonic—and revealing.[28] In the course of condemning the relative lack of dissent from William Willoughby's "doctrinaire justifications of the integrated administrative structure" (63), Hyneman also notes numerous dissenters, including Francis W. Coker (1922), W. H. Edwards (1927, 1928), Millspaugh (1937), Harvey Walker (1930), and the Institute of Government Research at the Brookings Institution, which produced the report discussed above. He quotes Leonard White's (1936, 16, 20) labeling of Willoughby's principles as "hopes, assertions, and opinions" (64–65).[29] "My complaint," says Hyneman, "has been directed against a betrayal of the intellectual [and ethical] obligations of a learned profession" (74). His pungent view of that betrayal, quoted in this chapter's epigram, is a strong indication that efforts by Brownlow and others to preserve a myth of professional unity had decisively failed.

This heterodox chorus, whose origins are in the early 1920s, continued through the war years. Writing in 1951, Wallace Sayre observes that the decade did not begin with unanimity. He cites both John Gaus's 1938 review of Luther Gulick and Lyndall Urwick's 1937 "Studies" and the volume of essays, *Frontiers of Public Administration*, edited by John Gaus, Leonard White, and Marshall Dimock, which emphasizes the engagement of public administration with social and political values. Sayre also places in evidence against orthodoxy books by Chester Barnard, Schuyler Wallace, Arthur Macmahon and John Millett, and Pendleton Herring, among others. "In these, and in other sources, was to be found evidence that *the values of public administration were not yet settled and finite*" (Sayre 1951, 2, emphasis added).

Philip Selznick (1943), in one of the earliest critiques of Max Weber's ideas on bureaucracy, which were just being published in English, argues that Weber fails to understand that hierarchical administration would set up new sources of personal influence by administrators themselves. Along with Friedrich, Selznick's intuitions foreshadow the problem of congressional agency, which we take up in chapter 5: "Action which seeks more than limited, individual results becomes *action through agents*. It is the activity of officials acting as agents with which the discussion of bureaucracy is concerned" (1943, 51).[30]

In the same year, David Levitan provides clear evidence that a scholarly discourse was well under way and that an alternative to "orthodoxy" (his term) could be found in the literature. Criticizing overly narrow interpretations of seminal works, Levitan (1943, 354) argues that "the men who were responsible for the development of the institutional approach [Wilson, Willoughby] themselves realized the importance of the relation between the administration and the broad underlying philosophy of a government. The emphasis on administration as concerned with techniques and means rather than with ends has been so great that sight is often lost of an equally definite aspect of their philosophy of administration."

On this aspect, Levitan (1943, 355) quotes Leonard White—"The general character of administration has always been governed by the physical basis of state organization, by the prevailing level of social and cultural organization, by the development of technology, by theories of the function of the state and by more immediate governmental and political traditions and ideals"—and Schuyler Wallace—"There exists a tendency on the part of many of those who deal with administration to concentrate upon some particular aspect . . . and to ignore or neglect its relations to the process of government as a whole. . . . Those who deal with administration generally do not look upon the study of that subject as requiring the study of government as a whole—much less as necessitating a broad consideration of the economic, social, and psychological characteristics of the society in which they are operating."[31]

Scholars were beginning to take up the theme of democratic *control* of administration. Says Charles Hyneman (1945, 310): "The essential feature of democratic government lies in the ability of the people to control the individuals who have political power." Levitan, while contesting the notion of neutral competence, endorses the validity of a politics-administration dichotomy.[32] He notes, however (1946, 573–574), that "administrative officials do and should assist and advise in both executive and legislative policy determination and are often called upon to give directions to and assume the initiative for initial policy formulations" in the spirit of representative bureaucracy. "The dichotomy has need of correction in so far as it creates two imaginary worlds where administrative policy formulations and executions diverge entirely from each other. But the correction does not lie in the direction of creating another imaginary and arbitrary world where they must become an indistinguishable unity."

"COLLAPSE AND DISINTEGRATION"

However vigorous the field's pre–World War II discourse might seem in retrospect, it was to become even more so beginning in the late 1940s, as the attacks by Waldo, Simon, and Dahl produced their liberating effect.[33] The focus of contention was the fundamental directions of the field itself, and an extraordinary heterodoxy began to emerge. Public administration became "vast and sprawling" (Siffin 1956, 367), without a central analytic framework. "Our values," argues Wallace Sayre, "have moved from a stress upon the managerial techniques of organization and management to an emphasis upon the broad sweep of public policy—its formulation, its evolution, its execution, all either within or intimately related to the frame of administration" (1951, 4). Indeed, as Sayre notes, there were competing values: legislative dominance (Hyneman 1950), administrative autonomy (Long 1949), seamless policy making (Appleby 1949), popular sovereignty (Levitan 1943), representative bureaucracy (Kingsley 1944), and decision making (Simon 1976).[34]

Intellectual developments within a field that now had a formal professional identity in the American Society for Public Administration (ASPA) nevertheless seemed to take three principal directions: a continuation of the search for "essentials" that grew out of traditional public administration; a turn toward the normative foundations of public administration, arguably in reaction to the seeming aimlessness of the search for essentials; and finally a concern for intellectual legitimacy, which is reflected in the theoretical and methodological preoccupations of the field.[35]

The context for these avenues of inquiry consisted of developments outside the field that began to heavily impinge on the field's intellectual agenda, methods, and influence. These developments include the "discovery" of public management by American public policy schools and by European administrative reformers (and the resulting globalization of public administration discourse) and intellectual developments in the field of administrative law (which are discussed in chapter 4), in the disciplines of sociology and psychology, and of particular significance for our argument, in specialized domains such as public choice theory and the economics of organization and information. The cumulative effect of this flourishing heterodoxy was a growing sense within public administration not of robust intellectual health but of crisis and drift—a sense that, incidentally, has never really dissipated.[36]

Where's Waldo?

The earliest expression of this sense of crisis is that of John Millett (1956, 176), who depicts "a somewhat chaotic condition" in the field following the Brookings report of 1937, Herbert Simon's 1946 assault on proverbs, and Dwight Waldo's 1948 book. Matters simmered until Waldo, without a trace of irony, declared a "crisis of identity" within the field in 1968 and suggested that public administration was at the point "of possible collapse and disintegration" (Waldo 1968, 3, 4).[37] Arguably the most articulate expression of emerging angst is that of Vincent Ostrom (1973), who declaims that the profession prescribes bad medicine owing to its flawed classical paradigm. To Kent Kirwan (1977), the crisis is the intellectual vacuum created by the rejection of the field's dichotomy-related positivist orientation on the part of those associated with the Minnowbrook conference and the "new public administration." Though all three critiques identify the same root cause—the "Wilson-Weber paradigm"[38]—their solutions varied dramatically: to Waldo it was professionalism, to Ostrom the replacement paradigm of the Virginia school of political economy, and to Kirwan a "prudential" approach that identifies the values at stake in solving administrative problems.[39]

This perception of crisis in the field was not entirely an internecine matter. Following World War II, argues Gerald Garvey (1995), popular attitudes toward administration shifted. As explored further in chapter 4, legislators and professional elites no longer saw bureaucracy as the principal way to reconcile accountability and capacity. The second Hoover commission (which was created to consider, in the light of the New Deal and World War II expansions of public responsibilities, what the government should and should not do, that is, to consider ends, not means) exemplifies that loss of faith, and it was gone "certainly by 1960" (Garvey 1995, 96). Subsequent public management reform commissions were plainly antagonistic toward bureaucracy, with the Clinton administration's National Performance Review providing a definitive counterpoint to the faith in administrative management expressed in the Brownlow committee report forty-five years earlier. Public administration's parochial intellectual struggle was thus exacerbated as it began to grasp its loss of legitimacy with the public, policy makers, and disciplinary scholars.

That loss of legitimacy was not entirely debilitating, however. Even while the perception of crisis was sharpening and motivating alternative visions of the spirit of public administration (Stillman 1990; Frederickson 1997), the mainstream continued to flow.

Grasping the Scheme Entire

Scholars whose careers began before World War II continued to add to a literature conceived in the traditional spirit. A selective survey of the most prominent works reveals their continuing wisdom and insight if not the kind of intellectual precision that was becoming de rigueur in the disciplines.

As he had for three decades, for example, John Gaus continued to contribute some of the keenest insights. "The fact is," he writes in 1950, "that administration is an aspect, a process, of every phase of government, from the first diagnosis of an emerging problem by a chemist in a health department to the final enforcement in detail of a resulting statute and regulation" (165). Thus we must "steer between the extremes of a vague, general, ambiguous comprehensiveness without savor or focus, and a refinement and specialization that detaches us from the tang and urgency of human action" (166). In one of the field's best known utterances, Gaus insists that "a theory of public administration means in our time a theory of politics also" (168). Expanding on that idea a few years later, he argues that "we have for a half century been expanding our use of formal and informal citizen and client participation in . . . program planning. . . . So widespread is this practice that new conceptions of the nature of the modern state are being formulated from the resulting experience, and have already begun to influence us" (1955, 7).

Charles Hyneman's *Bureaucracy in a Democracy*, published in 1950, is an incisive, analytical work. His concern is with maintaining adequate democratic direction and control of a bureaucracy that might otherwise act in a manner inimical to the public interest. His book is about "how to relate the federal bureaucracy and the power it possesses to the institutions and ways that are essential to democratic government" (12), especially representative institutions. His formulations are worth noting in some detail. "As I see it," he says (43),

> the questions which are crucial to the direction and control of administrative officials and employees relate to the following matters: determination of the governmental activities in which the administrative departments and agencies shall engage (description or definition of the tasks which the bureaucracy shall perform); setting limits to the scope and intensity of the bureaucracy's effort to carry out different governmental activities (usually accomplished by determining how much money shall be available for carrying on each activity); prescribing the conditions under which and the way in which activities shall be carried on; creating and regulating the organization by which activities are carried on; determining what individuals shall have what authority (by selecting, placing, and removing individuals and transferring authority among them); making clear to individuals what their respective tasks and respective obligations are; investigating the conduct of individuals and organizations; and taking action to make sure that things are done the way they are supposed to be done.

Hyneman readily acknowledges the counterarguments. "Those writers who argue most effectively for administrative freedom from the political branches rest their case primarily on three lines of reasoning" (48). The first is the importance of impartial devotion to constitutional mandates as against the threat of partiality and unequal treatment. The second is that administrative officials "can sense more accurately than elected officials what kind of government the American people want" (48). Third, they value popular participation in administration, so that the administrator obtains better information than either the president or Congress as to what "different sectors of the population" really want and will insist upon; "I am sure that the administrative official cannot obtain from the political branches of the government all of the guidance he needs" (52). But, he insists, the other methods for obtaining guidance must supplement, not replace or supplant, political direction. "The American people have authorized nobody except their elected officials to speak for them" (52).[40]

In contrast, Arthur Macmahon (1955) addresses issues relating to the manager's role. "The essence of rational structure for any purpose frequently lies in recognizing how far administration is an argumentative as well as a deliberative process that goes on within the frame of legislation" (40). He continues: "What is the administrator's duty in the light of public interest when, in one way or another, the agency in which he serves is specialized?" (47). The answer, where there is discretion, is "to take the broadest possible view that is consistent with the intent of the law" (48). The administrator's "distinctive general public are those who are affected indirectly but substantially by what is done or not done under that particular law" (48). He must also consider interactions with other public purposes. Finally, he must consider "long-run interacting effects" (49). The safeguards against misuse of discretion or poor judgment concerning legislative intent "lie in attitudes that should be diffused throughout administration" or a "perspective of public interest" (50).

Addressing the issue of "essentials" directly, Fritz Morstein Marx (1957) lists four: "(1) the essential of rationality, (2) the essential of responsibility, (3) the essential of competence, and (4) the essential of continuity" (34). Rationality, he argues, has numerous aspects or meanings: the pursuit of purpose (administration itself is a means to an end); source of cohesion as opposed to "countless clusters of personal influence" (36); application of knowledge; application of reason; as a gatherer of intelligence. Morstein Marx concedes that "ultimately, [rationality] is controlled by its conscious premises or its unconscious predispositions" (40), and he cites as examples the British and French administrations and any colonial administration. But he also sees institutionalized rationality as "putting proposed policy to the acid test of cause-and-effect relationships" (42). Concerning responsibility, he argues that "in structures as elaborate and hence as rich in opportunities for obstruction as is large-scale organization, control could not accomplish co-ordination in the interplay of human wills" (43). Control requires as well "well-formed habits of deference sustained by reason" (43).

In his *Ideal and Practice in Public Administration* (1958), Emmette Redford discusses how the public interest might be identified. He quotes Pendleton Herring (1936): "The *public interest* is the standard that guides the administrator in executing the law. . . . This concept is to the bureaucracy what the 'due process' clause is to the judiciary" (23, Herring's emphasis). What is the reality of the public interest? One reality is that there is a direct expression of the interests of organized groups.[41] Herring insists upon "a working relationship between the bureaucrats and special interests" that "will enable the former to carry out the purpose of the state and the latter to realize their own ends" (24–25). Will a broader public interest be thereby ignored? "Usually, as Herring recognizes, policy making will go beyond mere identification and involve some balancing of group interests involved" (Redford 1958, 111).

But this does not exhaust the possibilities for identifying the public interest. A second approach, according to Redford, recognizes the public's interest in collective goods. "Developments have occurred which create a public need" (112). However, "the generally-shared interest may be compromised with the interests of subgroups which do not share evenly, or perhaps at all, in the prevailing common purpose. Or it may be fostered by subgroups which, in addition to sharing the common purpose, also have particular interests which will be protected or advanced by action for the common welfare" (113). There is, third, a public interest in fair and effective government, including public administration. This leads to the creation of mechanisms for insuring this, for "constitution making" (113). Redford recognizes the threats to the public interest from organized interests. But "protection cannot be found in administration alone. The protections must be found in society, in administration, and in the operation of the government as a whole" (119).[42]

In *Democracy and the Public Service* (1968), Frederick Mosher sets up his problem within a different framework. "Reliance on popularly elected representatives," he argues, "is one step removed from direct participative democracy. A second step occurs when officers so chosen select and delegate powers to other officers, appointed and removable by them. . . . A third step away from direct democracy is taken with the designation of personnel who . . . are protected from removal on political grounds" (3). The central problem is, "How can a public service so constituted be made to operate in a manner compatible with democracy?" (3). Traditional protections against immorality in administration—checks and balances, decentralization, federalism, and others—are less than effective, even negative, as could be career systems and expertise. Mosher endorses Paul Appleby's (1952, 212) two solutions: expose more areas of administration to general political responsibility and hierarchy, not as a basis of authority but as "a means to broaden the perspective for, and the responsibility of, decision."

Evaluating such contributions, the Englishman William Siffin (1956, 367) sees three lines of development: "administrative organization, administrative processes, and general administrative theory or 'administration generally.' "[43] The first, in his view, is almost sociological in emphasis (see for example Max Weber in Gerth and Mills 1946, Chester Barnard, and Philip Selznick) although drawing on many social sciences. The best exemplars of the latter are the works of Dwight Waldo: "The student seeking a penetrating and sophisticated introduction to the background and current status of public administration as a subject of study in the United States will find no substitute for these" (Siffin 1956, 369). John Gaus is also favorably cited, as are Paul Appleby, Norton Long, Carl Friedrich, Leonard White, Herman Finer, and David Truman. "One is impressed and encouraged by the fact that [public administration] is marked not by the dominance of method and technique, but by broad scholarly approaches whose significance lies in their contribution to the recognition of an essential synthesis of administration and government, of policy and execution" (Siffin 1956, 371).

Scholars in the emerging era of heterodoxy during and following World War II began to put forth a variety of nontraditional perspectives on the responsibility of public managers. These perspectives (discussed at greater length in chapter 7) were given prominence at the Minnowbrook conference and in the Minnowbrook-inspired New Public Administration movement, in the Blacksburg Manifesto, and in "the spirit of public administration" (Frederickson 1997). They are nontraditional in that they are normative and antipositivist in spirit and claim to be attuned to changing social conditions, progressive, respectful of minority and unpopular views and, therefore, a good deal more democratic in spirit than traditional public administration. Similar perspectives enjoy continuing popularity within the profession.

These kinds of normative doctrine are, however, constitutionally atheoretical, and many are openly contemptuous of republican institutions. The role of public administration "is not to cower before a sovereign legislative assembly or a sovereign elected executive," says Gary Wamsley and co-authors (1990, 47). "Administrative discretion," argue Michael Spicer and Larry Terry (1993b, 244), "may be justified on the constitutional grounds that it sometimes enables public administrators to modify, delay, or resist the directives of political leaders in a lawful manner." Says H. George Frederickson (1997, 229) in advancing a New Public Administration, public managers "must resist, thwart, or refuse to implement policy that runs counter to the founding documents or to American regime values."

If, however, public managers take it upon themselves to "manage for inclusion" (Feldman and Khademian 2000) and attempt to give back to "the people" powers that the framers assigned to the separate powers, they will almost surely upset the balance of interests struck between Congress and the president, a balance that is, after all, public management's constitutional root, even after judicial review. Public management forswears legitimacy within the separation of powers when it seeks to second-guess and reorient the deliberative results of the political branches and the constitutional reasoning of the judiciary.

The Deepening Crisis

Despite efforts to reinvent Charles Hyneman's secular priesthood with inspirational raiment and ritual, the atmosphere of crisis continues to deepen. Whereas Dwight Waldo, Wallace Sayre, and others once celebrated the advent of heterodoxy in public administration, heterodox developments came to be regarded as a "perils" for the field, as "centrifugal forces" that threatened to further fragment what was left of the field's identity. Donald Kettl (1990, 1993), who became the most persistent commentator to warn of new dangers from within and without, identifies three such forces: the increasing popularity of the implementation perspective, the public management movement associated with the growth of public policy graduate schools, and the intrusion of economic models into political and organizational studies.

Common to each of the new approaches, according to Kettl—straining to glimpse a silver lining—is the effort "to reconcile the different sources of administrative power: delegation . . . expertise . . . and politics" (1993, 421). These new forces are scarcely an advance over the cumulated insights and wisdom of traditional thinking; or rather, they represent a healthy continuity in thinking about governance despite the diversity of origins. These are truths, however, that scholars who embrace the new "out with the old" orthodoxy are precluded from seeing.

Over There

Something "new" was percolating in Europe as well during the 1970s (Aucoin 1990; Pollitt 1990; Kickert 1997), a rapidly growing intellectual movement under the rubric of "public management." Formerly, argue Jan Kooiman and Martijn van Vliet (1993), public management was not a well-developed concept but a fusing of ideological, practical, and scientific ideas. Unlike its American counterpart, the awakened European interest in public management was a political rather than an academic invention. It was directly inspired by the economic crises of the mid-1970s and influenced by the complex challenges of the postwar welfare state. For intellectual capital, Europeans could draw on a fifty-year-old field in America (Kickert 1997), as New Zealand drew on American political economics.

Some European students of bureaucracy and management, like the Waldonians, sought to repudiate their own seemingly entrenched paradigm: the legalistic thinking that had continued to dominate training and practice since the nineteenth century (Kickert 1997). In France especially, owing to the influence of Michel Crozier, Erhard Friedberg, and others, the concept of *management public* gained a following, and the *Institut de Management Public* was created in the 1960s (Crozier and Friedberg 1980). There was an awakening interest in public administration in Germany and latent interest in Great Britain, although these seedlings would later bear fruit (Lynn forthcoming). Desmond Keeling's *Management in Government* (1972) was published when the New Public Administration movement was still in its infancy in America.

Although the substantive orientation of this new European interest in public management was not toward the "best practices" or craft orientation that was increasing popular in the United States (Lynn 1996), "the appeal of the recent managerialist literature lies in the fact that it has been packaged in ways which have addressed issues from the perspective of managers rather than from the perspective of the theorist" (Aucoin 1990, 118). At the same time, European approaches reflect more traditional concepts of administrative science and public administration (Pollitt and Bouckaert 2000). Peter Aucoin (1990) sees two sets of such ideas at work, whose juxtaposition recalls the Friedrich-Finer debate of 1940–1941. One is a private-sector-oriented managerialist ideology first conceptualized by Christopher Pollitt (1990) and manifest in the administrative reforms of the British prime minister Margaret Thatcher, which asserts the primacy of management over bureaucracy. The other, more political, perspective is inspired by public choice theory and the economics of contract (Lane 1993), which establishes the primacy of representative government over bureaucracy. These two sets of ideas lie, in Aucoin's analysis, in sharp tension: managerialism requires a politics-administration dichotomy, Virginia school public choice theory repudiates it.[44]

"There has been an increasing degree of cross-fertilization throughout advanced political systems," Aucoin notes in 1990, "and some considerable spread of these ideas to less advanced political systems" (119). A year later, Christopher Hood (1991) coins a term that becomes a banner for the globalization of public management: New Public Management (NPM). The term is meant to characterize a neo-Taylorian, neocameralist approach to managerial reform, originating with the Thatcher government in Great Britain and with managerialist reforms in New Zealand and Australia. NPM refers to a simulacrum of the allocation of resources by competitive markets that suits neoconservative times: managerial, customer oriented, performance driven (Pollitt 1990; Hood and Jackson 1991; Kickert 1997).

Impressed by the apparently global nature of public management reform and by the family resemblance of its motivations and strategies, academics began creating new international forums for professional discourse on the subject in the 1990s. As Klaus König (1997, 226) notes, "management has become the . . . *lingua franca* in an increasingly internationalised administrative world. It signals that public administration implies planning and coordination, staff recruitment and development, personnel management and control, organisation, and so on, and that allowances must be made in all these respects for the scarcity of resources."

The American field of public administration might find reasons to be cheered by this internationalized discourse. In a sense, it completes a circle begun in 1887 by Woodrow Wilson, who used European precedents as background for his ideas about public administration in the United States. It turns out that both traditional thinking and the scholarly dissent of recent decades resonate in numerous ways with the widening, reform-oriented discourse. In the United States, however, momentum continues to mount behind the argument that the ground is shifting under the field of public administration and that, to avoid collapsing into a rubble of irrelevance, the field must be repositioned on new foundations (Frederickson and Smith 2003; Kettl 2002; Salamon 2002). Unfortunately, what these foundations might be remain as elusive as ever, obscured by a thick overgrowth of controversy, heterodoxy, and crisis. If anything, the field as a self-conscious and self-confident domain of inquiry has regressed.

Fortunately, or so we argue, the requisite foundations already exist. The overgrowth of controversy having been penetrated, we turn to saying what those foundations are.

RESTORING THE FOUNDATIONS

During public administration's first half century, its leading contributors identified and began to confront "the abiding, recurrent problems of governance in liberal democratic regimes" (Pollitt and Bouckaert 2000, 134). Their awareness of the deeper issues at stake in building the American administrative state, of the dilemmas of balancing governmental capacity and democratic control in a formal separation-of-powers regime, is fully evident in the ideas discussed in this and the previous chapter. Even the phrasing betrays intellectual vigor and insight, zest and style: "fine tact" (Finer 1935), "mother wit and logic" (Gulick 1933b), "managerial uncleanliness" (Juran 1944), "wholesome and zealous" (Friedrich 1940), "the tang and urgency of human action" Gaus (1950), "cozenage and barratry" (Hyncman 1939).

Initially, as chapter 2 demonstrates, public administration discourse centered on administrative reform. It was driven by the requirements of mobilizing support for change and of motivating and informing the decisions and actions of policy makers. A premium was placed on proposals that were concise, practical, and unequivocal, on ideas that, experts agreed, addressed the problem and promised success. Within a generation, however, a second, primarily academic discourse emerged that was more about ideas per se than about the programmatic demands of reform. This second discourse was driven by the requirements of conceptual clarity, theory development, and the accumulation of empirical knowledge. A premium was placed on intellectual precision, rigor, and the transparency of methods: on deepening appreciation and understanding of ideas themselves.[45] The point was for experts to disagree, and they did.

If the Waldonian "orthodoxy" has an identity, then, it is primarily in the discourse surrounding civic life and administrative practice. Properly understood, the ideas and doctrines labeled "orthodoxy" are the pragmatic responses of the designers of the administrative state to the specific practical challenges. Such pragmatism was codified into workable programs that address municipal, state, and national policy needs. These founders of the administrative state were attempting to create institutions that would be responsive to the requirements of an increasingly ambitious public policy in ways that comport with our constitutional scheme. The idea that administration is primarily the province of the executive department is a precept for the design of administrative arrangements rather than a contribution to democratic theory. As Dwight Waldo (1984, 75) himself notes (with customary ambiguity —he is accusing Millspaugh of being "too severe"), Wilson, Goodnow, and Cleveland (not to mention Brownlow, Gulick, and Merriam) "were ardently seeking a scheme to save [democracy]. And if the President's Committee believes that 'without results Democracy means nothing' they are entitled to that interpretation. They may be right."

Why has the field of public administration allowed its own intellectual traditions to be distorted into unrecognizable forms, into a second, even more rigid orthodoxy? How can the field countenance the attribution to Wilson and Weber an influence they never had, the distortion of classical ideas, the tolerance if not embrace of the flawed critiques of Simon and Waldo, and the despair over a heterodoxy that is in fact a source of strength?

A likely explanation is that the prestige of the ideas and insights of civic engagement were undermined in the universities, where the field's future lay, by young, influential scholars who, because they pursued new directions in theory and research, were accorded considerable leeway. Perhaps some were offended by the hegemonic tendencies of Louis Brownlow and his activist colleagues. Just as first-generation academics helped establish the legitimacy of Progressive administrative reforms, second-generation academics attacked that legitimacy and, as the nation emerged from economic depression and world war, sought new directions. In the process, they laid waste to what had gone before.

In the light of developments in third- and fourth-generation thinking, there are ironies here. The paradigmatic aspects of the various "new public managements," for example, are no more sophisticated than those of the despised orthodoxy: the private sector is the model, there are principles of good public management, scientific analysis of performance and productive efficiency is essential. There is no less yearning among contemporary Mugwumps for a separation of public management from campaign-finance-addicted politics now than there was then for despoiling the spoils system.

Where, then, shall we turn? Our advice is to heed some wise counselors of an earlier era and restore the concept of responsibility in a republican sense to the center of our concerns. As we show in chapter 5, the tools of modern political economics can be used to show the constitutional efficiency of the administrative state they constructed.

Frederick Cleveland believes that the task of administration is "to supply the link which is missing between government and citizenship" (1913, 454). To do so, the exercise of administrative discretion must be transparently accountable to the people's representatives. What is unquestioned in early thinking is the connection between republican institutions and the public interest. While Progressive reformers often held politicians in contempt, they never sought to evade political oversight. Rather, the instruments that became the standard model of Progressive administrative reform—executive budgets, bureaucratic organizations, legitimizing principles of administration, merit and classification systems—were intended to ensure that citizens and their representatives had sufficient information to judge for themselves whether or not their governments were efficient in the sense of meeting community needs in a nonwasteful manner. In this way, balance among the separate branches of government could be maintained.

We cannot overemphasize the point that, among those whose primary institutional commitment is to effective public administration in a Madisonian world, very little has changed. In matters large and small, the field's traditional ideals and ideas find current expression. This observation suggests a number of questions for inquiry for both normative and positive scholars of public administration.

- Is the challenge of public administration to ensure that citizens trust their governments? We say that it is.
- Are the appropriate extent of detailed control of administration by statute, or the legitimacy of legislative delegations of authority, any less important now than they were to the Progressive reformers? Given the complexities of the measures that contemporary administrators must implement, they are more important.
- Are "principles of administration" still regarded as frameworks for competent performance of public responsibilities that will be regarded as a legitimate use of administrative power? We contend that the answer is yes.
- Is "scientific management" as much in vogue as it ever was? We submit that in the form of performance measurement and accounting, social impact statements, cost-benefit justifications for regulations, and the use of cutting-edge information technologies, it is indeed.
- Are today's elected officials any less concerned than were Theodore Roosevelt, William Howard Taft, and Franklin Roosevelt with maintaining hierarchical control over the uses of appropriated funds in order to ensure that they are

expended in accordance with the policy priorities of elected officials? Certainly not.

- Are the practice models of the General Accounting Office, the Office of Management and Budget, or the numerous management consultancies that market standardized products to public officials any less "rigid" than that of the New York Bureau of Municipal Research or the Institute for Governmental Research? More assumptions to address more contingencies make contemporary approaches more rigid.

- Is "efficiency"—now dressed up as "the elimination of duplication and overlap and of waste, fraud, and abuse"—any less politically salient than it has ever been? Such normative claims are ubiquitous in academic and political commentary.

The founding generations of public administration and management scholars laid hold of the central theoretical problem that continues to be at the center of public administration scholarship: ensuring responsible administration in a constitutional scheme that forces administrative authority to justify itself anew. Early scholarship identifies, if it does not resolve, two great tensions that lie at the heart of public administration: that between governmental capacity and the political control of that capacity, and that between individual justice and collective justice as criteria for responsible administration.

But there are three branches of government, not two, and three relevant intellectual traditions, not two. The legislature (and political science and public choice) and the executive (and public administration and management) are always in the forefront of democratic theory. But the tensions inherent in relations between the two cannot be resolved without the third: the judiciary (and administrative law). It is to the task of restoring the separation of powers that we now turn.

CHAPTER FOUR

Raising the Bar

Law and the Administrative Process

The main thing you need to know about delegation to practice law in
the federal courts can be said in one simple sentence: Congress may
and does lawfully delegate legislative power.   —*Kenneth Culp Davis*

Throughout its history, the field of public administration has been strikingly consistent in one significant respect: its "anti-legal temper" (Waldo 1984, 80). John Gaus (1923–1924, 220) notes that "the new administration . . . claims wide exemption from judicial review of its findings of fact." Says Leonard White (1926, preface), "The study of administration should start from the base of management rather than the foundation of law, and is therefore more absorbed in the affairs of the American Management Association than in the decisions of the courts." As Dwight Waldo (1984, 81) interprets the antilegal temper, "the lawyer suffers from a meager social outlook, the spirit of the New Management does not abide with him."

The most sophisticated reflection of the antilegal temper is that of John Dickinson (1927, 156), who makes the important distinction between administrative adjudication and "matters as to which the government is a direct party in interest, that is, the distribution of pensions or public lands, collection of the revenue, direct governmental performance of public services, and the like." Noting the prevailing skepticism toward legislative delegation by the courts, Dickinson argues that "the needs of the moment, the circumstances of the particular case, all that we mean and express by the word 'policy,' have an importance that professional lawyers do not always allow to them" (150–151). He asks (156): "If . . . we . . . imply that the main purpose of the technical agency is to adjudicate according to rules, will we not have abandoned the characteristic and special advantages of a system of administrative justice, which consists in a union of executive, legislative, and judicial functions in the same body to secure promptness of action, and the freedom to arrive at decisions based on policy?"

Currently only a handful of public administration scholars (see for example Bertelli 2004; Cooper 2000; Moe and Gilmour 1995; O'Leary 1993; Rosenbloom 2003) focus on the legal aspects of administration. The role of administrative law is generally regarded as a specialized topic within the broader field of public administration—equivalent to personnel management and financial management—rather than a fundamental aspect of managing in the public sector. Most contemporary works on the current and future state of the field neglect not only the role of administrative law but also the implications of the separation of powers for democratic governance, which is the intellectual foundation of both administrative law and, we argue, public administration.

A significant consequence of this neglect is that the field remains isolated from intellectual and institutional developments that provide the kinds of insights that might help in overcoming its pervasive sense of crisis and irrelevance. In effect, public administration scholarship takes little cognizance of a field, administrative law, that is the primary source of ideas concerning how the separation of powers affects public administration. The negative consequences of this neglect are compounded by the fact (noted in chapter 1) that public administration scholars and practitioners have the power to put their views concerning the implications of that separation for public administration into actual practice. By ignoring these views, public administration contributes to its own powerlessness.

In this chapter, we review developments in the field of American administrative law from its inception to the present, developments that occurred while public administration, in its antilegal temper, slept. Our intention in recounting these developments, particularly the most recent ones, is to establish their fundamental relevance to a field, public administration, which shares with it a fundamental need to comprehend the separation of powers in a very nuanced way. With that convergence established, the intellectual and practical significance of the precept of managerial responsibility, which we describe in detail in chapter 6, will become clear.

FROM NONDELEGATION TO DELEGATION: AN OVERVIEW

Administrative law in the United States developed at the federal level as a set of default rules for the "contracts" whereby Congress delegated powers to administrative agencies through the language of enabling statutes (Bertelli forthcoming). By examining the development of American administrative law from this premise, we present a history of attempts to define public management itself, beginning with the earliest of these delegations.

Early decisions by U.S. courts first situated public management within the executive branch but granted it only so-called executive powers, placing the president at the head of administration. This situation prevailed until the 1880s, when Congress created the Interstate Commerce Commission, thereby reviving the question of the character of the powers that might be lawfully exercised by the executive branch. Through a series of decisions, the courts enunciated a *nondelegation doctrine*: no legislative powers could be delegated by Congress to the executive branch.[1]

As the twentieth century began, however, more and more regulatory power was assigned to the executive branch, and enabling statutes became less and less detailed, leaving the courts unable to conceive of nondelegation tests in practice. With the exception of three cases during the New Deal, the nonedelegation doctrine was never applied, though it was never officially extinguished either.[2]

By the 1960s, administrative law experts were suggesting that the president should be allowed to regain control over administrative management: in effect a call for presidential dominance of administration. Tensions over the delegation of legislative power would resurface in the Supreme Court during the 1980s, with the Court generally upholding reasonable resort to discretionary actions by administrative agencies unless Congress specifically disallowed such actions in statutory language. Thus Congress could dominate administrative agencies, but it would have to be specific in its intent to do so.

From their inception as an instrument of governance, administrative agencies exercised adjudicatory powers when they determined the status of regulated individuals, companies, or benefit claimants. This power was judicial, not executive or legislative, however, and the power of the courts in the "state of courts and parties" that emerged in the nineteenth century (Skowronek 1982) was not easily relinquished by the bar to administrative agencies. The competition for control over the judicial powers of administrative agencies has become the dominant theme in the development of American administrative law.

Thus, as noted by Dickinson, administrative agencies exercise a mix of legislative, executive, and judicial power, which differs under each enabling statute. In what follows, we describe the way in which the courts and legal scholars attempt to define and circumscribe these powers. Their efforts have both legitimized the special advantages of the "technical agency" and situated public management, *as a matter of law*, within the separation of powers.

The Origins of American Administrative Law

Delegation to administration in the United States began on July 31, 1789, when Congress granted the power to "estimate the duties payable" on imports, among other things (Pierce 2002, 8). The language of this first delegation instantly created the often noted distinction between *rulemaking*—the authority to set standards applicable to broad ranges of cases—and *adjudication*—courtlike dispensation of a single case. Can the customs service estimate duties as guidelines? How might it do this? Do those on whom customs duties are levied have rights of appeal? The process of administration, then, has extraordinarily legalistic qualities. Martin Shapiro (1981, 21) writes: "The congruence of administering and judging must be specially noted. Indeed, the observer who did not so firmly believe in the independence of judging might take judging for a special facet of administering. Both the judge and administrator apply general rules to particular situations on a case-by-case basis. Both tend to rely heavily on precedent, fixed decisional procedures, written records, and legalized defense of their decisions. Both are supplementary lawmakers engaged in filling in the details of more general rules. Both are front-line social controllers for more distant governing authorities."

These similarities make administrative action a topic of profound interest for the bar, and it is the bar's interest and efforts to protect it that drives the story of American administrative law.

Administrative law scholars and practitioners often refer to public administration as "administrative process" (see for example Landis 1938). This usage brings the tension between the individual justice of due process values and the collective justice of agency policy making into sharp relief. This tension becomes stronger in practice, moreover, because American courts, like their English counterparts, are strong institutions. From John Marshall's battles with Thomas Jefferson through the codification movement of the Jacksonian period, the common law courts asserted themselves as something that could transcend democratic politics.[3] In 1826, James Kent's *Commentaries* (1971) ushered in the "treatise tradition . . . to propound the orthodox view that law is a science and that legal reasoning is inherently different than political reasoning" (Horwitz 1992, 10).

The court's strength is exemplified as follows. In 1864, just after Lincoln's defeat of McClellan in an election that was a referendum on no less than the union itself, Chief Justice Taney—a strong Marshallian federalist except in matters of race and slavery, as the *Dred Scott* decision demonstrates—wrote the opinion in *Gordon v. United States*, 117 U.S. 697 (1864). The case dealt with the reviewability of decisions by the Court of Claims, amended by statute the previous year to provide for judicial review by the Supreme Court. Taney, denying appellate jurisdiction and rebuking Congress, writes, "Congress may undoubtedly establish tribunals with special powers to examine testimony and decide, in the first instance, upon the validity and justice of any claim for money against the United States, subject to the supervision and control of Congress, or a head of any of the executive departments" (*Gordon*, 699). Nonetheless, "whether this court can be required or authorized to hear appeal from such a tribunal . . . is a very different question" (*Gordon*, 699). He continues: "The existence of this court is . . . as essential to the organization of the government established by the Constitution as the election of a President or members of Congress. . . . The position and rank . . . assigned to this court in the government of the United States, differ from that of the highest judicial power in England, which is subordinate to the legislative power, and bound to obey any law that Parliament pass, though it may, in the opinion of the court, be in conflict with the principles of Magna Charta or the Petition of Rights" (*Gordon*, 705).[4]

But the oddity about *Gordon* is that the case was presented to the Court on December 18, 1863, and docketed for argument on the second day of the forthcoming October term. Chief Justice Taney passed away on October 12, 1864, and the case was not argued until January 3, 1865. As Justice Waite observes in *United States v. Jones*, 119 U.S. 477, 478–479 (1886), "the opinion published as an appendix to 117 U.S. 697 must have been prepared by him before the decision was actually made." In *Jones*, the court was confronted with the standing of *Gordon* as good law. Justice Waite notes that "at the next session of Congress after this decision the objectionable section was repealed by the act of March 17, 1866. . . . From that time until the presentation of this motion it has never been doubted that appeals would lie. Indeed, immediately after the repealing act went into effect, and before the adjournment of the term then being held, a set of rules regulating such appeals was promulgated by this court, and it is safe to say that there has never been a term since in which many cases of the kind have not been heard and decided without objection from any one."

In odd microcosm, *Gordon* represents the grappling with the separation of powers that went on throughout the nineteenth century. The courts, as Taney's opinion suggests, achieved and maintained authority both separate and against that of Congress. Congress retained its authority through the ability to pass corrective legislation, and the interbranch strategic interaction that characterizes contemporary American politics was born and bred. The place of public administration, however, has taken much longer to define, as our preceding chapters detail. At law, the separation of powers questions over administration began with a relative lack of controversy as a matter of executive government.

Presidential Dominance

In *Williams v. United States*, 42 U.S. (1 Howard) 290, (1843), the Supreme Court dealt with the issue of subdelegations within the executive. It had been contended that an 1823 congressional act "expressly prohibits the advancing of public money in any case whatsoever, except under the special direction of the President" (*Williams*, 296). The extreme antifederalist Justice Daniel wrote for the majority: "Such an interpretation of the law this court may by no means admit. . . . It can never be reasonable to ascribe to [Congress] a conduct which must defeat every beneficial end they could have in view and render the government an absolutely impracticable machine" (*Williams*, 297). "The President's duty," the opinion continues, "in general requires his superintendence of the administration; yet this duty cannot require of him to become the administrative officer of every department and bureau. . . . This cannot be, 1st, Because, if it were practicable, it would be to absorb the duties and responsibilities of the various departments . . . in the personal action of the one chief executive officer. It cannot be, for the stronger reason, that it is impracticable—nay, impossible" (*Williams*, 297).[5]

In 1855 President Fillmore asked Attorney General Caleb Cushing the following question: "Are instructions by Heads of Departments to officers, civil or military, within their respective jurisdiction, valid and lawful, without containing express reference to the direction of the President?" (quoted in Goodnow 1906, 41). In *Williams* and in *United States v. Eliason*, the Supreme Court held that an action taken by the head of an executive agency was tantamount to an action taken by the president himself.[6] Cushing, who would later help negotiate for the United States a right of way across the isthmus of Panama, writes, "The Constitution provides for the subdivision of the executive powers, vested in the President among administrative departments. . . . What those 'executive departments' shall be, either in number or in functions, the Constitution does not say" (quoted in Goodnow 1906, 41). Cushing answers the president's question affirmatively: "It could not, as a general rule, be otherwise, because in the President is the executive power vested by the Constitution, and also because the Constitution commands that he shall take care that the laws be faithfully executed; thus making him not only the depository of the executive power, but the responsible executive minister of the United States" (quoted in Goodnow 1906, 42).[7]

Cushing's reasoning evoked comparative themes prominent in early American jurisprudence. In the most common form of legislation, he writes, "in which an executive act is, by law, required to be performed by a given Head of Department . . . I hold that no Head of Department can lawfully perform an *official* act against the will of the President; and that will is by the Constitution to govern the performance of all such acts. If it were not thus, Congress might by statute so divide and transfer the executive power as to utterly subvert the government, and change it into a parliamentary despotism, like that of Venice or Great Britain, with a nominal executive chief utterly powerless,—whether under the name of Doge, King, or President, would then be of little account, so far as regards the question of the maintenance of the Constitution" (quoted in Goodnow 1906, 43).

Thus early administrative law in the United States, such as it was, conflates administrative action with faithful execution of the laws and, correspondingly, with the powers of Article II. Though the courts never overruled an 1887 case requiring the personal judgment of the president in approving an army officer's dismissal following a court martial, they have circumvented it (Pierce 2002, 110).[8] An important example came in 1897 as the Supreme Court continued to express a restrictive view of judicial meddling with executive administration. In *White v. Berry*, 171 U.S. 366 (1897), a gauger in the Treasury Department had been removed from office for what he perceived to be political reasons after the passage of the Pendleton Act. His suit was technically voided.[9] However, Justice Harlan (the "Great Dissenter" who would support the Interstate Commerce Commission against the trusts) writes: "If the assignment of some one to duty as gauger . . . in the place of the plaintiff, did not work his removal from office, a court of equity ought not to assume to control the discretion which under existing statutes the Executive Department has in all such matters. Interference by the judicial department in such cases would lead to the utmost confusion in the management of executive affairs" (*White*, 366, 378). As we discuss in chapter 5, the Court's patronage jurisprudence turned away from this view in the 1970s.

In 1951, Congress directly addressed the subdelegation problem in Title 3, sections 301–303, of the United States Code by providing that the president "is authorized to designate and empower the head of any department or agency in the executive branch, or any official thereof who is required to be appointed by and with the advice and consent of the Senate, *to perform without approval ratification or any other action by the President,* (1) any function which is vested in the President by law, or (2) any function which such officer is required or authorized by law to perform only with or subject to the approval, ratification, or other action of the President: *Provided,* That nothing contained herein shall relieve the President of his responsibility in office for the acts of any such head or other official designated by him to perform such functions" (3 U.S.C., section 301, 2000; emphasis in original).[10] This statute effectively curtailed the judicial development of subdelegation doctrine. But, nondelegation remained an issue.

The Proverbs of Nondelegation

The separation of powers is born of a fear of the tyranny possible, or even probable, when those who make the laws also facilitate their implementation and execution. Such concerns can be found in the writings of John Locke and the Baron de la Brède et de Montesquieu, James Madison, and Thomas Jefferson, as well as the jurisprudence of the U.S. Supreme Court.[11]

Justice John Marshall, whose federalism defines the courts as expositors of constitutional law, writes for the majority in the 1825 case of *Wayman v. Southard*, 23 US (10 Wheaton) 1 (1825): "It will not be contended that Congress can delegate to the courts, or to any other tribunal, powers which are strictly and exclusively legislative. But Congress may certainly delegate to others, powers which the legislature may rightfully exercise itself" (*Wayman*, 15). Nonetheless, the Court reasons, "the line has not been exactly drawn which separates those important subjects, which must be entirely regulated by the legislature itself, from those of less interest, in which a general provision may be made, and power given to those who are to act under such general provisions to fill up the details" (*Wayman*, 16).[12]

A change had been effected—one that came to be called the "nondelegation doctrine"—in another opinion by Justice Harlan in the 1892 case of *Field v. Clark*.[13] In upholding the president's authority to modify import duties, the Court draws some lines between executive and legislative power and, in making these distinctions, implies that the courts have the power to make such determinations: "What the President was required to do was simply in execution of the act of Congress. It was not the making of law. He was the mere agent of the law-making department to ascertain and declare the event upon which its expressed will was to take effect" (*Field*, 693). In dissent, but concurring in the judgment, Justice Lamar, who had served as special consul to Russia on behalf of the Confederacy, presents the nondelegation doctrine: "That no part of this legislative power can be delegated by Congress to any other department of the government, executive or judicial, is an axiom in constitutional law, and is universally recognized as a principle essential to the integrity and maintenance of the system of government ordained by the Constitution. The legislative power must remain in the organ where it is lodged by that instrument" (*Field*, 697).

Of the period between 1892 and 1935, Kenneth Culp Davis (1977, 34) writes: "So the Court reiterated the nondelegation doctrine, but along with the reiteration, it sustained one delegation after another." He continues, "the verbiage gradually developed that a delegation was lawful only when accompanied by a sufficient 'standard.' "[14] Nonetheless, Davis concludes, "sometimes telling the agency what to do is the practical equivalent of instructing it: 'Here is the problem. Deal with it' " (34–35). Regardless of Davis's pragmatism, the Supreme Court has not allowed the nondelegation doctrine to die quietly. In 1935–1936, it invalidated three New Deal statutes as standardless under the nondelegation doctrine.[15] In a concurrence in one such case, A.L.A. Schechter Poultry Corp. v. United States, Justice Cardozo sounds a fearful warning: "This is delegation running riot."

Nevertheless, nondelegation is most likely not the law today, though it emerges from time to time. Even in 1946, when a district court in California relied on the cases decided one decade earlier, it was reversed by the Supreme Court.[16] However, in the 1980s, three cases find justices, in dicta or dissent, heralding a revival of the nondelegation doctrine.[17] In Industrial Union Dept. v. American Petroleum Institute, 488 U.S. 607 (1980), Justice Rehnquist writes: "The Court should once more take up its burden of ensuring that Congress does not unnecessarily delegate important choices of social policy to politically unresponsive bureaucrats" (Industrial Union, 686). Concurring in Loving v. United States, 517 U.S. 748 (1996) Justices Scalia and O'Connor opine that "legislative power is nondelegable" (777). "Congress can no more 'delegate' some of its Article I power to the Executive than it could 'delegate' some to one of its committees. What Congress does is to assign responsibilities to the Executive; and when the Executive undertakes those assigned responsibilities, it acts, not as the 'delegate' of Congress, but as the agent of the people. At some point the responsibilities assigned can be so extensive and so unconstrained that Congress has in effect delegated its legislative power; but until that point of excess is reached, there exists not a 'lawful' delegation, but no delegation at all" (emphasis in original).[18] But delegable it has proven to be.

Delegation Running Riot

As we have seen, some constitutional law with regard to the delegation of powers has existed for some time. Nonetheless, as Frank Goodnow (1902, 6–7) observes, "the general failure in England and the United States to recognize an administrative law is really due not to the nonexistence in these countries of this branch of the law but rather to the well-known failure of English writers to classify the law." Of course, Goodnow is referring to A. V. Dicey's parliamentary supremacy argument, which holds that parliament could delegate no legislative power since it is the only holder of that power on behalf of the people. Such a rule has roots in Locke: "The power of the legislative, being derived from the people by a positive voluntary grant and institution, can be no other than what the positive grant conveyed, which being only to make laws, and not to make legislators, the legislative can have no power to transfer their authority of making laws and place it in other hands" (Locke, *Second Treatise on Government*, section 14). Nonetheless, writes Frederick Maitland (1948, 505–506), "if you take up a modern volume of the reports of the Queen's Bench division, you will find that about half of the cases have to do with rules of administrative law."

In *Law and Social Order in the United States*, James Willard Hurst (1977) observes that the contributions of the Congress and the executive branch to American administrative law follow the pattern depicted in figure 1. Beginning with the Customs Service delegation in the first Congress, legislation regarding the execution of laws was substantial, while administration added few rules beyond those written in statutory delegations. However, Hurst writes, by the end of the nineteenth century, "the regulatory component of statute law became much more prominent, and added considerably to the volume of legislation" (36). As a result, he continues, "the focus changed from enabling organized action to injecting more public management or supervision of affairs and providing more sustained, specialized means of defining and enforcing public policy" (36).[19] The sea change would occur in the decade between 1905 and 1915. Hurst observes that "by the 1920s, it was plain that the bulk of lawmaking was by legislation or by executive or administrative action under statutory delegation" (38).

Then came the New Deal and the explosion of statutory law to fuel a burgeoning welfare state. "By the 1950s," writes Hurst (1977, 41), "lawyers with business clients and individuals with demands on the increasing service functions of government had to turn more to administrative rule books than to statute books to locate the legal frame of reference for their affairs."

It is not surprising, then, that public administrationists would begin their most earnest activity toward developing a profession in the 1905–1915 period. That history is often thought to have begun in the 1870s, when the civil service movement challenged the Jacksonian conception of executive government and the Progressive movement moved for reform in nothing less than American political culture.[20] David Rosenbloom (1994, 5) observes that "the short ballot, primary election, referendum, recall, and direct election of senators was of great importance" to the reformers of the era. Also critical was "installing merit systems in local and state governments and strengthening regulations to take public employees out of partisan politics" (6).

But the parallel history of the response of the judiciary, and very importantly, the legal profession itself, is quite different. Indeed, that history represents a mirror image of the development of public administration as a profession and structure of

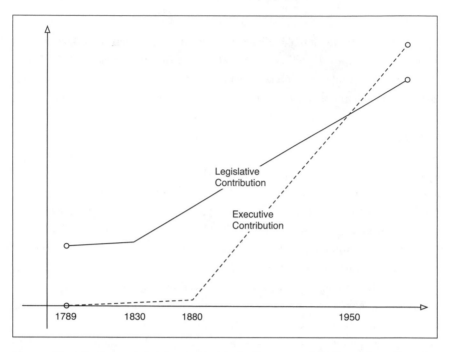

Figure 1. Contributions to Administrative Activity by Congress and the Executive, 1789 to the Present

governance. Some lawyers, such as Elihu Root, were sympathetic to grants of broad authority to administration. In his presidential address to the American Bar Association in 1916, Root (1916, 749–750) says: "Before these agencies the old doctrine prohibiting the delegation of legislative power has virtually retired from the field and given up the fight. There will be no withdrawal of these experiments. We shall go on; we shall expand them, whether we approve theoretically or not, because such agencies furnish protection to rights and obstacles to wrongdoing which under our new social and industrial conditions cannot be practically accomplished by the old and simple procedure of legislatures and courts as in the last generation." Nonetheless, Root admonishes that "the rights of the citizen against [these agencies] must be made plain" (750).

An example of the rights questions at issue during this time is the question of a regulatee's or citizen's right to be heard before an agency. In *Londoner v. Denver*, 210 U.S. 373, 386 (1908), an agency assessed the costs of street paving, allowing written objections but no hearing. In an opinion by Justice Moody, who had prosecuted Lizzie Borden in Massachusetts before his elevation, the court holds that a hearing is required: "Even here a hearing in its very essence demands that he who is entitled to it shall have the right to support his allegations by argument however brief, and, if need be, by proof, however informal." In a second foundational case, *Bi-Metallic Inv. Co. v. State Board of Equalization*, 239 U.S. 441, 445 (1915), Justice Oliver Wendell Holmes Jr., after dissenting in *Londoner*, penned the Court's holding that in a case concerning property valuations for the entire land base of Denver, Colorado, no hearing is required: "Where a rule of conduct applies to more than a few people, it is impracticable that everyone should have a direct voice in its adoption. The Constitution does not require all public acts to be done in town meeting or an assembly of the whole. General statutes within the state power are passed that affect the person or property of individuals, sometimes to the point of ruin, without giving them a chance to be heard. Their rights are protected in the only way they can be in a complex society, by their power, immediate or remote, over those who make the rule."

Concerns over rights such as these ushered in an era of opposition to administrative authority by lawyers and many judges, an opposition that James Landis (1938, 4) calls a "chorus of abuse and tirade." Richard Pierce (2002, 11) notes that to the present day "the bar sometimes continues its efforts to undermine administrative power . . . by arguing in support of increasingly elaborate, expensive, and time-consuming procedural formalities to govern agency decision making." He conjectures that "there may simply be an inevitable tension between the nation's need for an efficient and effective bureaucracy and the bar's desire for constantly increasing procedural formality."

Finding Rules outside the Statute Book

Regulatory bureaucracies were simply not popular with the legal establishment, despite the support of some key legal voices such as Elihu Root, Felix Frankfurter, James Landis, and others. After concluding his service as solicitor general in the Harding administration, Representative James Beck (1933, ix) writes, "Uncle Sam has not yet awakened from his dream of government by bureaucracy, but even wanders further afield in crazy experiments in state socialism." He continues, "possibly some day he may awaken from his irrational dreams, and return again to the old conception of government, as wisely defined in the Constitution of the United States." Beck resigned from the House of Representatives in disgust in 1934 and died two years later.

Morton Horwitz (1992, 216) locates the ire of conservatives like Beck in a challenge to their "delegation theory," under which "separation of powers theory created the framework for administrative action." He continues, "under this view, the legislature would decide all questions of policy and establish clear standards and goals. The

essential task of bureaucratic officials was to find the most efficient means to implement clear, legislatively elaborated ends." "The courts' role," Horwitz says, "was to
police this relationship by limiting administrative authority to clear delegations of
power from the legislature."

In the 1935 oral arguments in *Schechter Poultry*, we see the tension among the
branches concerning delegation theory in an exchange over the question of judicial
review. Stanley Reed, the solicitor general in the Roosevelt administration, and
Justice James McReynolds, one of the anti-Roosevelt "four horsemen of reaction"
and widely recognized as arrogant, ill-tempered, and anti-Semitic, though surely
conservative, debated the president's authority under the National Industrial Recovery Act, the most sweeping legislation of the New Deal. Part of their debate is given
here (Kurland and Casper 1975, 863):[21]

> *Mr. Justice McReynolds:* Is there any provision for a court review . . . any opportunity to
> be heard as to their reasonableness or otherwise?
>
> *Mr. Reed:* There is no provision for court review. But the government is of the opinion,
> of course, that the codes are subject to attack in cases such as this.
>
> *Mr. Justice McReynolds:* Yes, but can the code provisions be tested in the courts, in any
> way? Has a man the opportunity to go into the courts if he thinks those codes infringe
> his rights?
>
> *Mr. Reed:* There is no machinery provided when it passes from the approval of the
> President by which a test of the code can be made in the court, as in the Federal Trade
> Commission Act.
>
> *Mr. Justice McReynolds:* Well do they not have, in the case of the carriers under the In-
> terstate Commerce Act, some opportunity to be heard in court before the order is ef-
> fective?
>
> *Mr. Reed:* Some opportunity to be heard? I do not recall that in the language of the
> statute.
>
> *Mr. Justice McReynolds:* In the case of both the Interstate Commerce Commission
> and the Federal Trade Commission?
>
> *Mr. Reed:* Both of those are subject to court review.
>
> *Mr. Justice McReynolds:* Yes, and is that not the general rule—that there must be some
> chance to test it in court?
>
> *Mr. Reed:* I should say it had been done more often that way than otherwise.

Indeed, the 1880 Interstate Commerce statute was written in a very detailed
fashion, but by 1914 the attitude had shifted, and the statute directing the formation
of the Federal Trade Commission delivered an extremely broad delegation. This
shift was in no small part due to the difficulty the Interstate Commerce Commission

had in performing its duties under all of that detail. In his influential Storrs Lectures, James Landis (1938, 68–69), who had served as chairman of the Securities and Exchange Commission (SEC) and became a great champion of administration, writes of the problem: "Detailed regulative provisions encumber the Interstate Commerce Act. Indeed, that Act has ceased to have the appearance of a consistent document and resembles rather a regulative code." The political scientist Samuel Huntington (1953) calls it and the plight of the commission a case of marasmus. "The result of using such a technique," continues Landis (69), "is to call over and over again for Congressional amendments. Hardly a Congressional session concludes which has not passed some amendment of a minor or major nature to the Interstate Commerce Act." This *legislative-centered* delegation theory—with a strong and meddlesome principal—is an attempt to directly operationalize the politics-administration dichotomy.

An alternative might be called *bureau-centered* administration and is the theory behind the New Deal agencies. Of his own SEC, Landis (1938, 69) notes, "with broad rule-making powers vested in the Commission, amendment becomes necessary only when the administrative state is faced with primary problems affecting its powers. Such delegation of power means, of course, that the rules will be found outside the statute book." Thus Landis foreshadows the primacy of the agency in determining the rules relevant to practice, as shown in Figure 1, from the 1950s to the present. With the passage of the Federal Register Act in the 1930s—mandating publication of proposed rules in a central outlet—the administrative contribution to administrative law became as public as statutory law.

Landis, then, proposes a pragmatic delegation theory, to replace that based in separation of powers. "The chief virtue of this modern tendency toward delegation," he tells his Yale students (1938, 69), "is that it is conducive to flexibility," which he calls "a prime quality of good administration." The theme of discretion in public administration had come to intersect with influential thinking in administrative law, foreshadowing an era, which culminated in the Administrative Procedure Act of 1946 (APA), when public administrationists and administrative lawyers forged a compromise that has had lasting effects. Unlike Congress—the cornerstone of law making in the old delegation theory—"the administrative is always in session," writes Landis (1938, 69), summoning Montesquieu's ghost but defining a new problem: A centralized agency "gives some assurance against the entry of impertinent considerations into the deliberations relating to a projected solution." Agency capture and "iron triangles" had come to define a modern version of the problem of conflating legislative and executive powers in a single source.

Somewhat ironically, a bureau-centered theory of the administrative process has

significant advantages for the legislature. "Those with . . . an insight into the difficulties attendant upon bridging the chasm between the phrase 'Be it enacted' and
law in the sense of controlling human affairs," writes Landis (1938, 70), "recognize
that it is a lot easier to plot a way through a labyrinth of detail when it is done in the
comparative quiet of a conference room than when it is attempted amid the turmoil
of a legislative chamber or committee room." Still, this pragmatic lesson left the bar
uneasy, because a form of justice in executing the laws based on administrative
process was heavily dependent on expertise with what seemed to be a removal of the
judicial review prong of the old delegation theory.

Of Marxism and Whippersnappers

In 1934 the American Bar Association (ABA) formed a Special Committee on
Administrative Law, chaired by the venerable Harvard professor and former botanist
Roscoe Pound. Though Pound was "among the earliest thinkers to observe that . . .
the complexity of industrial society . . . undermined [the nineteenth-century Progres-
sive] identification of generality with predictability," he made an "abrupt about-face"
in his service to the bar on this committee (Horwitz 1992, 219). Pound considered the
administrative process to be Marxist, telling the Allegheny County Bar Association in
Pittsburgh a frightening story: "Professor Paschukanis, economic and social advisor
of Soviet Russia . . . told us that in the soviet state . . . there were no laws but only
administrative orders and ordinances. The professor is not with us now. . . . If there
had been law instead of administrative orders it might have been possible for him to
lose his job without losing his life" (Pound 1940, 127).[22] In 1936 Pound's committee
concludes—in contrast to Dickinson's seeming acceptance—that the developing
administrative state brings with it two grave concerns: first, judicial, legislative, and
executive functions were being combined with abandon; and second, independent
control of administrative action was often absent.

Pound worried that "administrative absolutism" would, over time, completely
undermine the rule of law. We had come 180 degrees from the concerns of Caleb
Cushing in 1855: The executive now had too much power. Writes Morton Horwitz
(1992, 222), "the rise of administrative regulation thus represented a renewed threat to
common law conceptions of legality, which had already resisted the earlier challenges to codification." The Pound committee challenged the bar to take action lest
the bureaus overtake the place of the courts in American government. The four
horsemen of reaction on the Supreme Court were drawing similarities between the
SEC and the Star Chamber, whose actions hastened the English Civil War (*Jones v.
Securities and Exchange Commission*, 298 U.S. 1, 28, 1936).

What had ripened was bitter conflict between the *collective justice* goals of the bureaus and commissions and the *individual justice* orientation of the courts. Horwitz (1992, 222) observes that courts "sought to insist upon judicial ideals of justice in the individual case even for systems of economic regulation devised to provide only rough justice over a vastly expanded number of cases." In the Pound committee, one sees the old legal formalism of the nineteenth century, A. V. Dicey's parliamentary superordination, and the "state of courts and parties" (Skowronek 1982). In Landis, one finds the scientism of public administration and scientific management and the legal realism and, ironically, Pound's own "sociological jurisprudence." The Gettysburg of this conflict would come in 1939 with the introduction of Senate bill 915 by Senator Mills Logan, which Louis Jaffe would call "a bill to remove the seat of government to the Court of Appeals for the District of Columbia" (Jaffe 1939, 1232).

This Ungodly Combination

In 1936, before the battle over the Walter-Logan bill, a contemplative Justice Harlan Fisk Stone (1936, 16–18) suggested that "the time has come for a more ready recognition that the procedures worked out by administrative bodies have realized [a balancing of individual and collective justice] largely without the coercive intervention of the court, and that they have set up standards for the appraisal of the specialized experience with which they are concerned, which courts could have formulated, if at all, only more tardily and with greater difficulty." Stone was a Republican appointed to the Court by President Coolidge. He came to support New Deal programs and wrote the famous "footnote four" in *United States v. Carolene Products*, 304 U.S. 144 (1938). He died reading a dissent into the record. Though Stone saw the need to condone, at law, the administrative process, the bar took the opposing course in the Pound committee report.

To compete with the Pound committee, President Roosevelt established the Attorney General's Committee on Administrative Procedure, chaired by Walter Gellhorn. Gellhorn and Kenneth Culp Davis, through their work on the committee and afterward, would situate themselves among the most important administrative law scholars in American history. Gellhorn and Davis were very much in favor of administrative discretion and the view expressed above by Justice Stone. They studied each agency and commission carefully and generated a report in 1941, which became a key source for understanding the administrative state in the decades that followed. Before their work could be completed, however, the bar would make its most aggressive step toward judicial dominance of the administrative process in sponsoring the Walter-Logan bill.

That bill would have imposed courtlike proceedings on the decision-making activity of nearly every agency except the Interstate Commerce and Federal Trade Commissions, perennial favorites of those supporting the bill in Congress. Administrative agencies would have been required to hold hearings and justify their decisions with substantial evidence and facts, and judicial review would have been available to anyone "significantly" affected by administrative action (West 1985, 75). Representative Emmanuel Celler, a conservative Democrat who would represent his Brooklyn district for fifty years, told his colleagues on the House Judiciary Committee that the nearly universal judicial review required under the proposed legislation myopically reflected conservative frustration with burgeoning administrative policy making. In his experiences with the Department of Labor, he says, "I have been confronted with mere 'whippersnappers'—young students just out of law school—who apparently are given undue authority in originating, if not effectuating, final decisions." Nevertheless, he contends that Walter-Logan "would simply mean that . . . judges would substitute their views for those of the administrative officers. . . . This would involve endless litigation. Anyone aggrieved could bring action and tie into knots the activities of the agency for months and months" (quoted in Shepherd 1996, 1605).

Celler's remarks would identify the rub between the bar and congressional positions for years to come. It was the difference between "administrative process" and "public management." If procedures were to become increasingly judicialized, then the administrative process would move ever slower. What lay in the balance was, of course, administrative *responsibility* as we define it. Then solicitor general (and later maverick justice) Robert Jackson (1940, 146–147)—writes of the tension: "Those who dislike [regulatory] activities . . . rightly conceive that if they can destroy the administrative tribunal which enforces regulation, they would destroy the whole plan of regulation itself." Said Walter Gellhorn of Senator Logan, cosponsor of the bill, over forty years later, "When I saw him he would get really red in the face and say, 'Oh, it's ha-a-a-rd to do.' All we're trying to do is end this ungodly combination of judge, jury, and prosecutor! We're seeking to require due process. Now who can be against that?!?" (Davis and Gellhorn 1986, 515).

The Walter-Logan bill passed both houses but was vetoed by President Roosevelt. In his veto message, Roosevelt excoriated the bar for attempting to destroy the regulatory state: "Many of the lawyers prefer the stately ritual of the courts, in which lawyers play all the speaking parts, to the simple procedure of administrative hearings which a client can understand and participate in. Many of the lawyers prefer that decisions be influenced by a shrewd play upon technical rules of evidence in which the lawyers are the only experts, although they always disagree. Many of the lawyers still prefer to distinguish precedent and to juggle leading cases rather than to get down to the merits of the efforts in which their clients are engaged. For years, such lawyers have led a persistent fight against the administrative tribunal" (Horwitz 1992, 231). Echoing Justice Jackson's reading of the judicialization initiative, Roosevelt concluded that "great interests . . . which desire to escape regulation rightly see that if they can strike at the heart of modern reform by sterilizing the administrative tribunal which administers them, they will have effectively destroyed the reform itself" (Horwitz 1992, 232).[23]

In vetoing the bill, Roosevelt was counting on the report of his Gellhorn-Davis committee to support the very concept of public management through an endorsement of the administrative process. That committee would issue a majority report, written primarily by Gellhorn and Davis, and a minority report that represented the views of conservatives, leaving D. Lawrence Groner, a D.C. Circuit judge serving on the committee, in Davis's words, "off by himself, way off at the right end, nobody joining him" (Davis and Gellhorn 1986, 513).

In distinguishing the reports, writes Horwitz (1992, 232), "the most significant structural difference . . . was over the question of whether a general code of administrative procedure would straitjacket the agencies." The majority rejected any code of rules that would suppress the potential for creative agency solutions to public policy implementation problems. Ironically, it was the minority report that would serve as the basis for the structure of review that would become law under the Administrative Procedure Act.

But the 1941 report would be eclipsed by Pearl Harbor, and reforms of administrative procedure would languish during World War II, though executive governance, as in World War I under President Wilson, would increase its influence. Ralph Fuchs (1941, 352–353), a member of the commission, knew of the diversions presented by the international crisis and placed the report in context:

> To an increasingly evident extent, the system of administrative justice which we have worked out and which it is now proposed to improve, is an alternative not only to a more highly judicialized system but also to a swift-moving executive system. We have resorted to the executive system before in time of war; we have gone back to it now on a considerable scale during the national emergency [of the Great Depression]. . . . Were the times more settled, we could rest reasonably secure in the belief that the system of executive justice would again pass largely out of existence. . . . We have no assurance that the system of safeguarded administrative justice can be our main governmental reliance in the future. . . . In this situation, and not in the inner disposition of anyone that may be in power now or in the future, lies the greatest danger to our democratic way of life.

George Shepherd (1996, 1641–1642) argues that a number of factors during the war period contributed to the emergence of the minority view as the Administrative Procedure Act. Wartime agencies received more authority than ever from Congress and the president to administer wartime concerns, with Roosevelt even suspending the publication of the *Federal Register*. Agency performance, however, was not unequivocally positive. Price controls seemed ineffective and stateside shortages abundant. During the war, Republicans captured forty-seven new House and nine Senate seats. Yet this new conservative force was not enchanted by the notion of turning administrative oversight over to a judiciary that, after three Roosevelt administrations, had seen a steady increase in liberal appointees. The bar saw changes, as did the Department of Justice. Carl McFarland, a conservative who joined the minority report during his service on the Gellhorn-Davis committee, became chair of the Administrative Law Section of the ABA. Francis Biddle, McFarland's colleague on the Gellhorn-Davis committee, became attorney general in 1941 and served until the end of the war. Though he endorsed the minority report, Biddle sensed the importance of reforms at the earliest opportunity (Shepherd 1996, 1647).

McFarland's ABA committee drafted the APA in 1943; Representative Pat McCarran (D-Nevada) introduced it as H.R. 5081, and Senator Hatton Summers (D-Texas) simultaneously did so with S. 2030. Upon its passage in 1946, the law was considered a victory for both bar and administration interests. "Differing assessments of the APA," writes William West (1985, 76), "may be attributable in part to differences in the backgrounds and perspectives of those who wrote them." He continues, "students of government or public administration are more likely to view due process requirements as burdensome than are legal commentators, who are apt to consider such procedures as indispensable in many contexts." Though West rightly suggests that the normative tension between administrative and judicial process as the primary check on public management continued, the act did impose trial-type hearings when enabling statutes require adjudication—what courts do—"on the record after opportunity for an agency hearing" (5 U.S.C., section 554). When the agency's mandate is to engage in rule making—what Congress does—however, the APA is much more lenient on the matter of judicial review (5 U.S.C., section 553).[24]

Examining the legislative histories of three important acts during the 79th Congress (1946)—the APA, the Legislative Reorganization Act, and the Employment Act—David Rosenbloom (2000) shows qualitative evidence for the view that, after the New Deal, Congress was forging a "legislative-centered public administration." On this view, administrative agencies had come to be considered "extensions of Congress" when performing legislative functions such as rule making (134). Members of Congress, on behalf of their constituents, have "very broad supervisory authority over federal administration," while judicial review can keep in check executive discretion, which emerges when Congress does not delegate powers with specificity and protect constituents against "harmful executive action" (136, 138).

By contrast, Mathew McCubbins, Roger Noll, and Barry Weingast, publishing collectively as Mcnollgast (1999), also provide evidence (by analyzing congressional roll-call votes) that the failure of the Walter-Logan bill, and the subsequent success of postwar measures such as the APA, can be explained as an outcome of the dissolution of Democratic Party unity beginning in 1938. The APA, they argue, was a "grand compromise" on the two issue dimensions central to New Deal policy making: "Republicans achieved some of their desires on individual rights, while the northern Democrats got most of their way on economic policy" (191). Under the APA's provisions for judicial review of agency action, established New Deal agencies would be insulated from presidential control.

Northern Democrats, seeing losses in congressional seats throughout the early 1940s and fearing President Truman's defeat in the 1948 election, saw the APA as a way to protect the gains they had made during the New Deal era. Republicans knew that "procedurally unfettered" agencies would not be insulated, since the APA would give courts no grounds to review their actions (Mcnollgast 1999, 193). A new president and a Republican Congress could undo a portion of the administrative state without running up against the many federal judges appointed during the Roosevelt administration. The reason for the compromise, they conclude, is a variant of the "deck stacking" thesis (McCubbins, Noll, and Weingast 1987; 1989), that is, "the desire of New Deal Democrats to 'hard wire' the policies of the New Deal against an expected Republican, anti–New Deal political tide in the 1940s" (Mcnollgast 1999, 180).

Whatever the explanation for its passage, the APA changed the focus of federal administrative law.

CODDLING A MONSTER

The general trend in the years following the APA, Morton Horwitz (1992, 233) writes, is characterized by a "declining faith in the ability of experts to produce scientific, neutral, and apolitical solutions to social and legal questions." This increasing distrust, he argues, led to a reemergence in formalism and proceduralism throughout the next fifty years of administrative law. The Court began to chop away at the expertise model of administration developed from the civil service reform era through the New Deal. A critical, and suggestively ironic, example of the assertion of judicial power against the expertise of public management came in the Supreme Court's opinion in *Universal Camera Corp. v. NLRB*, 340 U.S. 474 (1951).

In 1947 the Republican "clean sweep" in Congress congealed sufficient distaste for the actions of the National Labor Relations Board to facilitate the passage, over President Truman's veto, of the Taft-Hartley Act. On judicial review, the act stipulated that courts base their decisions on "substantial evidence on the record as a whole." Reversing a circuit court decision by Judge Learned Hand, Justice Frankfurter, a key advocate of the New Deal and flexible public management in the 1930s, announced that "the substantiality of evidence must take into account whatever in the record fairly detracts from its weight. This is clearly the significance of the requirement [in section 706 of the APA] that courts consider the whole record" (*Universal Camera*, 488).[25] Several courts had previously refused to look beyond evidence that was consistent with the finding of the administrative agency. Writes Horwitz (1992, 236), "the Court was, in effect, deciding that the APA itself had significantly expanded the scope of judicial review of *all* administrative determinations."[26]

By 1955 the second Hoover commission on the organization of the executive branch of the Government, created by President Eisenhower, was recommending that an administrative court be established with divisions in the substantive areas of tax, trade, and labor, echoing a proposal advanced by the Pound committee in the 1930s. Attorney General Herbert Brownell recoiled at the thought: "These changes would substantially 'judicialize' the administrative process, with disastrous results to efficient and effective government" (Pierce 2002, 17). Nevertheless, the Hoover commission's sentiment and judicial action in cases such as *Universal Camera* catalyzed the bar once again, and by 1956 it had established a code of administrative procedure.[27]

The code was a move back toward the Walter-Logan bill from the more moderate APA and would be introduced, in the main, as amendments to the APA in S. 1663 during the 88th Congress. One provision that courts follow federal evidence rules in "civil, nonjury cases" is considered in Kenneth Culp Davis's definitive *Administrative Law Treatise* "nothing but a cross-reference to meaninglessness" (see Pierce 2002, 18).[28] The bill would even have deleted a provision in section 10 of the APA that prohibited judicial review on grounds of "abuse of discretion" of "action of the President and State Department in conducting foreign policy, the President's refusal of a pardon, the President's appointment of X to an office instead of Y, the discharge of a cabinet officer . . . and a host of other determinations that have never been reviewable and are not suitable for judicial review" (Pierce 2002, 19).

The New Criticism

In September 1959, Louis J. Hector resigned as a commissioner of the Civil Aeronautics Board (CAB). In a memo to President Eisenhower, Hector changed the debate over public administration from the protection of process rights to the *in*competence of agencies. "As I stated in my letter of resignation to you," writes Hector (1960, 931), "my experience on the Civil Aeronautics Board has convinced me that an independent regulatory commission is not competent in these days to regulate a vital national industry in the national interest." Hector levied charges of inefficiency and lack of coordination at the CAB and other governmental authorities in policy implementation. He continues: "As a lawyer, I have been disturbed at the inability of an administrative agency, such as the CAB, to give a true judicial hearing to parties who come before it in litigated cases. The agencies are long on judicial form and short on judicial substance" (931). As a remedy, Hector (as the ABA had done many times) "would recommend . . . transfer [of] the judicial and appellate duties of the CAB to a true administrative court" (932).

Calling Hector's claims "the 'new criticism,'" FTC chairman Earl Kintner (1960, 965) asserts that "it purports to abandon the attack on governmental regulation of business as such, and to decline to inveigh against the 'headless fourth branch of government' because it offends the pristine concept of separation of powers." Instead, Kintner continues, "the basic contention is that the administrative agencies simply do not do the job assigned to them." Hector was ushering in an era of distrust of the *expertise* of public administration, not simply of its formal structure within constitutional governance.

This new criticism, moreover, does not express a similar conservative distrust of expansive government through regulations like those during the New Deal. Walter Gellhorn (1956, 8) notes that liberals had gradually shifted from a belief that "administrators could be relied upon for wise and just decisions," making judicial review a meddlesome force that could "rigidify administrative procedures or supplant the informed administrative conclusions." Nonetheless, Horwitz (1992, 241–242) argues that liberals began to fear the capture of administrative agencies by regulated interests, political overseers, and other forces. If claims could credibly be made that agencies use their expertise in a biased manner, Gellhorn (1956, 22) states, a resistance to judicialization might "limit the review of administrative rulings in a way that to all intents and purposes gives sanction to administrative fiat."

President-elect Kennedy did not embrace the administrative court proposal but did receive the advice of a commission chaired by James Landis to overhaul the executive branch toward the end of more control over the independent agencies in particular and the administrative state more generally. The Landis commission, according to Carl McFarland (1961, 390), proposed the selection of an executive "from the commission or board to manage the assistants of the commission or board and delegations to them"; it also proposed that "an executive office . . . select such executives and have general supervision over them" and that a "Code of Ethics and intra-agency organization" be constructed and implemented "through the Administrative Conference" of the United States.[29] McFarland, who had served on the Gellhorn-Davis and post-Pound ABA committees, in an article subtitled "The Voice of One Crying in the Wilderness," calls Landis's proposals "a program" that "would recast the image of the independent federal regulatory board or commission. It would more firmly . . . enclose the 'fourth branch' in the network of the Executive. . . . Its purpose is to galvanize a moribund sector of national governance into some degree of action. And there, of course, will be the rub. What action? For whose benefit? Who will be hurt? The objectors and the fearful will be many, and some of them will be powerful."

McFarland's characterization of public administration as moribund echoes Dwight Waldo's claim seven years later that the field had fallen into a "crisis of identity." With the omnipresent problems of civil rights at home and peace in the international nuclear age dominating foreign policy, public management was finally in the center of governance. Nathaniel Nathanson (1963, 40), who served as both a member of and consultant to the then ad hoc Administrative Conference appointed by President Kennedy, succinctly states that "the problems of our administrative process are in a sense a reflection of the problems of our society." Nathanson's conference was far from the watershed that intellectual leaders hoped for; although it produced thirty recommendations, few were followed. Indeed, the APA remained remarkably untouched until 1966, when section 552 was replaced by the Freedom of Information Act. By 1970 even the bar abandoned the administrative code that had made an appearance in the 88th Congress (Pierce 2002, 22–23).

The Beneficiaries of Procedural Delay

The "great society" envisioned by President Johnson as he successfully sought passage of multitudinous social welfare legislation not only enhanced the discretionary power of agencies but also created for beneficiaries a "new property" in the largesse of the government (Reich 1964). "This association of the expansion of welfare rights with widening procedural guarantees," writes Horwitz (1992, 246), "shattered the traditional Dicean connection between conservatism and proceduralism in the administrative state."

Conservatives, who fought for procedural checks against the agencies when business regulation was the central policy controversy in the administrative state, now came to argue that administration should be given substantial discretion to deal with the benefits of the social welfare state. When this force combined with anti–Vietnam War sentiment and the disaster of Watergate, trust in government began to erode, and public management, as the epicenter of policy implementation, was assaulted from all sides.[30] The striking switch of liberal support from administration to a court strategy to effectuate social justice interests (see for example Scheingold 1972), combined with the conservative backlash against "big government" created, by the end of the 1970s, the crisis in the separation-of-powers foundation of public management that is the rationale for this book.

But as the decade of the 1970s began, the pulling and hauling had really just begun. Kenneth Culp Davis (1969, 219), still the ardent supporter of the administrative process, advances informal rule making as the answer to the problems of responsible public administration: "Administrative rulemaking is the key to a large portion of what needs to be done. To whatever extent is practical and consistent with the need for individualized justice, the discretion of officers in handling individual cases should be guided by administrative rules adopted through procedure like that prescribed by the federal Administrative Procedure Act." Davis (1972, 16) is revolted by what he calls "an extravagant version of the rule of law" under which "legal rights may be finally determined only by regularly constituted courts." In contrast to our reading of the same work, he calls John Dickinson "the outstanding American writer to take this position," though it was more popular in Europe.

In his 1944 book, *The Road to Serfdom*, Nobel Memorial Prize–winner Friedrich Hayek considers the principle to require "that government in all its action is bound by rules fixed and announced beforehand—rules which make it possible to foresee with fair certainty how the authority will use its coercive powers in given circumstances and to plan one's individual affairs on the basis of this knowledge" (quoted in Davis 1972, 17). Hayek advances a view that would be embraced by conservatives such as Justice Scalia through "textualist jurisprudence," whereby the electorally responsible Congress would receive deference from courts when they are clear in their words but not when they are vague. Davis (1972, 17) does not mince words: "Whether such an absurdity could have been intended by Hayek or whether the statement was an inadvertence does not appear; Congress in deciding how to legislate cannot be bound by rules fixed and announced beforehand, nor can the President in conducting foreign relations, nor can the Supreme Court in breaking new constitutional ground, nor can the planner of a network of highways." The pragmatism in the thinking of Davis reflects that of traditional public administration: Davis is pragmatic about the state's role in the governance of human affairs. Courts generally agreed with Davis, and throughout the decade encouraged rulemaking with tempered passivity (Pierce 2002, 23).

An important test of judicial restraint came in 1978, when the Supreme Court decided the case of *Vermont Yankee Nuclear Power Corp. v. Natural Resources Defense Council*, 435 U.S. 519 (1978). That case considered regulation of the disposal of nuclear waste, which had led to an environmental position—held by interest groups such as the Natural Resources Defense Council—that the certification of new nuclear power plants should be ceased due to the proliferation of spent fuel. In making licensing decisions, the Atomic Energy Commission (AEC) sought to use the notice and comment procedure advocated by Davis (1969) to set standards for fuel disposal generally, rather than through adjudication—which is, of course, more tightly constrained under the APA. Under the resulting rule, the Vermont Yankee plant was approved. Environmentalists sued, and the D.C. Circuit Court, holding the rule-making procedure itself to be invalid, imposed "hybrid" rule-making procedures on the AEC (more specific than the language of section 553 of the APA) and voided the rule. The plant appealed the case to the Supreme Court.

The Supreme Court reversed in what then University of Chicago law professor Antonin Scalia (who had served a stint on the Administrative Conference) called a "remarkably self-denying opinion" (Scalia 1978, 345). Justice Rehnquist, for the Court, delivered the holding that "agencies are free to grant additional procedural rights in the exercise of their discretion, but reviewing courts are generally not free to impose them if the agencies have not chosen to grant them." He continues, "this is not to say necessarily that there are no circumstances which would ever justify a court in overturning agency action because of a failure to employ procedures beyond those required by the statute. But such circumstances, if they exist, are extremely rare" (*Vermont Yankee*, 524).

The Court's holding represented a victory in the case for conservatives, since the D.C. Circuit Court, through its hybridization of section 553, had imposed additional and costly requirements on the nuclear power industry. The hybrid standard, however, was not universally helpful to district courts. In *Atchison, T. & S. F. R. Co. v. Callaway*, 459 F. Supp. 188, 192 (D.D.C. 1978), the court writes: "It appears that no definitive guidance has ever been provided to the federal trial courts with respect to whether their role in ensuring strict compliance with NEPA's procedural mandate is limited to review of the administrative record or whether their role includes fact-finding outside of the administrative record. This uncertainty has been compounded in recent years . . . by the Supreme Court's decisions in *Kleppe v. Sierra Club* [427 U.S. 390, 1976], and in *Vermont Yankee*."

Scalia (1978, 405) sees it as judicial restraint within the separation of powers; if the courts were to grab the power to innovate and impose procedures on administrative agencies, Congress would be hard pressed to remove it. "The procedural foundations of the judicial process were laid long ago, and the basic role of the courts seems firmly established by both tradition and constitutional prescription. There is little legislative inclination, therefore, to adjust upward and downward the power of the courts, and even less inclination to achieve this by fiddling with procedures. Not so with the agencies. Their powers are for the most part neither constitutionally prescribed nor well-established, and their procedures are only recently formed. Thus, the tendency to alter procedures as a means of altering power is immeasurably stronger." Scalia's approval of the Court's restraint in *Vermont Yankee* begs the question of a constitutional role for public management within the separation of powers.

In political terms, much of the power that Scalia references came from the ability of courts to delay the activity of public managers through more procedures, and this posed a problem for conservatives. In the economic regulation model, writes Horwitz (1992, 245), "procedural restraints had traditionally been defended in the name of protecting private property rights against essentially confiscatory governmental policy." But the environmental movement and the Great Society had "created a new set of beneficiaries of procedural delay" in liberal interest groups and the clients of the social welfare state.

The New Deal legacy, then, is an important harbinger of the advancement of administrative law from pragmatic administration into the political theory of the separation of powers during the 1980s and 1990s. The question of the role of agencies in constitutional democracy—unanswered during the vitriol of the 1930s and 1940s—took center stage. In cases such as *Humphrey's Executor v. United States*, 295 U.S. 602 (1935), the Supreme Court "attempted to harmonize the administrative state with the Constitution by reference to the then-prevailing distrust of political institutions" (Pierce 2002, 25). Richard Pierce quotes the Court, which quotes Congress, "with obvious approval" in asserting that the Federal Trade Commission "was not to be 'subject' to anybody in the government but . . . only to the people of the United States" (Pierce 2002, 25, quoting *Humphrey's Executor*, 625). But, Pierce quips, "that dictum was patent nonsense. There are only three Branches of government; any agency must be 'subject' to some combination of the three" (Pierce 2002, 25). This is true, of course, even though the Court has rejected the notion of "three airtight departments of government," *Nixon v. Administrator of General Services*, 433 U.S. 425, 443 (1977).

As a result of the gap in the separation of powers for public management, the Court came to grapple with a "public choice" view of administrative governance: though *policy implementation* is technical and specialized, *policy making* is and should be political. To attempt to technically divine legislative intent from the deals struck by the diverse body of individuals in Congress would give short shrift to that diversity and the politics of coalition formation that produce the deals (Mashaw 1989; Shepsle 1992). So Congress would have to be specific in the language of its instructions to administrative agencies in order for courts to overrule agency action. Otherwise, "reasonable" agency action would stand, and it would be up to Congress to correct the agency's offending policy choice with new, and more specific legislation.

This was the rule established in the most cited case in Supreme Court history, *Chevron U.S.A. v. Natural Resources Defense Council*, 467 U.S. 837 (1984). Like the "rules fixed and announced beforehand" that Hayek suggests are the guide to governance, the *Chevron* principle would be a default rule on which both Congress and the administration could rely. If the composition of Congress changes, so could the direction of agency policy making. If an agency's mandate loses salience with Congress, it need not wait for congressional approval to act decisively.

Justice Stevens, writing for the Court in *Chevron* (865), situates the role of public management as subservient to Congress, which grants it authority through legislation. Regarding the agency's interpretation of the 1977 amendments to the Clean Air Act,

> the Administrator's interpretation represents a reasonable accommodation of manifestly competing interests and is entitled to deference. . . . Congress intended to accommodate both [economic and environmental] interests, but did not do so itself on the level of specificity presented by these cases. Perhaps that body consciously desired the Administrator to strike the balance at this level, thinking that those with great expertise and charged with responsibility for administering the provision would be in a better position to do so; perhaps it simply did not consider the question at this level; and perhaps Congress was unable to forge a coalition on either side of the question, and those on each side decided to take their chances with the scheme devised by the agency. For judicial purposes, it matters not which of these things occurred.

Justice Scalia (1989, 516) later quite lucidly explains his view of the rationale for *Chevron* in the separation of powers:

In my view, the theoretical justification for *Chevron* is no different from the theoretical justification for those pre-*Chevron* cases that sometimes deferred to agency legal determinations. . . . An ambiguity in a statute committed to agency implementation can be attributed to either of two congressional desires: (1) Congress intended a particular result, but was not clear about it; or (2) Congress had no particular intent on the subject, but meant to leave its resolution to the agency. When the former is the case, what we have is genuinely a question of law, properly to be resolved by the courts. When the latter is the case, what we have is the conferral of discretion upon the agency, and the only question of law presented to the courts is whether the agency has acted within the scope of its discretion—i.e., whether its resolution of the ambiguity is reasonable.

In his reading of cases preceding *Chevron*, Justice Scalia (1989, 516) argues that the Court "sought to choose between (1) and (2) on a statute-by-statute basis. Hence the relevance of such frequently mentioned factors as the degree of the agency's expertise, the complexity of the question at issue, and the existence of rulemaking authority within the agency." Firmly within the public choice view (see for example Shepsle 1992), Congress would have to legislate specifically to overcome the ambiguity of "intent." Scalia (1989, 516) continues, "all these factors make an intent to confer discretion upon the agency more likely. *Chevron*, however, if it is to be believed, replaced this statute-by-statute evaluation (which was assuredly a font of uncertainty and litigation) with an across-the-board presumption that, in the case of ambiguity, agency discretion is meant." So, like Hayek, Scalia values clear default rules.

What seems no watershed to Justice Scalia is indeed such for the field of public administration: public management operates under congressional dominance, in addition to the presidential dominance established through action on the recommendations of the Landis commission of 1960, the White House personnel office, and other elements of executive control (see Weko 1995). Far from the judicial conception of the administrative state as an executive apparatus (discussed above with the surveyed early- and mid-nineteenth-century cases), public management had become a tool for legislative policy making. It was born largely in the New Deal, matured through the 1950s, and by the 1980s had developed procedures that both liberal and conservative interests could exploit.[31] The jurisprudence of *Chevron* seems to allow the "monster" Louis Jaffe (1949) invoked on Justice Frankfurter's behalf before *Universal Camera* to be unleashed only when Congress is too disinterested, too divided, or too inarticulate to show in statutory language that it cares about what an agency does.

Throughout the 1980s and 1990s the Supreme Court turned to fundamental questions of congressional, presidential, judicial, and administrative authority. In addition to *Chevron* and *Lujan v. Defenders of Wildlife*, the Court examines, in *Industrial Union Dep. v. American Petroleum Institute*, 448 U.S. 607 (1980), the breadth of delegations; in *Chadha v. Im. & Nat. Serv.*, 462 U.S. 919 (1983), the ability of Congress to withhold "vetoes" when making delegations; in *Morrison v. Olson*, 487 U.S. 654 (1988), the power to create independent agencies; in *Northern Pipeline Construction Co. v. Marathon Pipeline Co.*, 458 U.S. 50 (1982), and *Commodity Future Trading Commission v. Schor*, 478 U.S. 833 (1986), adjudication outside courts established under Article III, such as the federal bankruptcy courts and agencies; and in *Motor Vehicle Manufacturers Assn. v. State Farm Mutual Automobile Insurance Co.*, 463 U.S. 29 (1983), the obligation of agencies to engage in "reasoned decision making." Each of these cases attempts to clarify the boundaries between public managerial discretion and other authority in the separation of powers.

Bureaucratic Waste

After a Republican sweep in the midterm elections of 1994, the incoming 104th Congress pledged to rise above an "era of official evasion and posturing" to form a "Contract with America," which would amount to "the end of government that is too big, too intrusive, and too easy with the public's money" (Gingrich and others 1994). The clear target of the new legislators was the bureaucracy, and the 104th Congress passed an unusual number of "regulatory reform" measures, most pertinently including the Paperwork Reduction Act of 1995, the Unfunded Mandates Reform Act of 1995, and the Small Business Regulatory Enforcement Fairness Act of 1996. Daniel Cohen (1998, 700) says of the reforms during his tenure in the Clinton administration's Department of Commerce: "The rhetoric of regulatory reform is based on anecdotal evidence and wide-ranging estimates of the costs of the regulatory system, with most such estimates paying little or no attention to the benefits achieved and making a series of untested, unusually politically motivated, analytical assumptions."

But it appeared that Congress was merely using its power over bureaucracy that had been solidified—if present for much longer—in the 1980s administrative law jurisprudence of the Supreme Court. Indeed, Cohen's rhetoric seems no less relevant to counteracting Emmanuel Celler's mention of whippersnappers in the Department of Labor in 1939, as his committee debated the Walter-Logan bill. Still, the Contract with America was a new attack on the administrative process, and its resonance with the New Public Management in Europe led to the importation of such ideas as discussed in the preceding chapter.

Unlike the "new criticism" following the Hector letter and the judicialization debates of the 1970s, the 104th Congress was attacking the administrative process on pragmatic grounds of its own, the kind of efficiency rationales advanced by the likes of Luther Gulick and Lyndall Urwick while the administration was building its legitimacy. The legislation seemed to imply a feeling by the new Republican majority that public management had achieved existential legitimacy but now had to return to considerations of efficiency and effectiveness. Cohen (1998, 700–701), on behalf of public administration, countered on the grounds of politicization: "There is nothing really wrong with the regulatory system as it exists today. . . . It is easy, however, to deride this system when hard choices are in fact made to the detriment of a particular constituency." Under a strict version of congressional dominance, public management becomes susceptible to the same coalitional politics that characterize the floors of the House or Senate. Thus public management has come to suffer from its own success.

Congress also chipped at the bulwark of the APA with a 1996 amendment included in the Small Business Regulatory Enforcement Fairness Act. Under the amendment, Congress could veto any "major rule," defined in terms of the effect it is expected to have on the economy, within sixty days of its enactment by an administrative agency.[32] The veto must be conducted through a joint resolution, with presentment to the president. One such veto occurred during the Clinton administration (Pierce 2002, 414).

CONCLUSION

The fundamental theme in the story of public administration as it developed in the law is the separation of powers. As chapters 2 and 3 detail, public administration's leaders kept intellectual pace with administrative law until the mid-1940s, when the critiques of orthodoxy and the advent of behaviorism in political science undermined the field's prewar stature. When the ABA argued that administrators could not properly deal with rights questions and that only courts could legitimately perform that role, public administration countered on that issue, and it eventually won with the enactment of the APA. The APA was a political compromise; the New Deal coalition had lost influence, Republicans had gained power in the postwar Congress, and Roosevelt's death left the politically weaker Truman in the White House. But the act legitimated the discretionary decisions of public administrators in those agencies that already existed.

In abandoning its foundations at the very moment of its largely unrecognized advantage over the bar in the APA, mainstream public administration was not only setting the stage for its permanent state of crisis but also conceding the power to define the scope and legitimacy of public administration to, ironically, the bar and the courts. The New Criticism spawned by the Hector resignation could have been answered by traditionalists, but they were being relegated to the sidelines. The new public administration heterodoxy provided no leverage against these critiques. The field and the question of its legitimacy in government became profoundly political, with public and legislative impatience over wasted resources and procedural delays providing fodder for interest group manipulation of administrative discretion (Lowi 1969). Scholars of political economy found analytical leverage in theories that situate control over public administration in the bargaining among the separate powers and organized interests. The theories of public administration scholars dissipated into a disjointed collection of largely normative arguments oriented toward helping bureaucrats unsuccessfully push the Sisyphean rock of moral autonomy up the mountain of legislature-and-court-dominated administrative practice.

Now more than ever, public administration needs an existential theory of its own. A good normative theory must account for separation-of-powers politics, but it must work within the legacy of the traditionalists to regain the legitimacy of public administration. In the next chapter, we describe the political economy view in more detail and develop a theory of public management that is inherently constitutional.

CHAPTER FIVE

A Theory of Politically Responsive Bureaucrats

The Constitution of the executive department of the proposed government claims next our attention. There is hardly any part of the system which could have been attended with greater difficulty in the arrangement of it than this; and there is perhaps none, which has been inveighed against with less candor, or criticized with less judgment.

—*Alexander Hamilton, The Federalist, No. 67*

The recruitment, selection, and retention of federal bureaucrats—that is, the personnel function of American public administration—has largely been relegated to the status of a mundane specialty within the larger field of public administration. In this chapter, we argue that, properly conceived, the personnel function is intended to address—and is only effective when it serves—certain constitutional imperatives. Moreover, we claim that, through the political branches, early public administrationists sought to make the connection between administrative personnel and the people. Unlike their pragmatic inquiry, we reach this conclusion by theoretically working "backward" from the personnel function to the Constitution, concluding with a general proposition that, in chapter 6, is cast as a precept of managerial responsibility. Our conclusions illuminate the importance of the founding narrative of public administration woven in the works discussed in the preceding chapters.

We begin by describing the central problems of administration by unelected bureaucrats in our constitutional scheme: the delegation of authority and the political control of the bureaucracy. We then briefly review the manner in which positive political theory has developed around these questions to provide context for what is to follow. Our normative argument then characterizes the personnel question as a problem between Congress and its agents in the executive branch and the independent agencies. The execution by one branch of government—be it the elected executive or a "headless" fourth branch—of laws made by a separate and distinct branch, namely the legislature, raises the two problems mentioned above, which have been the subject of much analysis.

The first problem, the *delegation of authority*, can be described as follows.[1] Given that administrative and executive agencies are potentially able to exert their authority in ways that thwart congressional intent, Congress takes care, when writing a statute authorizing administrative activity, to give the implementing agency or agencies an optimal level of discretion (see for example Bendor, Glazer, and Hammond 2001; Epstein and O'Halloran 1999; Huber and Shipan 2002; Shipan 2004; Huber and McCarty 2004). The second problem, that of *political control of the bureaucracy*, is addressed when Congress—knowing, as before, that its intent may be sullied by the policy implementation decisions of unreliable bureaucrats—designs a set of statutory safeguards to mitigate "agency drift" in policy implementation (see for example McCubbins and Schwartz 1984; McCubbins, Noll, and Weingast 1987).

As argued in the preceding chapter, administrative law has created a set of default rules that make the delegation problem easier for Congress to address. In what follows, we advance the claim that, though Congress addresses the political control problem in each statute it creates as well as in the internal organization of the legislature (Weingast and Marshall 1988), Congress likewise has a set of default rules of constitutional origin, and it is over these default rules that it may construct political control.[2] Such rules ensure that bureaucrats are reliable constitutional agents for congressional delegations of authority.

This argument and the style of this chapter are, readers will soon detect, different from the other chapters in this book. As noted in chapter 3, Frederick Mosher and Emmette Redford grappled with the same problem in a very different way. In this chapter, our underlying logic is based on formal reasoning. We employ the economics of contract and social choice theory to derive a theoretical solution, what we term a "mechanism," to the framers' problem of ensuring that executive administration reliably reflects the popular will. Because it must reflect essential realities of constitutional governance, this derivation is rather complex, and the solution is, in theoretical terms, "third best" rather than optimal. However, our solution "works," in that, under plausible assumptions, it constitutes a reasonable basis for prescribing public personnel policies that comport with the Constitution.

We might have adopted a different strategy for presenting our argument.[3] We might have omitted this verbally technical chapter entirely and asserted the theoretical solution in a footnote, or in a supporting argument, to the intuitive derivation of the same solution that we present in chapter 6, asking the reader to take our word for its validity. (Readers not wishing to journey into the theoretical heart of darkness presented below can do just that.) But those who stay the course will, we believe, see the value of our logical roadmap in two ways. First, we show how formal reasoning can be used to address complex problems of governance in ways that produce practical insights. Second, we strengthen the basic argument of this book: the intuitions of the field's first- and second-generation contributors not only shaped the evolution of the American administrative state but, at the same time, fashioned an interpretation of constitutional principles that was, mirabile dictu, theoretically coherent, even prescient.

CONSTRAINING MANAGERIAL CHOICE AND ACTION

Scholars have gained considerable insight into the political control of the bureaucracy by examining it as a principal-agent problem. Such problems arise when a principal (the legislature, in our case) anticipates the emergence of information asymmetries and conflicts of interest after entering into a contract with an agent (an administrative agency).

The U.S. Congress, for example, anticipates that the Food and Drug Administration (FDA), when reviewing the applications of pharmaceutical manufacturers for the approval of antihistamines, will come to know more about both the manufacturers and antihistamines than Congress itself. This fact presents Congress with advance warning of a *hidden information problem*, which, in the above example, makes the FDA better informed than Congress about the opportunities and capacity of government to regulate the pharmaceutical industry.

The FDA, in defiance of congressional intent, might also develop lax standard operating procedures for (or, alternatively, be overvigilant in) reviewing applications, creating the potential for approving dangerous drugs (or for failing to put safe drugs on the market). It is very difficult—or, at least, the over-the-shoulder monitoring of FDA operations is very costly—for Congress to observe this aspect of administrative effort, a situation that alerts Congress to an imminent *hidden action problem*. The reality of FDA regulation involves both problems, and Congress must do what it can to mitigate them (see generally Hart and Hölmstrom 1987).

In general, the principal-agent framework guides our analysis. As we show, however, the analysis becomes more complex due to the presence of two such relationships—between the people and Congress, and between Congress and its administrative agents—relationships that are not independent of one another. A theory of public management must understand the need to solve both problems. Such understanding begins with a consideration of how bureaucratic agents attain their positions in government.

Positive political-economic theory tends to divide the political and legal constraints on public administration into two categories, which echo the central points of the Friedrich-Finer debate. External checks on agency action may operate either on the set of feasible choices that public administrators face when managing public policies, programs, functions, or organizations; or on the specific actions those administrators take from among the feasible choices (see for example McCubbins and Schwartz 1984). Congress designs bureaucratic structures—for example, an agency's rule-making authority, governance, and internal organization—as well as administrative processes—for example, acts governing administrative procedure, hiring and compensation, and budget execution (McCubbins, Noll, and Weingast 1987; 1989). Bureaucratic structures affect how agencies identify the alternatives that are feasible, while processes and procedures affect how agencies go about choosing among feasible alternatives.

In a well-designed structure and where information asymmetries are narrow (the Social Security Administration, for example), the incentives of legislative principals and their administrative agents can be closely aligned. In a poorly designed structure and where information asymmetries are wide (such as the Central Intelligence Agency), administrators at all levels have more latitude to pursue goals other than those that are politically expressed through statutes and budgets.

Scholars emphasizing external checks on managerial discretion differ in their assessments of effectiveness. For example, Mathew McCubbins, Roger Noll, and Barry Weingast (1987, 1989) conclude that Congress has the incentive to "stack the deck" in favor of its constituents' interests through administrative procedures prescribed in statutes. Given a choice of agents, delegation studies in a variety of contexts find that an equilibrium results when legislators delegate authority to agencies that are most closely allied with their policy preferences (Bendor, Glazer, and Hammond 2001). Kathleen Bawn (1995, 1997) shows that, on the basis of expected agency preferences, including a preference for autonomy from legislative interference, legislatures attempt to create an optimal mix of technical delegation and political control. She contends that broad delegations occur where there is little conflict between legislators and elected executives on policy preferences and where there is considerable technical uncertainty over policy implementation with respect to matters on which the agency has expertise. Under broad delegation, legislatures must act ex post to rein in bureaus that drift. Similar incentives, furthermore, extend to the president. David Epstein and Sharyn O'Halloran (1999, 60) find that when bureaucratic capacity is high, "in equilibrium, the president will always choose an agency head with [identical] policy preferences. . . . Loyalty to the president's goals will be the primary factor in choosing executive branch officials."

These incentives are reversed when bureaucratic capacity is low. John Huber and Nolan McCarty (2004, 481) show that "bad bureaucracies are not only inefficient (that is, less successful at implementing the policies they intend), but also harder to control because their incompetence diminishes their incentives to implement the policies politicians describe in legislation." The implication is that legislators can more easily induce policy outcomes they prefer from competent bureaus that do not share the legislators' preferences than from incompetent ones that do. Legislators must be somewhat sophisticated in the knowledge of policies they maintain to achieve control, but Huber and McCarty (490) find that "the Politician can . . . best take advantage of a high-capacity Bureaucrat when strong *ex post* enforcement intensifies the relationship between actions and punishment. But the Politician has the least to gain from improving *ex post* enforcement when bureaucratic capacity is low." Furthermore, they show formally that "low-capacity bureaucrats bias policy choices . . . heavily toward their own ideal points. One way to eliminate those losses of political control is to try to politicize the bureaucracy by moving it to the Politician's ideal point." The quality of agents is thus important to external control.

In contrast, internal checks rely, by definition, on administrative self-governance by administrative agents who are expert in their domains, proactive, and relatively autonomous. They work best when agents are of a "high quality." The extent to which a reliance on internal checks puts the achievement of legislative goals at risk depends on a number of factors. Anthony Downs (1967), for example, asserts that "authority leakage" will follow from what might be called a "physics of hierarchy": more levels of hierarchy imply more leakage, which in turn increases the likelihood of policy drift. John Brehm and Scott Gates (1997, 196) identify three important constraints on the principal-agent model due to the characteristics of administrators and their agencies: officials' predispositions and attitudes; the type of production in which the agency is engaged (for example, information versus public goods); and contact with supervisors. Based on "overwhelming evidence," they argue that "the bureaucrat's own preferences have the greatest effect upon performance. First and foremost, bureaucrats control their own behavior."

These two perspectives, internal checks versus external checks, do not move the question of managerial responsibility beyond where it was left by Finer and Friedrich, however. Both are silent concerning the issues of management posed by the separation of powers; they simply assert that Congress can do certain things (primarily restricting discretion) to keep its administrative agents from drifting and that it cannot do certain other things. A view of constraints on administrative action that anticipates the rationale for our theory of public management opens the black box of legislative enactment to uncover interest group activity that underlies it.

From this interest-oriented perspective, the environment of public management is assumed to be explicitly Madisonian, that is, comprising factions seeking power. Interest groups are assumed to react to exogenous changes in the policy environment in which they operate (for example, the discovery of mad cow disease or of terrorist threats to commercial aviation) by altering their preferences for legislative constraints on administrative action. In the theory of congressional dominance, legislators count on favored groups to sound "fire" alarms when bureaus announce policies with which they do not agree (McCubbins and Schwartz 1984). Based on an informal version of the common agency model (Bernheim and Whinston 1986), a theory of interest group lobbying with interest groups as principals to a single governmental agent (such as an administrative agency), we argue (see Bertelli and Lynn 2005) that, in the provision of public services, a technological change that significantly alters the cost effectiveness of service provision can induce a revealed preference change among interest groups that will affect public policy.

If, for example, a lower-cost technology becomes available (for example, the discovery in the 1950s of psychoactive drugs that reduced the cost of serving seriously mentally ill patients by allowing community-based treatment), a common agency model predicts that, since groups will be similarly affected by this change, public policy shifts accordingly. If, on the other hand, individual interest group preferences change independently—as when, for example, a court decision privileges the position of one group (advocates, say, for the legalization of homosexual marriages) over that of another—groups' preference shifts may cancel each other out, leaving policy more or less unaffected.

Certain changes in the policy environment such as court decisions or statutory enactments modify the "influence technologies" of groups, that is, the specific manner in which they attempt to exert their influence on agencies (Bertelli and Lynn 2005). New laws may, for example, give an interest group standing to sue on clients' behalf, changing its influence technology from legislative lobbying to litigation. The resulting threat of suit may alter the way in which the agency perceives and responds to individual groups' support or opposition. Should an interest group anticipate a preference change, however, it would not choose a precedent-establishing technology such as litigation; litigation would not be used to "bluff" administrators.

The influence technology structure, then, constitutes an important departure from the pluralist notion of partisan mutual adjustment (Lindblom 1965). Multiple "means of influence" permit interest groups to choose among influence strategies and can greatly complicate interest aggregation in the purely pluralist sense. More-over, the existence of new influence technologies—the use of the Internet to mobi-lize mass pressure, for example—can create the incentive for groups to form, shifting the balance of influence on policy implementation (Olson 1965; Hansen 1985). The presence of a constellation of groups advocating for a particular policy change can bring about significant shifts, with clear implications for public management.

As a result of stakeholders' influence activities, government approaches what Douglas Yates (1982, 179) recognizes as the normative goal of a "strategic Madisonian approach to control: various controllers [interests] and bureaucrats would openly fight out major administrative issues and, in so doing, enhance the checking and balancing process envisioned by Madison." These strategic actors, neither obedient nor self-governing, are Madison's managers as contemplated by the precept of man-agerial responsibility (Bertelli and Lynn 2003).

In sum, scholars pay significant attention to how bureaucrats receive discretion and are overseen by political elites—legislators, elected executives, and interest groups. If, however, American public administration comprises a cadre of well-selected "agents" (and we fully define the optimal qualities of these agents in the following chapter) who can implement those laws enacted through the pulling and hauling among political elites, then those elites could rely on these bureaucrats such that checking, in equilibrium, becomes irrelevant. If the Constitution has an im-plicit role for public management, it must be this type of trust. We argue that traditional scholars' focus on the legitimacy of public administration, as chronicled in chapters 2 and 3, is constitutionally appropriate. While we clarify this basic argu-ment throughout this and subsequent chapters, we must first turn to the mechanism for selecting bureaucrats insofar as selecting and retaining a trusted cadre of admin-istrators is the linchpin of constitutional public administration.

THE PERSONNEL FUNCTION

A good textbook definition of the personnel function in American government includes four components: "First, it is the *functions* needed to manage human resources in public agencies. Second, it is the *process* by which public jobs are allocated. Third, it is the interaction among fundamental societal *values* that often conflict over who gets public jobs and how they are allocated. Finally, [it is] person-nel *systems*—the laws, rules, organizations, and procedures used to express these abstract values in fulfilling personnel functions" (Klingner and Nalbandian 2003, 1).

Personnel systems incorporate such things as merit selection, employee record keeping, grievance procedures, and employee relations, benefits, and training programs. As such, they constitute the central source for compliance with what we argue later in this chapter is a constitutional mechanism for selecting an optimal set of agents for the performance of policy implementation. In general, personnel systems incorporate structures that give potential employees information about the "payoffs" they can expect from taking a job in the public service, while providing the government with information about the characteristics of the job candidate. Before making this argument in detail, we first discuss some elements of the U.S. federal personnel system and its political-legal context.

Patricia Wallace Ingraham (1995) identifies three tensions omnipresent in carrying out the personnel function: neutrality against responsiveness, patronage against merit, and efficiency against effectiveness. These tensions are of importance to the analysis presented in this chapter. The personnel function, its management and processes, cannot therefore be fully understood without attention to the values and systems that make it the linchpin of the administrative state.

Neutrality versus Responsiveness

Achieving responsive competence with political neutrality has historically been a central theme in the personnel function; Paul Van Riper (1958, 112) notes a "latent antagonism between liberty and equality—so potentially explosive in a democracy." In the world of *Wayman v. Southard* (1825) discussed in chapter 4, one saw "no constitutional amendments; the body of administrative law was substantially untouched; the courts continued to mark the legal limits of administrative action . . . primacy of the Chief Executive in matters of administration stood intact . . . [and] the concentration of authority in the respective secretaries was denied by no one" (White 1954, 553–554).

Of "Jacksonian personnel administration," Van Riper (1958, 51) writes that "despite the rising tide of spoils, there constantly remained a stratum of the civil service which helped to maintain continuity and competence in administration. Even the most partisan of executives could comprehend the need to maintain a basic level of administrative efficiency by retaining a few key officials. Hence the comptrollers, auditors, and chief clerks of the departmental service in Washington frequently kept their positions through several administrations. So did a portion of the minor clerks, a number of the small group of scientific and technical personnel, and the officer corps of the army and navy. In the field agencies politics reigned, though not always to the exclusion of integrity and competence."

Van Riper (51) concludes that "the federal service was manned and managed by two personnel systems"; one is patronage, which dominated the Jacksonian era, and the other is expertise, which would overtake the former after the Civil War. In the postbellum era, "what had once been intended as an opening up of public office to the mass of citizens had all the earmarks of becoming the opening up of office to plundering by the politically privileged." He continues, "In 1883, contrasted to 1829, there was no new [political] class to turn to, nor any particular desire to turn the clock back to 1829." The Civil Service Commission, created under the Pendleton Act, could "systematically and rationally" fill offices, provide a "new measure of merit" through examinations, and instill the expertise model in American public administration.

The principal-agent model has great intuitive appeal for unpacking neutrality-responsiveness distinctions. In the business firm, Eugene Fama (1980) shows that separating ownership from control is efficient. Managers bear the risk of business decisions and face market discipline directly, but nonmanagement employees do not. In public administration, managers at the highest levels (and many more in a full-blown patronage regime) are appointed through a political process and, consequently, face the discipline of a political market. Political at-will employment at the top, then, creates incentives for, say, a cabinet secretary to temper decisions regarding the structure and function of the "internal market" within a bureau. Civil servants face this internal market, just as nonmanagement employees face the institutions that compose the firm.

Political control is thereby brought to bear on team production and metering problems (Alchian and Demsetz 1972) within the bureau through the political "ownership" of high-level appointees. Internal incentives, job design, and so forth are internal market constructs that, to a significant extent, lie within the choice set of public managers. Though a comprehensive patronage regime presents serious concerns as a personnel mechanism at a constitutional level, some degree of patronage can be helpful in addressing the agency problem between the Congress and its administrative agents.

Patronage versus Merit

Brought to the foreground by the Pendleton Act, weighing patronage against merit has been "the most basic and most persistent issue for the American civil service" (Ingraham 1995, xviii). Critical to the balance is the mix of civil servants and political positions within each agency. The Pendleton Act initially made approximately 10 percent of federal positions subject to competitive examination; by 1928 that number had risen to 75 percent (Huddleston and Boyer 1996, 26). As noted in chapter 2, the Pendleton Act was quite slow in creating an impact. William Jennings Bryan, a supporter of patronage, rekindled it at the highest levels of federal government when he became President Wilson's secretary of state (Van Riper 1958, 231).[4] Moreover, state and local systems were slow to adopt the practice of merit selection (Tolbert and Zucker 1983), though block grants from the federal government became an important incentive for states to fall into line. For example, the Social Security Act was revised in 1939 to require states to have merit systems to compete for distributive grants (Van Riper 1958, 343).

General legislation crowned an "almost convulsive movement to renovate the civil service system of our national government" (Van Riper 1958, 344). For example, the Position Classification Act of 1923 fixed salary structures in the agencies, which were ultimately replaced by the "GS" categories by the Classification Act of 1949. In that act, the Civil Service Commission was given the exclusive authority to approve departmental positions at the GS-16 and GS-17 "supergrade" levels, those who stood closest to political appointees of elected officials (Huddleston and Boyer 1996, 30). In 1940 the Ramspeck Act authorized the president to extend civil service to just under 200,000 federal positions previously without coverage (Van Riper 1958, 344).

President Eisenhower, who had run as a "politician above power," was urged by "the public administration community, good government groups, and civil service leaders . . . to bolster the presidential role in the appointments process" (Weko 1995, 107). Presidents Kennedy, Johnson, and especially Nixon would take up that recommendation. When Nixon "could not compete with policy networks for the loyalties of the men and women who were serving him, then he and his appointments staff would pull appointment decisions into the White House and find . . . 'men and women who are completely devoid of personal and political ambition, totally loyal to the president, politically sensitive, highly objective and analytical, and capable, result-oriented managers'" (Weko 1995, 112, quoting an unidentified aide to President Nixon).

Nixon's efforts did not, given Watergate and its aftermath, engender public confidence. But "reinforced by a series of scandals in Congress, the perfidies of Watergate soon broadened into the public mind to encompass the whole 'mess in Washington'" (Huddleston and Boyer 1996, 93). President Carter campaigned quite directly against the bureaucracy, and when Congress passed the Civil Service Reform Act of 1978, the supergrades were collapsed into a Senior Executive Service that centered official rank in the person, not the position, located appointment authority in the Office of Personnel Management, and stressed competitive compensation and mobility (Huddleston and Boyer 1996, 105–107). All of this movement has led the personnel function at this critical senior level to a "veritable mulligan stew of ideas: a little pay-for-performance here, a little political responsiveness there, with a splash of opportunity for career executives and a dollop of decentralization" (Huddleston and Boyer 1996, 138). Reform proposals currently abound to deal with the difficulties in managing the system that resulted from the tension between patronage and responsiveness (for example, National Commission on the Public Service 1989; Kettl and others 1996).

Though the redress of patronage had been an issue for Congress since the 1820s, it was first tied to a public employee's First Amendment rights in *Elrod v. Burns,* 427 U.S. 347 (1976). In that case, an action commenced by non–civil service employees of the Cook County, Illinois, sheriff's office, who were Republicans and were either discharged or threatened with discharge upon the election of a Democratic sheriff. A plurality of the Supreme Court concluded that there are two ways in which exclusively partisan firings violate the First Amendment. "Even a pledge of allegiance to another party," the justices reason, "however ostensible, only serves to compromise the individual's true beliefs" (*Elrod v. Burns* 1976, 355). "As government employment, state or federal, becomes more pervasive," the plurality opinion continues, "the greater the dependence on it becomes, and therefore the greater becomes the power to starve political opposition by commanding partisan support, financial and otherwise. Patronage thus tips the electoral process in favor of the incumbent party, and where the practice's scope is substantial relative to the size of the electorate, the impact on the process can be significant" (*Elrod v. Burns* 1976, 356).

A dissenting opinion by Justice Powell clearly shows the Court's division over the issue. "The Court holds unconstitutional a practice as old as the Republic," he writes, "a practice which has contributed significantly to the democratization of American politics" (*Elrod v. Burns* 1976, 376). Citing the work of David Rosenbloom among other scholars of public administration and politics, Powell argues that "patronage hiring practices have contributed to American democracy by stimulating political activity and by strengthening parties, thereby helping to make government accountable" (382). Powell opines further that patronage employees take on their positions willingly, and "may not be heard to challenge it when it comes their turn to be replaced" (380). Though the mix of patronage employees and civil servants in Cook County was "disproportionate," Justice Powell concludes that the Court "should not foreclose local options in the name of a constitutional right perceived to be applicable for the first time after nearly two centuries" (389).

Despite the difference of opinion, the Court further specified the conditions of the plurality in *Branti v. Finkel,* 445 U.S. 507 (1980). No public employee, the Court held, is required to prove coercion into changing political beliefs. Rather, it is sufficient to show discharge solely on the ground of political beliefs. If, however, the employer can show the appropriateness of requiring a particular partisan affiliation for effective performance of the duties of the office in question, an exception is permissible.

In *Rutan v. Republican Party of Illinois*, 497 U.S. 62 (1990), Justice Brennan, this time writing for the Court, extends the holdings of *Elrod* and *Branti* to promotions, transfers, and recalls on the sole basis of partisan affiliation. Justice Scalia, writing in dissent, expresses vigorous disagreement with the decision, and goes so far as to argue that *Elrod* and *Branti* be overruled.[5] "Suffice it to say," writes Scalia, "that patronage was, without any thought that it could be unconstitutional, a basis for government employment from the earliest days of the Republic until Elrod—and has continued unabated since Elrod, to the extent still permitted by that unfortunate decision" (*Rutan* 1990, 96). Scalia assails what he sees as an infringement of the separation of powers: "Though unwilling to leave it to the political process to draw the line between desirable and undesirable patronage, the Court has neither been prepared to rule that no such line exists (that is, that all patronage is unconstitutional) nor able to design the line itself in a manner that judges, lawyers, and public employees can understand" (*Rutan* 1990, 111). The crux of his claim is that "to oppose our *Elrod-Branti* jurisprudence, one need not believe that the patronage system is necessarily desirable; nor even that it is always and everywhere arguably desirable; but merely that it is a political arrangement that may sometimes be a reasonable choice, and should therefore be left to the judgment of the people's elected representatives" (*Rutan* 1990, 110).[6] Justice Scalia argues, then, that the efficiency and effectiveness of patronage is for the political branches to decide.

Efficiency versus Effectiveness

The final tension identified by Ingraham (1995) is that which requires a balancing of efficiency with effectiveness. This concern evolved gradually. In the beginning of the Republic, Hamiltonian "energy in the executive" was operationalized as "no administrative scheme at all; men who headed organizations simply performed their functions according to their own aptitudes and preferences, and these personal inclinations, as well as the nature of the relationship between chiefs and subordinates, determined administrative structure and procedure" (Crenson 1975, 72). By the time of the Civil War, writes Cindy Aron (1987, 96), "government offices functioned, in many ways, according to informal, personal, and irregular rules." As the administrative state expanded, formalization increased, but throughout the remainder of the nineteenth century, "a mixture of the idiosyncratic and the rational,

the informal and the bureaucratic, persisted within Washington agencies and presented federal workers with a variety of problems." Thereafter (as discussed in chapters 2 and 3), the scientific management movement and the advent of merit systems,
and (as chapter 4 suggests) administrative law began to shape the administrative
process and public management practice.

Another important issue for the balancing of efficiency in the provision of government services with effectiveness in policy implementation is reflected in the debate
over performance-based pay regimes. Graduated pay, and then step-in-grade systems
appeared after the Pendleton Act and persisted until the 1970s, when these regimes
encountered criticism for rewarding longevity, not performance (Perry 1986, 57).
Beyond issues of underfunding of the merit raise pool, the effects of pay inequity, and
the manipulation of ratings mechanisms—most employees were rated as "average"
(Perry 1986; Kellough and Lu 1993)—merit pay in public sector agencies has counterarguments from a variety of theoretical perspectives.

One position is that the current system is more or less efficient. Edward Lazear
and Sherwin Rosen (1981) show that when an employer makes rank-order com-
parisons among risk-neutral employees, rather than on the cardinal value of their
output, the resulting performance is equivalent to that generated by piece rates.
Such a system is known as a rank-order tournament, where employees compete for
moves to a higher-level position. Since it is less costly to measure relative ranks than
cardinal outputs, especially in highly discretionary civil service jobs, such a system
makes considerable sense. With risk-averse employees, the result is no longer equivalent to the strict pay-for-performance outcome, but, depending on the preferences
of the employee, it can be the preferred regime.

Salaries are, therefore, more like "prizes" (for winning the tournament) than
wages paid at the marginal product of labor, the standard condition for equilibrium
in the labor market (Lazear and Rosen 1981, 863). This interpretation follows from
the authors' treatment of the lifetime production of an employee as a linear combination of his or her average skill and "lifetime luck," where the former represents
human capital investment by the employee and the latter is some ability level that is
revealed over his or her working life (843). Salary rewards luck and acquired skill
from investment, the aptitudes and personal inclinations that drive administrative
structure and process in the Hamiltonian scheme.

The federal civil service system is very much like the system described by Lazear
and Rosen (1981), argues Andrew Whitford (2004, 13), in that its "step-level pay
gradations in hierarchies, with nontrivial probabilities for promotion, suffice to ensure the motivation for mobility on which a tournament relies." This leads him (18)
to conclude that "flattening" the bureaucracy (expanding the supervisory span of

control) makes organizations less efficient: "In flatter organizations with supervisors, subordinates competing in promotion tournaments face lower individual probabilities of advancement and reward; effort levels may fall in response and organizational performance, too."

A second argument is that the equilibrium generated by civil service is not simply reached through a market-clearing wage, as merit pay requires. Nobelist George Ackerlof (1982) argues that labor contracts are part compensation, part gift exchange. Suppose there are two types of employee, low performing and high performing, and that the firm in which they work pays a flat wage to all employees. Further assume that some employees are more productive than others. In equilibrium, Ackerlof shows, the higher-performing people, counterintuitively, buttress the productivity of the entire organization. Why? High-performing workers "give" higher productivity to the firm in "exchange" for lenience toward less-productive workers. It would not, then, be sufficient to argue that productivity is not rewarded, as in some arguments for merit pay. Rather, productivity is simply expected at a higher level than those that would be generated by strictly self-interested bureaucrats.

We argue later in this chapter that public service motivation actually captures elements of the civil servant's job milieu, such as the partial gift exchange. Economists have recently devoted considerable attention to the "motivation crowding effect." This notion posits that when intrinsic motivation is constant or increased by the creation of a scheme of external incentives (such as a payment schedule), worker effort increases and the principal (employer) is made better off. In other words, the extrinsic incentives "crowd in" intrinsic motivation. However, if those external incentives change bureaucrats' perceptions of their task such that intrinsic motivation is decreased, or crowded out, raising monetary incentives lowers the supply of output (Benabou and Tirole 2003; Canton 2003; Frey and Jegen 2001). This is startling in that it "suggests the opposite of the most fundamental economic 'law'" (Frey and Jegen 2001, 590). David Kreps (1997, 361) notes that "what is called intrinsic motivation may be (at least in part) the worker's response to fuzzy intrinsic motivators, such as fear of discharge, censure by fellow employees, or even the desire for co-workers' esteem."

Public service motivation may, then, be a product of the placement of an employee within a civil service environment, not simply an inherent predilection. Psychological experiments agree, suggesting that crowding out intrinsic motivation is attributed to individuals' perceived incongruity of monetary, or high-powered, incentives with self-determination and own valuations of task competence (Deci, Koestner, and Ryan 1999). Indeed, as we have seen, this is precisely the type of "failure" cited by commentators on the Civil Service Reform Act of 1978, which instituted performance pay reforms (Perry 1986; Kellough and Lu 1993). When the 1984 Performance Management and Recognition Act reinstituted step-in-grade, but with bonus eligibility, it reinstated the rank-order tournament and, arguably, reinvigorated the public service motivation of bureaucrats.

Against this backdrop, we turn to a derivation from the Constitution of the optimal mechanism for selecting the set of potential bureaucrats. Of central importance to our analysis is avoiding a simplistic model of a known agent to a congressional principal. To adopt such a model would be to treat mistakenly the complicated contemporary reality of the personnel function as the person-centered arrangement of the Jacksonian era. We begin our analysis by identifying governance in our Republic within a principal-agent framework that comprehends essential complexities in that relationship.

TWO LEVELS OF DELEGATION

We wish to tell a story that begins with the 1789 congressional delegation of authority to the customs service but a story that is sufficiently robust to cover delegations generally. Political theory considers one form of principal-agent problem, that of "the constitutional allocation of powers as a delegation from the people as principal to the segments of government as agents" (Shapiro 2002, 173). Administrative law, as we have seen, stresses "a second principal-agent relationship, the delegation of some of its legislative power by the constitutionally empowered legislature to the constitutionally defined executive branch or . . . to independent agencies." The framers' interest in the personnel function penetrates through the first relationship and into the second. What, then, does political economy have to say about the constitutional question of creating the incentives for "faithful execution of the laws"? As it turns out, quite a lot.

In the remainder of the chapter, we characterize the problems facing the framers regarding the development of a responsible administrative state by first explaining the case of a single delegation through the monopolistic screening model. Fortunately, the solution concept for that model is identical to the solution concept for a more general model—one in which society, not Congress, provides the goals of the delegation. To explain the solution to this constitutional-level problem, we discuss some key concepts in social choice theory. After analyzing the constitutional problem of responsible administration, we describe a solution concept and some necessary game theoretic concepts that, in our view, represent the essence of the personnel function. This result reveals the constitutional grounds for public management as an institution in the separation of powers.

We can state strategic versions of the questions to be addressed through the personnel function in the following manner:

1. If an ideal agent could be found to whom Congress could delegate the authority to execute a particular law faithfully, what would be the agent's characteristics?

2. Generally speaking, how can delegations be designed to entice individuals with these ideal characteristics to take part in governance, for example, by becoming civil servants, regardless of the subject of the delegation (that is, no matter what the mission of the agency)? In other words, how can public service careers be made attractive to the right sorts of people?

The first question is the ongoing congressional agency problem, while the second problem is one of constitutional design. In effect, the framers faced a policy design problem, and only by anticipating a resolution of the congressional agency problem could they formulate a structure for the role of delegated power in what would become the administrative state. We first examine the incentives present in the congressional agency problem. Then, given the optimal solution for Congress, we move "backward" to the framers' problem.

Congress's Monopoly

The congressional agency problem is a version of what the economics literature calls the monopolistic screening problem (Maskin and Riley 1984; Baron and Myerson 1982). This variant of the principal-agent model is concerned with the ex post problem of hidden information. In our setting, suppose that Congress wants to delegate a one-time task to a particular agency. The "effort level" of the agency after the delegation is made is, in this case, perfectly transparent to Congress. As the agency performs its delegated task, however, Congress has much more difficulty in assessing how comfortable the agency is in performing it. The agency may find its task to be both philosophically and politically satisfying, reducing its dislike of exerting effort in its pursuit of that task on the margin. Alternatively, the agency may find itself in conflict with the executive in implementing the delegated task, have no experience in the substantive policy area in which the delegation was made, and so forth. In the latter case, the agency's reluctance to exert effort increases.

This particular problem is monopolistic in that Congress would, in principle, need to offer a menu of incentive contracts to a number of agencies in order to "screen" them for the ideal type that it desires: the willing implementer. Monopolistic screening problems arise on a regular basis in legislative deliberations. For example, should federal mortgage lending agencies be supervised by the Department of Housing and Urban Development or by the Department of Justice? Should direction of intelligence collection agencies be the responsibility of the secretary of defense, the director of central intelligence, or a White House director of intelligence? Should the National Oceanographic and Atmospheric Administration be under the secretary of commerce, in the Department of the Interior, or an independent commission? Should the safety of meat production be the responsibility of the Department of Agriculture, the Food and Drug Administration, or the Department of the Interior? In addressing such questions, Congress is the sole (that is, monopoly) principal, but there are many feasible agents. Congress, then, wants to design a screening procedure to select the optimal one from all feasible agents.

It should be stressed that, in general, the menu of contracts will not be apparent in enacted legislation. That menu of contracts will have been visible in deliberations, discussions, testimony, and other opportunities for Congress to question interest groups, experts, or the bureaus themselves regarding their policy predilections, administrative efficiency, and so forth. It is an ongoing process, which is a central part of what Daniel Carpenter (2001, 14) calls the "forging of bureaucratic autonomy." Carpenter argues that as the bureaus of the American administrative state age, they become politically differentiated from the officials controlling them and develop capacities to carry out their preferences. In this process, bureaus gradually become politically legitimate, creating a "belief by political authorities and citizens that agencies can provide benefits, plans, and solutions to national problems found nowhere else in the regime."[7] On this base of legitimacy, bureaus, through the expertise of public managers, build "issue coalitions," with stakeholders both inside and outside government. Carpenter thus creates a vision of public management as the centerpiece of policy implementation.

A recent example is illustrative. Consider the whistle-blower protections in the Sarbanes-Oxley Act of 2002, passed in response to the collapse of Enron, WorldCom, and Arthur Andersen due to severe accounting misrepresentations. Under the act, corporate whistle-blowers have recourse to a federal review process if they are fired, and the Occupational Safety and Health Administration (OSHA) was the agency chosen to implement the program. In making the delegation, Congress believed that OSHA's track record with whistle-blower protection in safety matters gave it the right expertise for the job, even though the substance of their previous cases—say, dumping chemicals—is quite distant from corporate financial shenanigans.

Carpenter suggests that in public management we find information concerning the durability, authority, and capacity of agencies within substantive policy domains. In assessing that expertise, however, agencies also maintain and develop the capacity to thwart congressional interests. To protect against reprisals, agencies fared better when they built issue coalitions than when they simply relied on expertise, which is the premise of various civil service and other administrative reforms. Issue coalitions are a political constraint on agency drift such that bureaus are given more autonomy on the basis of coalitional agreements regarding the policies that they will actually implement. Of course, an agency that drifts too far is surely to be punished by the other members of the issue coalition. An incentive check is present, or in Madisonian terms, "ambition" is "made to counteract ambition." But can the incentives of bureau and Congress be aligned without resort to ad hoc political deals? Can this process be institutionalized? Formally, there is a way to do just that.

The solution to the monopolistic screening problem is a particular type of contract called a "revelation mechanism" (Myerson 1979). Without overlooking better alternatives, Congress can make delegation "contracts" that have three characteristics.[8] First, when the agency comes to understand its hesitance or reluctance in performing its delegated task, it must inform Congress of it. Second, the delegation includes some specific outcome—a "reward" for the agency—for any possible announcement. Third, in any scenario, the agency must find it most beneficial to make a truthful report to Congress, rather than to misreport. The third requirement is satisfied in the same way that principal-agent problems are typically solved, by making the incentives of the agent compatible with those of the principal.

Reconsider the FDA example stated earlier in this chapter. The revelation principle stated above requires that in congressional oversight hearings the administrator of the FDA would tell the truth about its procedures for approving new drugs. Suppose, however, there is a level of corruption in the process: that FDA officials are known by the administrator to receive noncash bribes, such as trips to Jamaica for informational meetings paid for by drug manufacturers in the hopes of favorable approval. Such corruption affects the level of effort the agency expends in screening drugs for the open market. How much of what he or she knows will the FDA administrator reveal to Congress?

The revelation principle again provides the answer. Due to the corruption, the FDA is in fact a "low-performing" agency, so if the administrator presents the agency to Congress truthfully, it will receive the budgetary allocation designated for low performers.[9] Though a lie that would give the FDA a "high-performance" budget level would, indeed, bring more budget, the administrator would face the difficult organizational problem of eliminating the corruption, rendering the FDA a truly high-performance agency. In doing so, the FDA would forgo the benefits from that corruption. If the administrator values the benefits from corruption sufficiently, he or she will report low performance, taking the lower budget and the Jamaican snorkeling excursions.[10]

The "personal" administration and patronage system developed during the Jacksonian period attempted to deal with the problem by creating incentives similar to those under the revelation principle, though the patronage system was more complicated than necessary. Patronage, interestingly, does reflect a constitutional theory of public management. By situating all administrative action under the president as executive agent, Congress had a single agent, namely the chief executive. The president thus inherited Congress's agency problem, and patronage screened in those who value loyalty above other objectives, achieving presidential goals. Recall the holding of Justice Daniel, appointed to the High Court by President Jackson, in *Williams* on the matter of subdelegation as facilitative of a patronage scheme. The electoral connection flowed through the president. As congressional delegations grew in number and scope, however, a patronage-driven personnel function would no longer serve constitutional needs. A more complete solution would be needed to save the president's neck from the electoral chopping block in the event of policy drift.

The monopolistic screening problem as formulated above involves congressional choice among multiple implementing agencies. If for example the FDA shows its (dirty) hand, Congress might choose the Consumer Product Safety Commission for the task, creating a market-based incentive for the FDA to improve its performance. It can easily be seen that where the FDA is the sole feasible implementing agency, the corruption can become organizationally routinized due to the failure of the revelation mechanism to clean up the agency. The reputation of the FDA in Congress would be known and poor, but for pharmaceutical approval, there would simply be no alternative implementing agency. Organizational sociologists would begin to call the corrupt FDA an "institutionalized organization" (DiMaggio and Powell 1991).[11]

The Department of Agriculture in the mid-1800s was such an organization. Its mission was to disseminate knowledge about agriculture but not to create it through research-related activities. "For the first four decades of its existence," writes Daniel Carpenter (2001, 179), the department "was conceived by its supporters and its overseers as the clerical servant of American farmers." Its employees were clerks who, in fulfillment of politicians' preferences of "distributive programs over scientific policy," passed out seeds directly to the agency's farmer clientele (181). Giving out seeds and information on growing them was good political pork. Though agrarian organizations were not enthusiastic about the department, they took the seeds. Agricultural scientists, however, left the agency in droves, "for the program that garnered most of the attention, prestige, and resources of the department was not a research venture but a seed giveaway" (183).[12] The department quite simply could not recruit, attract, and retain scientists as its mandate prescribed.

The type of agency in our FDA example—be it low performing or high performing—is the culprit, and it would seem an obvious target for administrative reforms, personnel reforms in particular. What characteristics, then, would a good administrator exhibit? That question is a central concern of this book. After analyzing the constitutional-level problem, we attempt to formulate a solution.

The delegation of policy implementation authority from Congress to the administration is vulnerable to both hidden information and hidden action problems. The FDA in our example not only develops a greater substantive expertise about both the pharmaceutical industry and its products but also adopts standard operating procedures that allow certain activities (such as communications with industry representatives) to be difficult for Congress, or anyone else, to observe or to reconstruct. As even the most casual reader of news accounts of bureaucracy knows, these hidden actions can be highly relevant to general issues of governance. Consider the OSHA inspector who overlooks a workplace hazard, only to have it claim lives. Or the inspector who, quite apart from judicial determination, fails to protect the corporate whistle-blower in the belief that the whistle-blower is complicit in a crime and deserves punishment. Given such possibilities, the revelation principle does not characterize the full solution to the congressional agency problem.

Congress can find more guidance in Roger Myerson's (1982) hybrid revelation principle for scenarios of hidden action and information. As before, the agency must report its degree of reluctance or hesitance to perform its delegated task to Congress as soon as possible, and it faces differing rewards (for example, through budget allocation) as a result of the report. However, the agency must not only exhibit a willingness to be truthful about the agency's condition but must also be willing to take the action that Congress expects from an agency of the type discussed above.

The latter requirement is known as "obedience." Without it, the agency could simply tell Congress what it must to maximize its budgetary allocation and take a minimally costly action after its accounts have been funded (see for example Niskanen 1971).[13] As we describe in the foregoing chapters, public administration's intellectual project was in significant part to reconcile expertise with obedience, though it was second-guessed by the courts all along the way. Throughout the history of the administrative state, the focus of the personnel function shifted from the presidential agency problem of the Jacksonian era to the congressional problem in the civil service era, to the presidential problem again with the Landis report and the Nixon administration's centralization, and finally back to Congress with the congressional dominance jurisprudence of the Supreme Court in the 1980s.

Principal-agent relationships frame the study of a special case of a larger problem that is especially important for public sector governance, the mechanism design problem. The second prong of what we identify as the framers' dilemma of routinized constitutional administration, this problem is one of creating a mechanism— a game for prospective bureaucrats to play that identifies for the public their type— for eliciting faithful execution of the laws generally, rather than effectuating the specific intent of a particular congressional coalition in the context of a given substantive delegation. As the reader surely anticipates, this problem is not easily solved.

A Primer on Social Choice Theory

Social choice theory is the study of the aggregation of individual preferences into some conception of social utility, which the government, according to the paradigm of economics, should seek to maximize. In the seminal work of social choice theory, Nobelist Kenneth Arrow (1963) makes the case for the importance of understanding social choice. "The rule of the single individual is the extreme of administrative discretion," Arrow writes, "the rule of a sacred code the extreme of rule by law" (1). These are the extremes of the arguments over administration presented in chapter 4. It is important, however, that we analyze those choices that determine the trade-offs between discretion and law toward the end of making the mix of both better for society.

This is prudent since, as Arrow states, "In dynamic situations the rule of a sacred code leads by insensible steps to dictatorship. The code needs interpretation, for conditions change, and, no matter how explicit the code may have been in the first place in determining how society shall act in different circumstances, its meaning becomes ambiguous with the passage of time." He continues: "It might conceivably happen that the job of interpretation passes to society as a whole, acting through some democratic process—'vox populi, vox dei.' Or it can happen that interpretation passes to the hands of the people individually and not collectively; in this case, as soon as differences of opinion arise, the religious code loses all its force as a guide to social action." Social choice theory provides a means by which the outcomes of these "conflicting tendencies in a democracy" can be understood and anticipated.

Abram Bergson (1938) and Paul Samuelson (1947) pioneered the use of a social welfare function to mathematically and completely represent the aggregation of individual citizen preferences and, implicitly, the government's predilections for distributing utility among the individuals whose preferences its social welfare function contains. When the government optimizes a social welfare function through the creation and implementation of public policy without distorting individual utilities, it is said that the social welfare function has been implemented.

Social welfare functions can be endowed with certain characteristics that speak to the quality of government: they may contain only the preferences of individual citizens (and not solely government considerations) to render them free of paternalism; they may admit social utility increases if individual utilities increase and vice versa such that they can be characterized as Paretian; they may represent each individual utility equally or symmetrically; and they may be characterized by an aversion to inequality among the individuals represented, or mathematically, display concavity in the individual utility arguments (Mas-Colell, Whinston, and Green 1995, 825–826). The institutions of representative democracy speak directly to such criteria. As one such institution, so must public management.

It is extremely difficult to observe the preferences of individuals for purposes of aggregation by government. Citizens must reveal this information.[14] At a constitutional level the mechanism design problem presents the framers with the problem of designing a means by which citizens will truthfully tell the government their preferences so that the government, in turn, can make public policy that comports with those preferences. The stability of government rests on the solution to this problem, a point that was crystalline to so astute a student of government as James Madison in *The Federalist, No. 51*: "In framing a government which is to be administered by men over men, the great difficulty lies in this: You must first enable the government to controul the governed; and in the next place, oblige it to controul itself. A dependence on the people is no doubt the primary controul on the government; but experience has taught mankind the necessity of auxiliary precautions."

MECHANISM DESIGN AND THE MIRACLE AT PHILADELPHIA

For Madison, voting mechanisms seemed insufficient to make government a benevolent optimizer of social welfare. Separation of powers specifies three optimizers and a web of checks and balances among them. The constitutional separation of the creation (Article I, sections 1, 6) from the implementation (Article II, sections 1, 3) of public policy creates the principal-agent problem discussed in the preceding section. That disjunction further creates the problem of selecting executive agents who will "faithfully" (Article II, section 3) implement duly created laws. The people, not merely the Congress-as-principal, have a stake in the qualities of those who implement those laws crafted by their representatives.

Article II, section 1, provides the people with a complex voting mechanism for aggregating their preferences over presidential candidates who will occupy the chief office of policy implementation, but the constitutional silence over the aggregation of preferences over any other individual involved in policy implementation is legendary in the field of public administration (Rohr 1986). Even the power of appointing agents is divided between the Senate and the president (Article II, section 2), severing the electoral connection between "public ministers and consuls" and the people.

We argue that this electoral connection is implicit, not in the language, but rather in the theory and construction of the Constitution. In the language of mechanism design, then, the American electorate's problem is to select those persons to staff the administrative state who have some set of characteristics that will make the overall social welfare function implementable. The solution to that problem—the creation of an institutional mechanism characterized by judgment, balance, rationality, and accountability—forms the basis for the administrative state and the default rules for delegations and political control mechanisms generally. The characteristics of the solution form the basis of our theory of public management among the separate powers. The primacy of the personnel function in the institution of public management then becomes clear.

The Theory of Mechanism Design

Stated very generally, the mechanism design problem describes a relationship among multiple agents, who each possess knowledge, expertise, or other characteristics that constitute some portion, but not all, of the elements required to solve a particular optimization problem. The broader social goal is to solve that particular problem by selecting the optimal contribution of each and every agent. More specifically, if the social objective is the faithful execution of the laws, and those laws cover a vast array of subjects—from the regulation of commerce to the administration of justice—then the set of potential agents who will implement a portion of those laws should include economists, lawyers, and a myriad of others who have relevant substantive expertise. Government, however, should not employ every economist or lawyer regardless of experience, training, or other qualifications but only those, and only in such number, sufficient to "optimize" the implementation of law and public policy. Numbers of bureaucrats are easily controlled through personnel procedures, but the characteristics of those bureaucrats beyond those on a résumé—their "type," in the language of the economics of contract—are more difficult to screen.

The standard solution to the mechanism design problem, the revelation principle that we have seen before, suggests that the administrative state should reward certain characteristics of bureaucrats more than others in order to invite participa-

tion in governance only to those potential bureaucrats who embrace specific constitutional values, which we define shortly. This principle quite simply aligns the
incentives of the administrative state with the interests of the polity. Our precept,
then, implies, for example, that a court should not substitute its judgment for that of
an agency unless it is clear that the agency is violating this principle (Bertelli and
Lynn 2001, 2003). An agency that is responsible under our precept will not require
court intervention so long as it remains responsible, justifying judicial deference.

A Primer on Game Theory

Before continuing, it is necessary to define two game theoretic concepts that are
essential to an understanding of the mechanisms discussed in this section.[15] Any
game—such as that between Congress and the FDA over policy implementation—is
completely defined by its players (Congress and the FDA), represented by their
preferences through utility functions, their strategies (Congress can provide a small
or a large budget; the FDA can identify itself as a low- or high-performance agency),
and the payoffs (budget levels and policy performance) that accrue to each player as
a result of taking the actions. The objective of each player in a game is to better itself
by selecting a strategy that will provide the greatest utility from those payoffs it
expects given the anticipated strategy of the other player. In this sense, an equilibrium strategy for one player is a best response to the strategies of the other player.
Solutions to games create an equilibrium in strategic interaction, and there are
many solution concepts that can be employed to determine equilibria that make
sense given the analyst's substantive knowledge of the game.

Two solution concepts are particularly relevant to the discussion that follows. A
dominant strategy equilibrium is a solution to a game in which each player's strategy
provides that player with the greatest well-being regardless of the strategy of the other
player. This is clearly a strong solution concept for substantive interpretation, since
players who myopically focus on their own welfare can reach dominant strategy
equilibria. Such players do not have to be very sophisticated. When players (such as
administrative agencies and Congress) are more sophisticated, an analyst can expect
them to engage in more complex thought about the expected payoffs from their
strategies vis-à-vis other sophisticated players. Their advanced knowledge allows
them to reach equilibria that less sophisticated players would not find. In certain
games, there are no dominant strategy equilibria, and the analyst must decide
whether the players are sophisticated enough to warrant another type of equilibrium
refinement. Refinements are legion, and in the event that the analyst cannot real-

istically employ an existing one, he or she may develop another that makes sense in the particular substantive situation being studied.

A refinement that addresses sophisticated public management issues is the Bayesian-Nash equilibrium. Bayesian players are assumed to have prior beliefs about other players. Congress, for example, knows that among the agencies to which it may delegate regulatory authority, the FDA (in our hypothetical example) might seem to be corruptible when compared to the Department of Agriculture. (The Department of Labor, Representative Emmanuel Celler once indicated, was filled with "whippersnappers" with no real expertise, so a commission of experts created by Congress in the enabling statute may appear more apt.) Past experience, hunches, stereotypes, and a host of other factors can account for these beliefs, but only their existence is assumed for analytic purposes. Furthermore, for Bayesian-Nash equilibrium, the prior beliefs are assumed to be shared by all players; the FDA knows for example that Congress thinks it is corruptible. Given these prior beliefs, each player imagines a probability distribution over the other player's strategies, or an ordering of which strategies are more likely to be played than others. Equilibrium strategies are simply best responses to the probability distribution of the other player's strategies—not, as before, to the strategies themselves.

When designing a mechanism for the personnel function, dominant strategy equilibrium would be preferred to Bayesian-Nash as a solution concept, since the former requires the designer—an early public administrationist—to assume less about the characteristics of potential bureaucrats than in the latter case. Unfortunately, a mechanism that implements dominant strategy equilibria is terribly difficult and under very weak conditions (which we explore in a moment) is impossible to design.

To "play" a mechanism—a game between the agent and the mechanism on behalf of the principal—an individual must give information about his or her preferences to the mechanism, which will return a payoff. In our case, the mechanism is simply the personnel function, whether it is housed in an individual bureau, in the independent Civil Service Commission created by the Pendleton Act, or in the White House Personnel Office. The potential bureaucrat gives information about his or her beliefs, motivations, and so forth to the mechanism, which returns payoffs—appointments, salaries, promotions, opportunities, prestige, and the like—to the bureaucrat in office. In doing this, the broader goal of faithful execution of the laws—represented by a social welfare function that includes all the substantive and procedural preferences of the polity—is optimized, creating the best possible outcome for the polity. Optimization in mechanism design may not meet the most idealistic goals of some members of the polity, but given the array of preferences among individuals, it represents the best that government can do.

Like social welfare functions, mechanisms have characteristics that make the outcomes they implement more desirable for the designer. Among these characteristics, the following are pertinent for our analysis.

First, a mechanism can be considered Paretian if it implements a social welfare function that is, itself, Paretian (as before, such a social welfare function admits social utility increases if individual utilities increase, and vice versa). If all that can be said is that the players expect the ultimate outcome to be Paretian, though future events may prove them wrong, then the mechanism is said to be ex ante Paretian.

Second, a mechanism is considered efficient if it implements a symmetric social welfare function (recall that such a function represents the preferences of each individual equally).

Third, a budget-balanced mechanism is one that implements a social choice function that is nonpaternalistic (again, such a function contains only the preferences of individual citizens and not separate government preferences). The term "budget balanced" is used because, as in our specific case, the information given to the mechanism serves no goal other than the general social objective. In other words, the bureaucracy itself, if it is a budget-balanced mechanism, only uses the information it receives about the preferences of individual bureaucrats for the goal of faithful execution of the laws. It is also the case that a mechanism that is efficient and budget balanced is Paretian.

Fourth, the incentives must be right for "good" potential bureaucrats to enter the bureaucracy, which, in the language of mechanism design, implies that the mechanism must be individual-rational. The benefits that such potential bureaucrats expect to gain from entering public service must outweigh the benefits that the individual anticipates receiving from another career choice.

SELECTING PUBLIC MANAGERS

Since we have fully specified the problem faced by the framers in regard to an administrative state, we have only to find a mechanism that is Paretian (efficient and budget balanced) and individual-rational and translate it into a set of general principles that guide the activities of bureau personnel. Indeed, the revelation principle provides the characteristics of satisfactory mechanisms in both the dominant strategy and the Bayesian-Nash cases (Myerson 1982). The primary goal is to design a mechanism, as in the monopolistic screening case, wherein potential bureaucrats find it most beneficial to tell the truth about their preferences and where this veracity is a dominant strategy equilibrium. When a mechanism has these characteristics, it is considered "strategyproof."

Unfortunately, the only strategyproof mechanism that can be designed is a dictatorship (Gibbard 1973; Satterthwaite 1975).[16] To see this, suppose that a bureaucrat can simply dictate a policy outcome, say the amount by which welfare caseloads will be reduced in a given period of time. Quite obviously, he can achieve his optimal caseload reduction. Moreover, this reduction is also Paretian because changing caseloads by even one case in either direction would reduce the welfare of at least one person, the bureaucrat. Since the bureaucrat, as dictator, always gets his optimal caseload reduction, that outcome is strategyproof in that none of his colleagues, nor his superiors, nor politicians, nor judges can manipulate that outcome by misrepresentations. Our bureaucrat, of course, gets no value from such misrepresentations, so he truthfully reveals the amount by which he wishes caseloads to be reduced. Telling the truth is his dominant strategy.

In a real-world bureaucracy that is patently not a dictatorship, what logically follows is that lying can manipulate outcomes. This result implies that if the only thing that can be assumed about potential bureaucrats is self-interest, then in a real-world agency, which is by no means dictatorial, one bureaucrat can always manipulate the personnel function to his or her advantage and to the disadvantage of others—candidates, bureaucrats, and citizens alike.

A third-best solution is available, however, and it is, we argue, what the founders of the public administration field intuitively understood. To reach that solution, logic requires that we forgo one of the valuable characteristics of mechanisms. But which one? To make matters worse, an additional result shows that it is impossible to achieve both efficiency and budget balance (Hurwicz 1975). Again, the analyst must consider the substance of the problem being confronted. Clearly, the Paretian properties of efficiency and budget balance cannot be compromised in a democratic society.[17] However, if we can assume that potential public servants have sufficiently similar characteristics such that they can form prior beliefs about one another, and the government about them, then the requirement of dominant strategy equilibrium can be relaxed in favor of Bayesian-Nash equilibrium.

This is almost possible. But under very weak conditions, the individual-rational property fails in every such mechanism, so potential bureaucrats never know with certainty that they will be better off in public service than in other careers (Myerson and Satterthwaite 1983). Despite this fact, a mechanism can be constructed that is efficient, budget balanced, and individual-rational in expectation. This means that potential bureaucrats anticipate that they are better off in government when they enter public employment, though they may be later proven incorrect. Resting the equilibrium on expectation will require, in reality, some monitoring of disenchant-ment during civil servants' tenures in office. Since this mechanism was developed by Claude d'Aspremont and Louis-André Gérard-Varet (1979), it is known as the d'AGVA mechanism.

The d'AGVA mechanism operates as follows. First, the applicant for public em-ployment tells the mechanism (that is, the personnel office) about his or her prefer-ence, a statement that need not be truthful—for example, his or her earning poten-tial in a similar position in the private sector or the perquisites of that private sector job (Allison 1983). Then, quite unlike the revelation mechanism, the bureaucrat is rewarded with a payment equal to the expected change in social welfare that would occur if the candidate had lied about his or her type and proved to be something else—for example, the mechanism will compute the social welfare loss of the in-flated wage and fringe package given to the dishonest candidate, who would have in fact received less in the private sector than he or she reported. In other words, payment depends on the amount of damage that the candidate's lie could inflict on the execution of laws. Given that the payment scheme relies on the behavior of all other candidates, each candidate shares the damage from the lies told by a single candidate, which achieves budget balance and eliminates the possibility of any spoils to the government. No one wants to bear the costs of another's lying, but the mecha-nism ensures that they will.

The interdependence of candidates and incumbent officials is the key to under-standing the d'AGVA mechanism. When a candidate gives the personnel office information about his or her type, say during a job interview, it is an effective request that the bureau calculate a package of benefits that depends upon the bureau's expectation of the distribution of types across all other candidates and incumbents in service. The bureau must make those benefits available truthfully. Each of the other candidates and incumbents, by participating, acknowledges a willingness to share the costs of the benefits packages given to everyone else.[18] If we consider these acknowledgements to be revelations of "public service motivation" (see for example Perry and Wise 1990), then no one without such motivation will enter public service. We should expect, as this literature has empirically discovered, that such motivation is strong among public servants.

It is critical to recognize that public service motivation is effected by a bureau's representation and the candidate's acceptance of the sharing arrangement of conse-quences of his or her colleagues' actions. Pay inequity—from merit schemes, for example—may upset that arrangement. Jeffrey Pfeffer (1995, 90) notes that "it may be the distribution, rather than the absolute amount [of remuneration], that is most consequential for understanding the effects of rewards on behavior." Perfomance-

based pay creates inequities that run afoul of the incentives in rank-order tournaments as well as the Ackerlovian partial gift exchange. Edward Lazear and Sherwin
Rosen (1981) show that in a rank-order tournament like the federal civil service, most
balance low probabilities of promotion with salary differentials (or, by extension,
nonmonetary differentials such as prestige). If a promotion is hard to get, say, because there are very few positions at the next level of the hierarchy (a failing in the
design of a personnel system), employees must be motivated to seek promotion by a
large pay or prestige distinction between their current position and that of the next
level.

A well-designed d'AGVA mechanism will screen potential public servants with
no theoretical expense imposed on government in finding out whether government
service is "good" for them. When bureaucrats take their positions, they enter a rank-
order tournament that induces promotion on prestige as well as pay. Their public
service motivation, screened in by the mechanism, reveals a willingness to seek the
prestige-based promotion, rendering pay differentials less important.

The personnel system is the keeper of core governmental values—judgment,
balance, rationality, and accountability—for all of the decentralized hiring procedures. The importance of these values to the precept, and their consistency with
the traditional values of publication, are explicated in the next chapter.

CHAPTER SIX

Managerial Responsibility

A Precept

A formal system of responsibility is . . . essential; it is unsafe to rely wholly on official codes and a sense of inner responsibility; but, on the other hand, a formal system in itself is inadequate.

—*Leonard D. White*

Defined by Alexander Hamilton as "due dependence on the people in a re-publican sense," the concept of managerial responsibility has been central to public administration's claim to constitutional legitimacy from the beginning of the Re-public. Using formal reasoning, we argue in chapter 5 that managerial commitment to a precept of managerial responsibility comprising judgment, balance, rationality, and accountability constitutes a mechanism that ensures an optimal character for public management among, not in addition to, the three branches of gov-ernment.

Although it produces a precept of managerial responsibility that agrees with the Hamiltonian insight that executive government must be both energetic and safe, our argument is essentially Madisonian and produces important contrasts with that of Alexander Hamilton, contrasts that are further dealt with in the next chapter. James Madison's scheme of government emphasizes the control of faction and power in the belief that "the great security against a gradual concentration of the several powers in the same department consists in giving to those who administer each department the necessary constitutional means and personal motives to resist encroachments of the others" (*The Federalist, No. 51*). Jeremy Rabkin (1987, 199) summarizes Madisonian logic: "Power is widely distributed [and] 'ambition' is 'made to check ambition' so there is less need to rely on 'enlightened statesmen' and 'higher motives.'"[1] Madison's scheme requires responsible statesmanship from everyone in government: legislators, elected executives, administrators, and judges. A precept of managerial responsibility sets boundaries on administrative actions that ensure the requisite "sense of responsibility" on the part of public managers.

The idea of managerial responsibility as a constitutional mechanism was intuitively grasped by public administration's traditional scholars. "It is the office of the administrative organizer," says Woodrow Wilson in his 1887 essay, "to fit administration with conditions of clear-cut responsibility *which shall insure trustworthiness* (213, emphasis added). Writes Carl Friedrich (1940, 19), "Responsible conduct of administrative functions is not so much enforced *as it is elicited*" (emphasis added).[2] In a similar spirit, Herbert Spiro (1969, 87–88) stresses the importance of "the manner in which institutions and processes structure political responsibility and thereby facilitate responsible conduct on the part of individuals." That this mechanism efficiently resides in the personnel function is something that early public administrationists, and even proponents of patronage regimes, understood but did not systematically ground in a theory such as that offered in the preceding chapter. Few of these scholars were able to give conceptual precision to the term; most of their efforts define responsibility normatively or schematically rather than analytically.[3] We begin this chapter by reviewing these efforts, then show how the axioms taken from that literature relate directly to the precept.

MANAGERIAL RESPONSIBILITY IN TRADITIONAL DISCOURSE

In Woodrow Wilson's (1887, 213) acknowledgment that power requires responsibility, he argues that Americans need not fear that professional administration of public affairs will lead inevitably to imperious government by bureaucracy. The bulwark against this bad outcome, in Wilson's view, is responsible conduct by administrators. The focus of responsibility is accountability to the citizens rather than a *Rechtsstaat* or English-style noblesse oblige.

Although owing little to Wilson's prescient argument, the theme of responsibility runs continuously through the literature as a shining thread from then onward (Bertelli and Lynn 2003). The following examples are representative.

- "From about 1912 on," says Jane Dahlberg (1966, 236), "the New York Bureau almost continuously devoted its energy to the inculcating of the idea of executive responsibility into our governing institutions, evolving a philosophy of executive responsibility" that is, she argues, consistent with Alexander Hamilton's concept of power commensurate with responsibility.

- While law narrows the possible range of governmental action to make it more predictable and controllable, John Dickinson (1927) asserts that it is impossible to lay down a rule for everything a government has to do. He insists that the control of necessary discretion requires some entity other than law. That entity has been found, he says, "in political responsibility of government to the governed" (277).

- Any answer to the dangers of bureaucracy, argues John Pfiffner (1935, 19), harkening back to Hamilton and Wilson, "combines power with responsibility."

- Argues Harvey Walker (1937, 99): "Public administrators cannot be permitted to construe laws in their own way. . . . If the laws are executed by administrators irresponsible to and even contemptuous of the public will and desires, democracy is only a name." More explicitly, Walker claims that "another limit to the exercise of the control function lies in the necessity for preserving a sense of responsibility in the heads of line departments" (132).

- "A responsible administration," says Leonard White (1939, 578, quoted in Levitan 1946), "cherished and strengthened by those to whom it is responsible, is one of the principal foundations of the modern democratic scene." Later (1942, 215) White argues that "a formal system of responsibility is, nevertheless, essential; it is unsafe to rely wholly on official codes and a sense of inner responsibility; but, on the other hand, a formal system in itself is inadequate."

- "The problem of the responsibility of administrative officials in a democracy," says David Levitan (1946, 566), "is the very crux of the problem of the maintenance of the democratic system. . . . The very continuance of the democratic system depends on our ability to combine administrative responsibility with administrative discretion. Both are indispensable for the maintenance of a democratic service state."[4]

As these and numerous other passages suggest, contributors to the traditional literature grasped the importance of responsibility to both the viability and the legitimacy of the institutions of America's constitutional republic. The importance of a sense of responsibility is a logical implication of the realization that discretion is essential to good administration in the modern American state and that responsibility in the exercise of that discretion *in a republican sense* is prerequisite to achieving good government (Gulick 1933b; Redford 1958; Willoughby 1927). "We find," says Gaus (1936, 35), "that problems of discretion and of responsibility are intermingled from the very beginnings of public administration in the modern national state." In his *Ideal and Practice in Public Administration*, Emmette Redford (1958, 41, 43) argues that "though administration is permeated and circumscribed by law, discretion is vital to its performance. . . . Discretion is necessary in administration [because] law is rigid, and policy must be made pragmatically." The overriding goal, he argues, must be *"the constitutionalization of administrative practice"* (150, emphasis added).

Responsibility in Principle

The above formulations assume, with Hamilton and antebellum courts, that responsibility for administration is located primarily in the executive department and that responsibility *in* administration is, therefore, its primary obligation. This concept was not uncontested, however, as proven by differences among the Founders and by administrative experience throughout most of the nineteenth century. Who is responsible for public action? The answer to this question is necessarily associated with one's theory of democracy.

Traditional public administration generally accepts the Founders' notions concerning representative government as inscribed in the Constitution and subsequently amended and emended by legislatures and interpreted by courts. Whether or not responsible administration is possible under this scheme is an issue upon which views differ. Carl Friedrich (1935, 22) argues that "no government offers as favorable a setting for the development and maintenance of a responsible bureaucracy as a constitutional government with a separation of powers such as that of the United States." At about the same time, Marshall Dimock (1937b, 34) reached the opposite conclusion: "The fixity of our written constitution, the multiplicity of our governing units, and the failure to provide for responsible leadership and administration make our constitutional system a difficult one within which to build principles of public administration."

The predominant view, however, is that, compared to pre–Pendleton Act governance in an America of courts and parties, administrative responsibility should be relocated more explicitly in the executive branch.[5] During most of the nineteenth century, responsibility was diffused among officials at all levels of government, while courts generally considered public administration to be merely "execution of the laws." As discussed in chapter 2, Mugwumps and Progressives feared a responsibility vacuum and sought to locate responsibility itself more clearly in the executive branch of government. When Congress began to regulate monopolies, administration gained new powers that spanned the branches (Rohr 1986). As chapter 4 indicates, the Supreme Court sought to reconcile the view of administration-as-execution with one of administration-as-discretion by announcing the nondelegation doctrine. Advocates for executive responsibility were undeniably successful over subsequent decades in strengthening the roles of senior officials at all levels of government. Nevertheless, the separation of powers ensured that concentrations of executive power did not exceed limits set by legislatures and courts. There was no "imperial executive."

Does responsibility, then, rest with the executive, legislatures, and courts? Or does it rest with mechanisms of direct democracy entirely outside of the constitutional scheme? This question remains a leitmotif of American politics. "Responsibility for administration," writes Gaus (1936, 29), "becomes one of the major stakes of domestic political strife as governmental services become public" (compare Aberbach and Rockman 1988). Gaus's important insight is that, in theory, the location of responsibility is endogenous to the functioning of the constitutional mechanism. "Administration," as Gaus puts it (1947, 124–125), "is intermingled with the entire process of government, and with the environment in which the people affected by the government exist."[6] Later, following a survey of the many perspectives and desiderata associated with the problem of administrative responsibility, Arch Dotson (1957, 726) concludes that "the problem of administrative responsibility is a problem of the entire political system."[7] This cannot be overemphasized. As we discuss in the following chapter, it relates directly to the propriety of administrative reforms.

It must be acknowledged that altogether different conceptions of responsibility can be derived from theories of democracy that would alter or disavow the primacy of "the entire political system." During the Minnowbrook conference, for example, it was argued that postpositivist and existentialist philosophies provided a theoretical rationale for administrators to be guided by their own values, by the requirements of self-actualization or mental health, toward the goal of keeping the way open for social change that promotes the self-actualization of others (Marini 1971, 187). Managerial responsibility in such conceptions is not to the political-legal environment—not, for example, to "clients" or constituencies selected by statutes or interested stakeholders—but to moral principles applied to anyone in the polity who, in the view of morally sovereign administrators, might actively pursue principled social change.

Postpositive, postempirical, and postmodern views of administration contain an irony. By invoking an administrator's own moral principles as the bases for responsible conduct, such views are formally equivalent to the views of those traditionalists, like W. F. Willoughby, for whom administrators comprise a fourth branch of government and whose conduct, if it is to be responsible, must be guided not by political calculation—Willoughby was no less scornful of legislative preeminence than contemporary postmodernists—but by "stable and enduring principle." Adherents of these equivalent views will invoke different principles, of course; postpositivists favor social equity, participation, and authentic discourse, while "dichotomists" such as Willoughby favor efficiency in meeting community needs.[8] Both would place administrators beyond the reach of the constitutional mechanism.

John Rohr makes an altogether different kind of argument on behalf of an extraconstitutional logic of managerial responsibility. The House of Representatives, Rohr argues (1987, 145), as did the anti-Federalists during the founding period, "presents a serious defect in the Constitution [because] it is at odds with what the founding generation thought representation should be. This defect is serious and perennial."[9] The solution to the representation problem is representative bureaucracy. If it can be made more representative of the American people than the House of Representatives, "the administrative state . . . heals and repairs a defect in the Constitution of the United States" (148).[10]

But what is a representative bureaucracy? If representation is merely descriptive—a Latina member of the Consumer Product Safety Commission to "represent" Hispanic consumers—then it does not do the trick. Descriptive representation relies on social facts, even those that hold temporally, not on the Constitution. Representation must be substantive for Rohr's argument to work, and this creates in the bureaucracy a secondary legislature, congealing preferences and gaming with the other branches. As we suggest in chapter 3, it is but a short step from arguments such as this one to the argument, at the core of the Blacksburg Manifesto, that the public manager is morally obligated to correct a defect in the constitutional scheme and to a doctrine of bureaucratic nullification of acts of Congress. Such an extreme position is, however, both dangerous and patently unnecessary if public managers, no matter what their descriptive characteristics, are bound by a precept of managerial responsibility, a mechanism that engenders trust in the executive. Such representation passes through the political branches and restrains factions, as Madison would have us ensure. "The problem of [democratic] control," argue the authors of the 1937 Brookings Institution report (U.S. Senate 1937, 10), "ramifies throughout the entire governmental structure. It does not stop even there; it goes back to the people."

The legitimacy of one set of principles as compared to another is, of course, a matter for argument. Governing principles must be chosen through deliberation, not invoked as a deus ex machina, at least in a democracy. The Constitution establishes Congress as the maker of laws, and the mechanisms of deliberation, debate, and the conditions for choice by the two houses that compose it are a centerpiece of the story of American political development (compare Krehbiel 1998; Rohde 1991;

Cox and McCubbins 1993; Rosenbloom 1983; Lowi 1993). The executive branch, much less subordinate echelons of public management, cannot simply assert a claim to that role. Administrators can share such powers only by dint of a formal and reviewable delegation by the legislature. To argue that public administration should arrogate to itself constitutional powers that it does not formally possess is not only feckless but also perilous. Thugs, scam artists, and ayatollahs might just as well use such a perspective to their partisan advantage as feminists, postcolonialists, or post-empiricists. Many believe that Presidents Reagan, George H. W. Bush, and especially George W. Bush, in their expansive interpretations of their war powers, attempted just that.

We argue that axioms derived from constitutional values deserve greater claim on our attention than autonomous "personal" or "professional" values that, while worthy in some ethical systems, lie beyond the constitutional compact that binds our government to the people. Unless they explicitly reject the stricture "in a republican sense"— such a rejection may, of course, be their unspoken point—postmodernists ought to appreciate the fact that the precept *will* provide the kind of public management that they advocate. Even more significant, an institution of public management under the precept is endogenous to separation-of-powers governance. Its practitioners—that is, managers with the requisite sense of responsibility—will be induced to choose public service through the mechanism we present in chapter 5 and will be held accountable by Madisonian checks and balances, not by a gallery of watchdogs of varying influence or by arbitrary and uncertain reliance on a public official's higher motives.

Responsibility in Practice

Despite being assigned a central role in the theory of constitutional governance, responsibility has been more a catchword than a fully developed concept. The traditional literature can be confusing because the distinction between where responsibility should be located and the requirements of responsible conduct is seldom drawn. Gaus's earliest (1923–1924, 228) pronouncement is typical: "In the past few years this country has seen a tremendous development of interest in improved organization of administration as well as some substantial accomplishments in developing responsible administrative leadership." Noting the importance of the discussion of "responsibility and accountability of the agencies of administration," Wallace Sayre (1951, 5) argues that these discussions have a common concern: how to reconcile the great, unprecedented growth of administrative power with democratic government. Harold Laski (1923, 96) says simply: "The implication of the positive State is surely the responsible State."

As public administration's academic discourse has evolved, however, more attention has been devoted to the conceptualization of administrative practice, and a
diversity of views has emerged.[11] Friedrich (1935, 37) distinguishes between functional or objective as contrasted with general and subjective responsibility. "Subjective elements appear wherever the possibility of relatively voluntary choice enters in,
and here political responsibility is the only method which will *insure* action in
accordance with popular preferences" (emphasis in original). Thus a "psychological" factor supplements "objective" responsibility in the form of dedication to a
career in public service. "All the people want is 'good' execution of this task" (37),
Friedrich argues; there is no "will of the people" with regard to objective tasks or
functions of government (38). In a broadly comparative analysis, Gaus (1936, 40)
argues that in "the new administration" responsibility is an evolving concept and
currently multidimensional: not only political and constitutional but also professional, which ensures an "inner check" on official conduct.[12]

The axis of tension in this discourse was to be fully revealed in the debate over the
sources of administrative responsibility between Herman Finer and Carl Friedrich,
discussed in chapter 3. Finer (1941, 336) argues that responsible administration in a
democracy can only be ensured through external control, as under the Interstate
Commerce Act: "The servants of the public are not to decide their own course; they
are to be responsible to the elected representatives of the public, and these are to
determine the course of action of the public servants *to the most minute degree that is
technically feasible*" (emphasis added). Friedrich, in contrast, takes a dim view of the
ability of courts and legislatures to control administration. He argues that any movement toward democratic responsibility requires that officials have the right orientation toward their work.[13] The checks on abuse of administrative discretion are, in
Friedrich's view, expertise and professionalism: the administrators' preferences and
values.

We ask the reader to take careful note of the centrality of the Friedrich-Finer
debate to the legitimacy of public administration. The earliest practitioners of public
administration attempted pragmatic steps to remedy this problem, and the political
and judicial branches of the U.S. government have had to address those concerns
since 1789. Nonetheless, the notion of responsibility remained a debate for many
years, with efforts to conceptualize responsibility in practice multiplying in the 1940s
and 1950s.

Herbert Simon, Victor Thompson, and Donald Smithburg (1991, 513), for example, define responsibility vaguely as "responsiveness to other people's values" and
accountability as "the enforcement of responsibility." J. Donald Kingsley (1944, 282)
argues that "the essence of responsibility is psychological rather than mechanical."

True responsibility, he says (precisely anticipating a principal-agent model of governance), "is to be sought in an identity of aim and point of view, in a common background of social prejudice, which leads the agent to act as though he were the principal." Paul Van Riper (1958, 550) comments approvingly on Kingsley's notion of representative bureaucracy as a protection against arbitrary and inappropriate administrative action that fails to reflect the values of the society at large. Anticipating a component of our argument in the preceding chapter, he argues that "the concept of professionalism, through which professional standards and scientific objectivity become measures of administrative action, relies primarily on an internalized and voluntary pattern of behavior. Professionalism can often keep administrative discretion within bounds more severe than a legislature would dare to prescribe."[14]

Arthur Maas and Laurence Radway (1949) advance the following criteria: responsibility for exercising discretion in the formulation as well as execution of public policy, responsibility to organized interest groups, and responsibility to the legislature through the chief executive, involving coordination with other executive agencies. Charles Gilbert (1959) lists twelve values associated with administrative responsibility: responsiveness, flexibility, consistency, stability, leadership, probity, candor, competence, efficacy, prudence, due process, and accountability; he excludes efficiency and effectiveness.

Attempting a synthesis, Frederick Mosher (1968), echoing Carl Friedrich (1935), twists several of Gilbert's threads into two aspects of responsibility. The first is *objective responsibility*, akin to accountability or answerability: policies, as the expressed will of the people, are to be carried out whether or not the administrator likes or approves of them. Objective responsibility, Mosher argues, is essential to the reliability or predictability of governance. The second aspect is *subjective or psychological responsibility*, reminiscent of identification, loyalty, and conscience. Responsibility, in other words, has both extrinsic, or political, and intrinsic, or professional and personal, dimensions. The responsible administrator is guided both by politics and by conscientious professionalism, and the personnel function selects individuals predisposed to such a conception of responsibility.

While the dual nature of administrative responsibility is responsive to the central issue raised in the Friedrich-Finer debate, Mosher's dichotomy provides little precise sense of how responsibility might be defined in constitutional terms (Bertelli and Lynn forthcoming). Fortunately, a more robust notion of the content of managerial responsibility can be discovered in the classical literature of public administration, which addresses issues of state building through administrative action with requisite specificity.

A probing analysis of that literature reveals an appreciation of the basic values inherent in the administrator's role. In rejecting administration as "simple commands," for example, Marshall Dimock (1937b, 40) argues that "the only kind of effectiveness which is acceptable to a democratic people is that which is produced by *those who can be trusted*" (emphasis added). In his exploratory essay on administrative responsibility, Rowland Egger (1965, 314) goes even further, invoking Peter Laslett's (1956) concept of the "face-to-face society," a concept akin to the "issue network" and distinct from the "territorial society," arguing that "the important ethical consideration of the face-to-face society is the public trust which it exercises in behalf of the general territorial society." What are the ingredients of trust? They can be found in classical writing, albeit not in codified form.

AXIOMS OF RESPONSIBILITY

Four aspects of managerial responsibility that are prominent in the traditional literature, we argue, should be taken as axiomatic when theorizing about public administration because they resolve the tensions inherent in the separation of powers consistent with our discussion in the preceding chapter. They represent the basis of constitutional government as it relates to public administration.

These logically related qualities of action are not principles in the sense of injunctions for action and practice that, like the widely criticized pre–World War II "principles" identified with Luther Gulick and William Willoughby (for example, unity of command), might or might not conflict or be definitive in given situations. Nor are they, like the elements of POSDCORB (planning, organizing, staffing, directing, coordinating, reporting, budgeting), a taxonomy or classification of managerial functions or activities interrelated as parts to a whole. Nor are they, finally, qualities of action such as those mentioned above—efficiency, effectiveness, professionalism, responsiveness, flexibility, consistency, stability, leadership, probity, candor, competence, efficacy, prudence, and due process—which, while laudable, are not fundamental to constitutional governance.

Rather, the four elements of the precept constitute axioms—or rather an axiomatic system necessitated by Madison and intended to govern managerial selection of specific actions and choices.[15] That is, conceptualized as they are in the following discussion, these elements are the most basic that can be incontestably related to the constitutional scheme.

Judgment

Managerial judgment is fundamental to constitutional public management since, through its exercise, public managers reveal information on the basis of which legislatures, presidents, judges, and citizens can decide to award or withhold trust. The central importance of administrative judgment is well recognized in traditional public administration, whose scholars also insist on its essentially subjective, and thus type-revealing, character.

Judgment—which we take as synonymous with autonomy or discretion—was conceptualized, and its significance recognized, early in the history of public administration. According to James Hart (1925, 28): "By discretion is meant the exercise of choice involving not the scientific application to the facts of objective standards but a subjective evaluation of the advisability of alternatives." John Comer (1927, 14), in a similar vein, says that "government by rule and law has become, in large part, government by the wish and discretion of administrative officers." Luther Gulick (1933a, 61) notes that "discretion, the use of judgment, is the right to choose within a constraining framework of necessity." And in an essay honoring Frank Goodnow, Charles Thach (1935, 275) argues that "the conclusion seems irresistible that a part, at least, of the true significance of the law must nowadays rest on the judgment of the enforcing agency itself."

Early formulations of judgment (or discretion) focus on the regulatory and quasi-judicial functions of government. Both Frank Goodnow (1900) and John Dickinson (1927), however, recognize that administration encompasses more general programmatic, business, and technical responsibilities, where the scope for judgment is wider. In the aftermath of the New Deal, scholars broadened the reach of the concept even further. As if responding to Herman Finer, Walter Van Dyke Bingham (1939, 4) insists that every administrator, no matter how explicit the legislative mandate or precise executive guidance, possesses a "zone of latitude within which his own philosophy, his own basic policies are determinative" (quoted in Lepawsky 1949, 61). According to Schuyler Wallace (1941, 89), "the exact degree of autonomy which should be granted to each operating unit, the work of which is neither purely routine nor quasi-judicial in nature, will and should be determined by reference to the primary purpose of Congress in establishing the unit, or by reference to some ideal purpose more comprehensive than that of Congress."

In a similar vein, Roland Pennock (1941, 33) observes that "what is new is that such discretion is now frequently reposed in agencies of government having many more persons and far larger material interests within their ambit than was the case with the policing authorities of earlier days."[16] Observes Charles Merriam (1945, 149): "Within the circle of larger policy, [the manager] develops smaller areas of policy of his own" (quoted in Lepawsky 1949, 61). David Levitan (1946, 582) argues that "the administration of the modern service state is not a job for automatons. It requires men of vision and ingenuity. It requires the vesting of broad discretion in officials and an ability and courage on their part to use that discretion wisely."

Managerial judgment is, therefore, fundamental to a constitutional scheme in which legislative delegation to executive departments is inevitable. The qualities of that judgment are another matter.

Balance

Managerial judgment must exhibit balance if the administrative state is to constitute a trusted institution of governance. Trust, again, is engendered among public administration's remarkably broad constituency, namely legislators, presidents, judges, and citizens. Managers must incorporate into their strategies and decisions the substantive and procedural preferences of the polity. If administrators systematically attempt to corrupt the constitutional process by acting selfishly on behalf of particular interests or ideologies instead of formulating a balanced view, their own rewards from public service will be correspondingly diminished; they will come to find that public service is a less satisfactory avenue to their goals than pursuing particular interests and ideologies in some less compromised manner, such as through lobbying or electoral politics. Those remaining in public service will be those who achieve high satisfaction from their efforts, inspired by Madison, to control distortions in public policy attributable to unbalanced factional activity and concentrated power.

Traditional scholars develop a nuanced understanding of balance (or what Gulick [1933a, 57] terms "balance and proportion") as an administrative imperative. In their work one finds the clear implication that a goal of responsible administration is the balancing of collective justice, defined by legislatures and the interplay of interest group forces, and individual justice, to which individual citizens are entitled under the Constitution. Following Goodnow, Ernst Freund (1915) distinguishes between powers directly affecting private rights and the administrative powers concerned with the management and operation of public services (see Fairlie 1935). John Fairlie (1935, 31) quotes Judge Cuthbert W. Pound of the New York Court of Appeals (from an unpublished lecture): "In a narrower sense, and as commonly used today, administrative law implies that branch of modern law under which the executive department of government, acting in a quasi-legislative or quasi-judicial capacity, interferes with the conduct of the individual *for the purpose of promoting the well-being of the community*" (emphasis added). Leonard White, like Freund, regards administrative law as concerned with the protection of private rights, while "the objective of public administration is the efficient conduct of public business" (see Fairlie 1935, 36).[17]

The ideal of balance was also expressed in more practical and tactical terms. Fritz Morstein Marx (1940, 286) argues that administration requires "a profitable blend of judgments, political and professional, staff and line, general and special." Administrators, he later writes (1959a, 102), should "give careful thought to the legislative balance of power, the enunciated or anticipated preferences of the chief executive, and the probabilities of public reactions. Ideally, political and administrative thinking should blend into a joint process." Arthur Macmahon (1955, 47) writes that "we may say of legislation generally that the pressures in a pragmatic democracy, sanctioned by majorities and guided by an instinct for equilibrium, are constantly writing a kind of balancing bias into one law or another." The act of striking a balance is termed "adjustive activity" by Emmette Redford (1969, 188): "In the concept of administration as adjustive activity, administration is an extension of the political process of adjustment among interests."[18]

To achieve balance, Marshall Dimock (1936a, 8, 9) argues that "the law related to the subject must, of course, be considered, but in addition the economic situation, the pressure of political parties, and vested interests must be given consideration [as they constitute] influences acting upon the actual administration of government. . . .There is a great deal of repetition, parallelism, and uniformity in the conduct of public business." He continues (11–12) in a vein that anticipates the precept: "Public administration is not merely an inanimate machine, unthinkingly performing the work of government. If public administration is concerned with the problems of government, it is also by the same token interested in fulfilling the ends and objectives of the state. . . . Public administration is planning."

The public manager is not obliged to weigh in the balance interests that are neither represented in nor of concern to the face-to-face community. Their purview is circumscribed by legislative and judicial mandate. Public administration, however, cannot be conceived as a secondary legislature. Insofar as judgment must be exercised within that purview, constitutional principle requires that it be balanced.

Rationality

Essential to constitutional governance, to ambition counteracting ambition, is that administrators have the personal motives to resist or forestall the encroachments of the other departments. As expressed in *The Federalist, No. 51*, "The interest of the man must be connected with the constitutional rights of the place." Constitutional governance assumes, in other words, that public managers actively seek rewards from public service in the executive department. By acting in an intendedly rational way, that is, with due regard for means-ends relationships and nonwasteful solutions to public problems, public managers will enhance those rewards. Acting irrationally, or nonrationally, they will elicit discouraging signals, and encroachments, from the political environment.

In this context, rationality has a commonsense interpretation. It "has something to do with thinking, reason, and reasoning processes. An action seems rational if it is agreeable to reason—if it is not absurd, preposterous, extravagant, or foolish, but rather intelligent, sensible, self-conscious, deliberate, and calculated" (Howard 1971, 287). Or as John Pfiffner puts it (1960, 128), the managerial decision maker "saves face by supporting his decision with reasons which possess face validity." In this light, says Pfiffner, rationality is even more demanding than narrower scientific or engineering notions of rationality in that "it takes into consideration a greater variety of data."[19]

As we note above, rationality has additional, explicit motivations within our separation-of-powers scheme. In political contests between the executive and the legislature, the transparent reasonableness of a political strategy confers an advantage on its proponents. When decision making in either branch lacks transparency, justified suspicions arise that the process is not to be trusted. With the maturing of administrative law, the demonstrable rationality of managerial decisions has become an important criterion for judicial determinations concerning whether or not deference to administrative actions is warranted. The axiomatic significance of rationality infuses classical thinking. According to Stephen Skowronek (1982, 286), state building during the Progressive Era represented a "drive toward administrative rationality grounded in scientific principles of public administration." Fritz Morstein Marx (1940, 42) puts it precisely: institutionalized rationality is "putting proposed policy to the acid test of cause-and-effect relationships." J. Roland Pennock (1952, 797) includes "susceptibility to rational explanation" as one of two meanings of responsibility (the other is accountability).

Rationality in this sense is "conditioned upon an attempt to obtain the relevant facts and, upon deliberation, and upon consideration of, and due regard for, the consequences." Management, says Dwight Waldo (1955, 7, 11), "is action intended to achieve rational cooperation in an administrative system," and "the central idea of public administration is rational action, defined as action correctly calculated to realize given desired goals."[20]

A rational choice among alternatives, in the philosopher Stuart Hampshire's (2000, 40) view, is an institutional process as well as a cognitive process. It is "argument and counterargument, with the just and fair weighing of conflicts of evidence, and of conflicts of desires." In other words, rational decision making is done by "systematizing the process of securing and sifting relevant information so that the factors involved in arriving at a policy decision can be stated and the consequences of alternatives can get analyzed and balanced" (Leiserson and Morstein Marx 1959, 46). Morstein Marx (1959a, 40) argues that "ultimately, [rationality] is controlled by its conscious premises or its unconscious predispositions," and as Stokes put it, "the goal is systems rationalization, or the search for rationally motivated consensus on the basis of the normative implications of systems designs or interventions."

For public managers who are motivated to fulfill the constitutional scheme, the reasonableness of their actions and judgments is the most compelling default position.

Accountability

Accountability is the entire purpose of public management as an institution among the separate powers. Given a good record of managerial expectations and ex post performance, the incentives inherent in the constitutional mechanism for constructing and maintaining public administration will produce high levels of accountability over time. The administrative state becomes a reliable pool of agents for congressional delegations and judicial deference, and their encroachments on the executive will be minimized.[21]

In traditional literature, "accountability" is often used as a synonym for "responsibility" and "answerability." For our purposes, it is more specifically defined as "those methods, procedures, and forces that determine what values will be reflected in administrative decisions" (Simon, Smithburg, and Thompson 1950, 513). In further definition, Leonard White (1955, 222) refers to "accountability for substantive achievements," to accountability for maintaining long-term capacity for "production and service," and to "public acceptability of the agency and its program."

Emmette Redford (1969, 193) terms external guidance "directive activity," that is, activity that establishes purposes, organizations, and rules of administration. Directive activity involves "setting the preconditions of administration on the basis of some measure of [political] consensus on what will be expected of it." Directive activity is definitive when the intent of positive law is clear. When it is ambiguous or incomplete, the public manager must exercise judgment concerning what accountability may require. While no regime of rules can eliminate possibilities for self-interested behavior by subordinate officials, "management guided by [the value of responsibility] abhors the idea of arbitrary authority present in its own wisdom *and recognizes the reality of external direction and constraint"* (Millett 1954, 403, emphasis added).

In the spirit of the precept, the accountability of public officials must not be a hidden or purely subjective aspect of their behavior. As J. Roland Pennock (1952, 797) puts it, "responsibility involves the identifiability of particular individuals or groups who are the effective causes of whatever the government does." Voters, he maintains, should be able to "identify the responsible authorities." So, too, should legislators and judges. Therein lies the power of the precept as a mechanism to, as Carl Friedrich puts it, elicit responsible conduct. Accountability is not an ideal for regimes or governments so much as it is an ideal for the individuals who serve in official capacities, which is chief among the theoretical implications of the preceding chapter.

A PRECEPT OF MANAGERIAL RESPONSIBILITY

We argue, in summary, that public administration and management should comprehend normative standards of action that together are the axiomatic foundations of purposiveness: a precept of managerial responsibility that constitutes a mechanism of constitutional governance. This precept should be invoked as a matter of course at every hierarchical level of executive government in which office holders perform managerial roles.

The commonsense logic of the precept is easy to summarize. Judgment is the sine qua non of responsible administration, necessitated by the delegation of legislative authority. Public managers are agents and, like the carpenter who constructs your kitchen cabinets, make expert judgments in fulfillment of objectives. In our republican scheme, these objectives are electorally connected to the citizens. The content of managerial judgment consists of balance: acceptance of responsibility for identifying and reconciling the inevitable conflicts among interests, mandates and desires: habitual resort to the relationship between action and consequences to ensure transparent justifications for managerial action. Balanced and rational judgments sum to accountability: individual commitment to the exercise of judgment that is balanced and rational and that, aggregated over all public managers, becomes the institutionalized acceptance of the separation of powers. Irresponsible public management, then, is management that disavows accountability and that acts without authority or in an arbitrary, self-serving, ill-informed, or nontransparent fashion.

It is not accidental that this standard echoes that for the review of agency action under section 706 of the Administrative Procedure Act of 1946: "The reviewing court shall . . . hold unlawful and set aside agency action, findings, and conclusions found to be . . . arbitrary, capricious, an abuse of discretion, or otherwise not in accordance with the law . . . contrary to constitutional right, power, privilege, or immunity . . . in excess of statutory jurisdiction, authority, or limitations, or short of statutory right . . . without observance of procedure required by law." Chapter 4 describes the political and legal struggles associated with reaching this equilibrium.

The spirit of this precept, which, as we argue, infuses the traditional literature, is well expressed by Reinhard Bendix (1947, 505). In attempting to define the requirements of democratic administration that necessarily involves bureaucratic organizations, Bendix avers that "in exercising . . . discretion in his direct contact with the public, the democratic administrator is ideally as concerned with administering a policy as he is with execution of a command. . . . Yet this policy continues to be subject to a multiplicity of influences to which the administrator must remain sensitive. . . . This implies that the democratic official does his duty in the continuous anticipation of checks on his authority, both from his superior *and* from his 'public' (which includes legislatures, pressure groups, affected individuals, etc.). He is trained in considering his office a *mandate of responsibilities*, which are subject to more or less continuous modification" (emphasis added). It is incumbent on the democratic official, Bendix argues, to presuppose that a legitimate policy emerges from ongoing political conflict—from the Madisonian interplay of faction and power —which is "a basic and worthwhile feature of the democratic process."

To accept political conflict as a crucible for responsible action is to reject the idea that the public manager is a self-governing, consensus-seeking agent of an exogenous system of values. That idea, most forcefully urged by Carl Friedrich, is also articulated in John Gaus's "inner check," in David Levitan's notion of service based on "deeply rooted personal values," in Minnowbrook's emphasis on correcting the constitutional scheme through embracing the public service goal of social equity through participation, in the Blacksburg view that public administrators should view themselves as a constitutional center of gravity and as guarantors of individual rights, and in the plethora of views that postulate public managers as risk-seeking entrepreneurs of public value. Even when such ideas refer to democratic theory, even the Constitution, they are not derived from the operation of constitutional institutions and do not constitute a mechanism of constitutional legitimacy. These ideas are invalid *in principle* because they explicitly or implicitly assume the professional and ethical autonomy (some would say sanctimony) of public managers and depend upon higher motives. As even a cursory glance at the Bill of Rights makes clear, such dependence is inimical to the Constitution.

To become a secular priesthood inspired by ex cathedra ideals is not an appropriate aspiration for the profession of public administration and management. The appropriate aspiration for public managers under our Constitution is to be public servants guided by a precept of managerial responsibility and thereby cognizant of their role in governing our republic.

CHAPTER SEVEN

Public Management

The Madisonian Solution

If angels were to govern men, neither external nor internal controuls on government would be necessary.

—*James Madison*

The separation-of-powers orientation of modern administrative law demands a constitutional justification for public management. We offer a theory of public management that draws its validity precisely from the separation of powers. That theory, expressed as a precept of managerial responsibility, operates through the long-neglected personnel function of the administrative state, a mechanism that screens, selects, disciplines, and promotes those who will come to hold managerial roles in public service. The personnel function becomes fundamental because implementing those outcomes intended by the legislature and approved by the courts creates incentives for choosing politically responsible public servants.

Our theory of public management, together with its implications for managerial practice, enters a crowded and variegated field of perspectives and prescriptions concerning what public managers should do and why. In this concluding chapter, we locate our theory of public management among this array of approaches and argue for its superiority.

We first review a number of representative perspectives on public management, noting their implications for constitutional governance. Next we compare contemporary thinking about personnel reforms to the mechanism we describe in chapter 5 and, in the light of this comparison, make some suggestions for how personnel reforms might be designed to further constitutional principles. Finally, we show how

"Madison's managers" are sufficient to ensure constitutional governance in a way that the other theories of managerial responsibility are not.

A PLETHORA OF THEORIES, STATED AND IMPLIED

As we note in chapter 6, the idea of managerial responsibility underlies the traditional literature, although one cannot find an authoritative conceptualization there. A similar concern for managerial responsibility has been a preoccupation of scholars and practitioners in posttraditional public administration. Characteristic of this era, these perspectives are heterodox, conflicting, even divergent.

Normative Perspectives

At the height of World War II, two remarkably prescient essays appeared in academic journals, each foreshadowing the awakening controversy over the administrative values that were attributed to the "new public administration" of John Gaus, Leonard White, and John Pfiffner. What was proposed, in effect, was a "new" new public administration.

In the first of these essays, Egbert Wengert (1942, 318) proposes that the intellectual agenda of public administration be changed in two ways. First, primacy should be given to the question, "What mechanisms exist, or can be developed, to create a genuine stake in the governmental process for the ordinary individual affected by it?" The official and the citizen, Wengert believes, should be viewed as continually related. Second, the role of hierarchy should be transformed from being coercive to being facilitative of communication, education, and learning.[1] "This notion might be labeled the 'engineering of consent,' with the understanding that there is no suggestion of manipulation but only of the creation of arrangements conducive to the maintenance of consensual relations, both within and without the administrative structure" (320). Sixty years later, questions concerning democratic administration would be no more penetrating than those posed by Wengert.

In the second essay, David Levitan (1942), foreshadowing the outcome of the Minnowbrook conference, questions the value of bureaucratic neutrality. To Levitan, neutrality means that civil servants shall not engage in partisan politics and that they shall be equally zealous in carrying out policies of whichever party is in power (that is, to abide by the decision of the majority). Taking issue, Levitan argues against "ideological indifference" (318): "There is a vital necessity, especially among the groups in the lower level of the hierarchy, for a renewed devotion to political ideas and for an infusion of a spirit of dedication to ideals and concepts" (318). He continues: "A civil servant in a democracy cannot properly discharge his duties and responsibilities unless he has a firm appreciation of the meaning of democracy, of the dignity of the citizen, and of the concept of being a servant of the people. . . .We should not expect them to look with equal favor on those who wish to accomplish the agency's purpose and those who wish to distort its purpose for party or group advantage" (319–320). Levitan argues for the importance of encouraging "deeply rooted personal beliefs" (321) in civil servants. Noting the importance of administrative interpretation, he argues that "what constitutes 'administrative feasibility' . . . depends on whether the official is more concerned with the plight of the unemployed citizen or with the smooth flow of papers" (322).

Levitan's concerns were to emerge as the "Minnowbrook perspective" (Marini 1971), then the "new public administration" (Frederickson 1971).[2] That perspective has six central themes: relevance, antipositivism, personal morality, innovation, concern for clients, and an antibureaucratic philosophy. "The new public administration," says Waldo (1984), "proposed to move in a liberal and, in a general and non-Marxist sense, leftist direction. It emphasized what were taken to be genuine democratic values and changes. Its central value—or at least its favorite phrase—was 'social equity' and its favorite means to achieve this value, 'participation' " (xvi–xvii). Skepticism or outright hostility toward the positivist, efficiency-oriented methods of policy analysis, as Kent Kirwan (1977) notes, motivates the search for alternative values.

In what is known as the Blacksburg Manifesto, a group of scholars at Virginia Polytechnic Institute and State University in Blacksburg advocate recognition of the problematic nature of the public interest. "The key to the legitimacy of a criterion [such as] the public interest, is . . . whether all those who have a stake in the matter at hand have had the opportunity to share in defining it" (Wamsley and others 1990, 40–41). The manifesto urges a "process that encompasses efforts to render faithful interpretations of the interests of all relevant stakeholders, including citizens at large" (41) in order to win their trust. The Blacksburg authors hold in contempt what they term "nonpartisan instrumentalism." The public administration, they argue, is morally obligated to correct a defect in the constitutional scheme. "Its role . . . is not to cower before a sovereign legislative assembly or a sovereign elected executive" (47). The people alone are sovereign. The public administrator is "trustee," not agent or instrument, expressing "transcendent purposes and moral commitment" (49, 50).[3]

Consistent with this genre, H. George Frederickson (1997) is concerned with the beliefs, values, and customs of those who practice public administration. With unacknowledged irony, Frederickson summarizes his view in terms of seven "first principles" that emphasize a broad perspective on governance, social equity, citizenship, and ethics. Linda deLeon (1998) sees Frederickson's approach as harking back to Minnowbrook, and it clearly echoes the Blacksburg perspectives as well. As noted in chapter 3, she quotes Frederickson's provocative view that bureaucrats "must resist, thwart, or refuse to implement policy that runs counter to the founding documents or to American regime values" (Frederickson 1997, 229). DeLeon comments: "This justification for bureaucratic disobedience, like the natural law justification for disobedience to an errant monarch, leads to some very difficult philosophical issues" (deLeon 1998, 410).

Yet another class of perspectives on managerial responsibility, albeit one that shares distrust of electoral institutions, is concerned with empowering citizens to play a more active role in all aspects of government that affect them. (For a useful survey of these perspectives, see deLeon 2005.) Linda and Peter deLeon (2002), for example, argue that public management should place the promotion of what they call the democratic ethos at the forefront of their concerns. Specifically, they urge the promotion of citizen and public employee participation within public organizations at all stages and levels of policy making to ensure that citizens and employees have direct influence over the organizational decisions that affect them. Doing so would promote personal development, governmental efficiency and effectiveness, citizen trust, and political democracy.

Perhaps the most extreme of the antitraditional perspectives is that of Guy B. Adams and Danny L. Balfour. In their *Unmasking Administrative Evil* (1998), the authors define evil as "knowingly and deliberately inflicting pain and suffering on other human beings" (xix), although, as Melvin Dubnick (2000) points out, they almost immediately abandon the "knowingly and deliberately" qualifications in favor of the view that evil is simply doing harm.

Administrative evil is a new form of evil that, according to Adams and Balfour, has been institutionalized by the modern administrative state. It is characterized by technical rationality, a culture that emphasizes the scientific-analytic mind-set and the belief in technological progress. What makes administrative evil so insidious is both that its perpetrators, ordinary public officials, lack evil intent and that it is masked as rational, progressive action. The predominance of technical rationality in the modern age so narrows the purview of professional (and even personal) ethics that individuals and organizations can act with utter disregard for the human consequences of their actions. The alternative to technical rationality, the cure for administrative evil, is not irrationality but a view of managerial responsibility according to which other modes of reasoning—particularly historical consciousness and critical reflexivity—enable the public manager to have an ear for other voices in administrative and policy processes. To do otherwise, to persist in implementing our precept of managerial responsibility, for example, is presumably to engage in evildoing.

What these antitraditional views have in common is their rejection of a constitutional view of administrative responsibility modified by the Hamiltonian clause, emphasized in chapter 1, "in a republican sense." The legitimacy of administrative autonomy is to reside in administrators' Delphic grasp of what democracy, the Constitution, and human well-being require, a grasp that precludes their craven deference to republican institutions.

Experiential Perspectives

An altogether different class of perspectives on managerial responsibility is based on experiential evidence. In spirit, these perspectives are traditional in that they are intuitive, positive, and inductive rather than ideological or normative.

In 1940, Roscoe C. Martin noted that public administration paid comparatively little attention to the "nature of the craft" of public management (Martin 1965, 8). As we discuss in chapter 3, the nature of managerial responsibility has been given only minimal theoretical or practical definition. Attempts to fill that void are made in the works of Joseph Juran (1944), Arthur Macmahon and John Millett (1939), Donald Stone (1945), Harold Stein (1952), John Millett (1954), Nicholas Nicolaidis (1960), and William Gore (1956) and in the work introduced by the Intercollegiate Case Clearing House, variously known as the "craft," "smart practice," or "best practice" perspective on public management (Lynn 1996; Majone 1989; Overman and Boyd 1994; Bardach 1998).

Best-practice perspectives are founded on "uncodified but richly textured folk wisdom and craft techniques" (Lynn 1996, 158). Most of these perspectives assume that the environment of internal and external constraints and the configuration of organized interests are given and focus on managerial behavior within that given environment (Moore 1984). Their focus may be inward, on the organizational environment, or outward, on the political environment.

Arguably the first book about public management with an experiential temper appeared in 1944. In *Bureaucracy: A Challenge to Better Management: A Constructive Analysis of Management Effectiveness in the Federal Government,* Joseph Juran ostensibly makes a plea for "scientific management" in the Taylor tradition. But in noting several "myths" about government, such as "one central agency" or the "genii back in the bottle" (63) (that moving agencies into a consolidated organization will create more efficiency); the "spectacular solution" (66) (that there is a single cure for what ails public management); and "the Presidential edict" (67) (that the president can make anything happen), Juran reveals a subtle grasp of managerial realities. Although not yet mistrusted, the managers of public bureaucracies confront the need to take action "which through professional pride will resist management uncleanliness, and which in the passing years will build up a lasting tradition of good management" (136).

Drawing on personal observation and experience, Donald Stone's 1945 paper is of particular note because his views anticipate the management ideas of the policy schools.[4] As is characteristic of traditional public administration, his focus is mainly on the organization rather than the political environment. Noting the public interest orientation of the public manager's role, Stone (1945, 212), echoing Chester Barnard (1968), argues that the executive's job is to "maximize his influence" throughout the organization rather than relying exclusively upon his formal authority and power of command, overcoming strong centrifugal forces in the process. He must be discriminating in using his power, however, or he will debase its value and find himself impotent in crucial situations. "His success . . . will be, in large measure, determined by his success in developing a body of commonly shared ideas" (213).[5]

In 1954, John Millett published what is, if Juran's idiosyncratic book is not, the first public management book with a contemporary tone. "Are administrative agencies . . . to be regarded as a 'fourth branch' of government?" he asks. "I believe that they have no such exalted status. Rather, they are a kind of subordinate echelon of government subject in our scheme of things to the supervision of legislature, chief executive, and judiciary. . . . The administrator in the public service is concerned with all three, and ignores any one branch only at his peril. So it seems to me that the politics of public administration is concerned with how administrative agencies in our government are kept subject to popular direction and restraint in the interests of a free society, through the operation of three coordinate branches" (Millett 1954, vii–viii). In summary, "the essential ultimate values of management in the public service are satisfactory service, responsible performance, and good government" (396).

The experiential perspective became particularly popular in the public policy schools, created beginning in the 1970s precisely to provide an alternative to traditional schools of public administration. As Mark Moore (1984, 2, 3, emphasis added), who was on the faculty at the founding of the John F. Kennedy School at Harvard, puts it: "Our conception of 'public management' *adds* responsibility for goal setting and political management to the traditional responsibilities of public administration. . . . Our conception of public management *adds* some quintessential executive functions such as setting purpose, maintaining credibility with overseers, marshalling authority and resources, and positioning one's organization *in a given political environment* as central components of a public manager's job."

The orientation of much of the later experiential literature became decidedly didactic, reflecting authors' determination to be useful to practicing managers. A representative contribution is that of Robert Behn (1991, 206): "For success—for results—the manager must put together policy, administration, and leadership" but, above all, leadership. Michael Barzelay (1992) "advances the argument that public management cultures must be transformed by infusing them with the spirit that has inspired recent corporate management reforms: motivating employee commitment, tapping employee knowledge, and unleashing employee ingenuity" (Lynn 1996, 82). For experiential authors, the criterion of managerial effectiveness is often "results citizen value" (Barzelay 1992, 119), "creating public value" (Moore 1995), or simply "results."[6]

Despite their verisimilitude, craft perspectives on public management simply fail to capture its place in governance. In concentrating on what managers do and how they do it, these perspectives are insensitive to constitutional principles, although they may inadvertently facilitate some of the values of the precept.

Management Reform Perspectives

Beginning in the 1990s, the increasingly intense interest in public management reform, like craft perspectives, is more traditional in the sense that it reflects pragmatic concerns for governmental performance. As it became a global phenomenon (termed the "new public management"), it was manifest, at worst, in a babble of slogans and panaceas: "steering, not rowing," "results, not process," "production, not politics," "empowerment, not power," "collaboration, not conflict" (Lynn 1998). At best, it contained thoughtful reflections on political structures and their implications founded on the conviction that "a stronger emphasis on performance-motivated administration and inclusion in the administrative canon of performance-oriented institutional arrangements, structural forms, and managerial doctrines fitted to particular contexts" (Lynn 1998, 232).

The legitimizing power of performance was perhaps best expressed by Jack Knott and Gary Miller (1987), who discuss a range of structural solutions to the problem of administrative responsibility. They call particular attention to proposals by Martin Landau (1969), Jonathan Bendor (1985), and Vincent Ostrom (1973), who argue, respectively, for redundancy, competition, and Madisonian checks and balances. Knott and Miller (1987, 274) conclude, however, that "there is no structure whose neutrality, expertness, or other characteristics can automatically legitimate the policy choices it makes"; they make the provocative claim that "an institution is justified by its outcomes, rather than the other way around." This view, that responsibility requires achieving good results, precisely anticipates the performance-based emphasis of the managerial reforms that have been de rigueur since the 1990s.

Two distinct reform initiatives in particular dominated the American public management agenda during the eight years of the Clinton administration (1993–2001). In August 1993, after deliberation originating during the administration of George H. W. Bush, Congress enacted the Government Performance and Results Act (GPRA), which instituted a performance-oriented planning and budgeting process throughout the federal government. The act requires agencies to collaborate with Congress in formulating and submitting annual performance plans and reports on program performance, both of which are then evaluated by the Government Accountability Office.

Concurrently, the Clinton administration, under the high-profile leadership of Vice President Al Gore, conducted its National Performance Review—later rechristened the National Partnership for Reinventing Government—which inaugurated what became known as the reinventing government (or simply "reinvention") movement. The reform agenda came to encompass a potpourri of initiatives and ideas, including managing for results, benchmarking, reinvention laboratories, and performance partnerships (Lynn 1999). Managed by the Office of Management and Budget, the Clinton administration initiative also recognized and supported quotidian government improvements, including interagency partnerships, improved human resource management, reduced internal regulations, improved travel management, procurement reform, improvement in support systems, downsizing, fiscal accountability, transforming organizational structures, and improved information technology.

Principled support for the movement was provided by David Osborne and Ted Gaebler's best-selling *Reinventing Government* (1992), a spawn of the earlier *In Search of Excellence*, by Thomas Peters and Robert Waterman (1982), which offers a universal "steer-don't-row" prescription and canonical principles that were to prove congenial to a new generation of reform-minded activists, including the practitioner-dominated National Academy of Public Administration and officials associated with the Clinton administration's National Performance Review. Linda deLeon and Robert Denhardt (2000) see three primary "theories" of public management in this agenda: a reliance on market models to allocate social resources, the transformation of citizens into customers, and faith in managerial entrepreneurship. Further, as Guy Peters (1997, 255) notes, "perhaps the one defining feature of reinvention is a disregard of some of the conventions associated with traditional public administration and an associated desire to rethink government operations from the ground up."

The reinvention movement was largely doomed with the election of President George W. Bush. The new Republican administration promptly launched a management reform initiative of its own, the President's Management Agenda, albeit with relatively little fanfare. That initiative includes five government-wide management initiatives (for example, strategic management of human capital and competitive sourcing); nine specific program initiatives (for example, better research and development investment criteria, broadened health insurance coverage through state initiatives); and the Scorecard and Stoplight Scoring System to track how well the departments and major agencies are executing the five initiatives. These initiatives are based on standards for success developed by the President's Management Council, after discussion with government and academic experts, including the National Academy of Public Administration. The initiatives were to be refined through experience and through a "diagnostic questionnaire" containing questions on four broad topics: program purpose and design, strategic planning, program management, and program results (Bruel 2004). Unlike the Clinton administration's initiatives, however, by the beginning of the Bush administration's second term, this agenda was only beginning to attract academic attention.

Where's Madison?

The diverse solutions surveyed in this section virtually all ignore the constitutional question that is the subject of this book. An issue in the historical disagreement between public administration, in its antilegal temper, and the bar—an issue not adequately addressed, if at all, by the authors of these alternatives—is whether the justifications for their implementation are sufficiently compelling to warrant principled legislative and judicial deference.

Our answers to that question vary. For example, to the extent that the political branches either explicitly authorize or implicitly endorse market-determined allocations of societal resources, a customer orientation or entrepreneurial initiative by public managers, as they most certainly have done in the case of GPRA and President George W. Bush's management agenda, there is nothing objectionable on constitutional grounds to these types of managerial reform. Nor are there constitutional objections to many of the ongoing efforts to improve the craft aspects of public management that were characteristic of the Clinton administration's approach to reinventing government.

The constitutional error in normative, experiential, and management reform schemes lies in the extent to which these schemes assume, for example, that all societal preferences are revealed in markets, thereby conferring legitimacy on all marketlike managerial strategies, that is, that market mechanisms are constitutional mechanisms. Such an assumption ignores the fact that the political environment registers societal preferences for collective goods and services; for the correction of various market failures; and for economic justice, social security, and the preservation of institutional balance. Failure to account for politically expressed preferences is irresponsible. In our constitutional scheme, such failure does not go unnoticed. As we argue throughout the book, it invites the kind of interventions by legislatures and courts that, unfortunately, are inconsistent with a Madisonian political optimum.

That kind of intervention in fact occurred in the case of one of the reinvention initiatives: performance-based organizations. Modeled after European public management reforms that separate administration from politics, the initiative identifies a number of public services that would be exempted from ordinary regulation and managed for high performance. The initiative lost most of its momentum because legislators became concerned with the potential for abuses of managerial discretion, and central overhead agencies answering to elected executives fretted over loss of control and weakened accountability (Lynn 1999; Roberts 1997; Caiden 1998).

Constitutional objections may be raised with respect to other aspects of managerial reform, such as strict adherence to agency-chosen performance measures in budgeting, the further delegation of legislatively delegated managerial authority to private sector partners, or the delegation of decision-making authority to citizen entities with no legal standing. Such measures may not accommodate the existence of faction and power in a manner that is constitutionally sufficient.

For example, judging the responsibility of public management by the performance of contractors fails to allow for the uncertainties inherent in collective goods provision, instead promiscuously distributing the risks associated with achieving both individual and collective justice. Unduly rigid performance-based judgment of managerial performance invites abuses of legislative and judicial determinations throughout the system, which is inimical to the elements of managerial responsibility incorporated in our precept.

More generally, should public management engage in wholesale redelegations of authority to citizen forums, "especially if undisciplined by legislative and judicial deliberation and approval, would arguably place in jeopardy fundamental rights and protections that citizens . . . have come to depend on" (Lynn 2002, 448)? To weaken or undermine Madisonian institutions might well lead to a society that is less just, resilient, tolerant, progressive, and effective in addressing its problems than obtains under the constitutional scheme.

If our argument is valid, then the most appropriate focus for public management reforms is not in the various measures to "make managers manage" according to performance mandates or in wholesale abandonment of managerial prerogative to unconstitutional institutions but, rather, in the personnel function itself, which, if operating properly, effects the strategy of "letting managers manage" in a way that respects rather than defies constitutional institutions.

REFORMING THE PERSONNEL FUNCTION

While reforms of public personnel systems are seldom the central focus of broader governmental reforms, they are hardly ever absent from reform agendas (Ingraham 2005). Because of our emphasis on the personnel function as the constitutional instrument of managerial responsibility, we turn our attention to contemporary ideas about personnel reform and their consistency with Madisonian principles.

Proposals for civil service reform can be analyzed on the basis of the key requirement of the precept of managerial responsibility: the maintenance of public service motivation. We saw in chapter 5 that high-powered merit pay incentives may undermine public service motivation, upsetting the equilibrium properties of the personnel mechanism by promoting expectations that will always be incorrect. That is, individuals may enter public service with intrinsic motivation, but in responding to merit pay incentives, that motivation may be driven out of their decision making. Thus we argue that it is inefficient to create strict merit pay systems because the incentives they create subvert the process whereby bureaucrats are recruited and selected for their Madisonian reliability.[7]

An example of unwise personnel policies can be found in the state of Georgia, where Governor Zell Miller signed legislation that rescinded all civil service protections for employees hired after July 1, 1996 (Kellough and Nigro 2002). Their employment henceforth would be "at will"; all decision making concerning hiring, firing, job definition, and so forth would be left to the discretion of the employer, but the employee might quit at any time and for any reason. Moreover, the Georgia merit system of personnel administration could be bypassed by all state agencies in subsequent hiring processes.[8] Around 2001, the Georgia state legislature authorized the GeorgiaGain program, which "included the establishment of a state-of-the-art performance management system, implementing performance measurement and evaluation procedures that supervisors and subordinates alike trusted, setting up a competitive compensation plan, and streamlining the state's position description and classification system" (Kellough and Nigro 2002, 146). Taken together, these reforms eliminate the process whereby employees compete for moves to higher-level positions (Lazear and Rosen 1981; Whitford 2004) in favor of high-powered incentives. The reforms make it less likely that public service motivation will be maintained among Georgia civil servants.

Comparing the responses of Georgia public employees to a 1993 government-sponsored survey (prereform) with their responses to the authors' own 2000 survey (postreform), J. Edward Kellough and Lloyd Nigro (2002, 156) find evidence of a decrease in public service motivation. For example, 17 percent of 1993 respondents responded affirmatively when asked whether they were "likely to leave state government within the next 12 months for another job." That number increased to nearly 26 percent in 2000. The percentage of respondents who said that their state employment offered sufficient opportunity for growth and development fell from 60 to 47 percent. A full 77 percent of prereform respondents said that performance appraisals were helpful in improving their performance, but less than 65 percent of the respondents felt that way after the reforms. Strikingly, 78 percent of prereform respondents felt that their job description was sufficiently informative "to establish clear standards and expectations used to evaluate [the respondent's] performance"; slightly more than 62 percent of the surveyed bureaucrats took the same position after the reforms.

The best-known proposals to reform the federal civil service also thwart the incentives at work in the personnel mechanism (described in chapter 5) by focusing on performance while claiming to promote public service values.

- Donald Kettl and others (1996, 4) call for the Office of Personnel Management to "be reinvented to define and promote the fundamental values of government service." They continue, "the central office needs to inculcate these values, promote high performance, collect critical data on how well the system works, and especially ensure adherence to the system's core objectives." They would expand the pool of potential agents: "The government needs a strong core, but it does not need to produce all of its goods and services itself. That work ought to be done by whoever can do the job best."
- The Volcker commission (National Commission on the Public Service 1989, 40–41) calls for attracting more high-quality candidates to the "talent pool"; improving the "public's trust" by focusing on the process of presidential appointments, attracting career executives, and decentralizing authority from the president into the agencies; and creating a "culture of performance" through performance-based pay and training. With regard to the Office of Personnel Management, the commission recommends fewer political appointees and the decentralization of the personnel function to the agencies where employees will work.
- At the Wye River Plantation in Maryland, a group of scholars and practitioners advanced the claim that although "human capital must be valued more

highly" than it had been, the key to success is to instill in employees the belief that "performance—high performance—should become a way of life and a critical part of the culture of federal service" (Ingraham, Selden, and Moynihan 2000, 54).

This human capital movement has become influential in government. A 2002 U.S. General Accounting Office report (9) describes three levels of achieving what seems to be a growing "cult of performance." At the first level, an agency's "approach to human capital is largely compliance-based; the agency has yet to realize the value of managing human capital strategically to achieve results; existing human capital approaches have yet to be assessed in light of current and emerging agency needs." Moving up a level, an "agency recognizes that people are a critical asset that must be managed strategically; new human capital policies, programs, and practices are being designed and implemented to support mission accomplishment." Finally, the most fully compliant "agency's human capital approaches contribute to improved agency performance; human capital considerations are fully integrated into strategic planning and day-to-day operations; the agency is continuously seeking ways to further improve its 'people management' *to achieve results*" (emphasis added).

But the putative advantages of this single-minded pursuit of performance are not so easily achieved within our constitutional scheme. First, as David Epstein and Sharyn O'Halloran (1999) and John Huber and Nolan McCarty (2004) show, the incentives of the legislature to delegate authority depend on the agency's level of competence. But the legislature has significant influence over public agencies' capacities to perform as well as over their objectives. Thus performance in the Wye River conference sense is necessarily established within (is endogenous to) the political process. Performance, in other words, is a moving target and, for that reason, a constitutionally pointless pursuit when the political context that determines the meaning of performance is ignored.

The rub can be exemplified in the following scenario. Suppose a bureaucrat has the incentive—say, because of a merit pay system—to achieve performance objective A. Now suppose that the objective is changed by the legislature to B. If the legislature is specific about its task—B is clear and distinguishable from "not B"—the high-performance bureaucrat will respond to incentives and achieve B. If, however, B is expressed in ambiguous statutory language, as citizens we want the bureaucrat to respect the wishes of our representatives and serve us when, as Justice Marshall opined in *Wayman v. Southard*, he or she is left to "fill up the details" of ambiguous legislation. Doing so in a constitutionally appropriate manner requires the public service motivation that the mechanism underlying the precept of managerial responsibility ensures in those selected and retained for public service. That motivation will be undermined if high-powered incentives such as pay for performance and at-will employment induce the pursuit of an apolitical concept of "performance."

Put differently, statutes send signals to bureaucrats about their performance expectations. Some statutes send noisier signals than others. If a statute mandates that standardized test scores, and only standardized test scores, shall be considered in making budgetary allocations across school districts in a given year, the signal is obviously clear. A statute that essentially mandates the Department of Homeland Security to reduce the likelihood of a terrorist attack generates, in contrast, a noisy or ambiguous signal. A performance orientation can be justified as a principle of public management only if there is, as a routine matter, little ambiguity in legislative authorizations. This is simply not often the case.

It is possible, however, for performance to be subsumed as a requirement of accountability. In the state of Texas, for example, all performance goals, objectives, and targets—numbering approximately 7,000—can be found in legislation. Though the state legislature did not produce all of these standards through floor deliberation, its agent, the Legislative Budget Board, has argued the points. The elements of the precept include rationality: the selection of means appropriate to the attainment of defined ends. When the legislature defines ends for the bureaus, performance becomes part of accountability, and modifying, delaying, or manipulating these goals is unlawful. In such a case, performance is appropriately a single-minded pursuit of goals selected by those with a democratic pedigree.

As we argue, the precept of managerial responsibility is effective in proportion to the depth of the pool of candidates that can be screened for optimal type. It works better when personnel officials calculate the costs of selecting the wrong people. Since agencies have more information relevant to this task than does a central personnel office, decentralizing personnel decisions is likely to lead to efficiency gains. Nonetheless, we believe that this selection task should be shared with a central office, since such an office must be the keeper of core governmental values—judgment, balance, rationality, and accountability—for all of the decentralized hiring procedures.

To reiterate, it is critically important that public service values not be displaced by high-powered incentives. We do not argue that performance incentives are inappropriate in all circumstances but rather that they be designed such that motivation is not crowded out. It is also important that public service motivation be held in higher regard than performance orientation in that it will ensure agents who are responsible to the legislature. If a cult of performance seems to be leading bureaucrats astray, the legislature will react by changing its delegation strategy or manipulating bureaucratic capacity, with the resultant instability and inconsistency that undermines optimal political performance.

MADISON'S MANAGERS

Among existing perspectives on public management, then, few alternatives to the precept rest specifically on constitutional authority, and none can be derived from the separation of powers.

John Rohr (1986, 181), for example, argues that public managers should use their discretionary power to maintain the constitutional balance of powers in support of individual rights: "Public Administration, like Congress, president, and courts, is an institution of government compatible with the constitutional design of the framers." He sees public management as a "balance wheel . . . intended to exercise all three powers of government" (182). Such balancing is achieved when public management chooses among the branches—president, Congress, and courts—to favor at any given time and on any given issue.

Rohr's theory of public administration is, therefore, a normative one: "There is no need to ridicule as lackeys those administrators who zealously support the president; nor to condemn as obstructionists those who oppose him. . . . By grounding our thinking about the Public Administration in the Constitution, we can transform erstwhile lackeys, leakers, obstructionists, and whistleblowers into administrative statesmen" (Rohr 1986, 183). But this normative theory misses the mark. Congress, as recognized by the administrative law jurisprudence of the 1980s, takes public management as its agent in delegating powers. Though Congress can, as Herman Finer (1935) recommends, legislate with specificity—a classic example is the Interstate Commerce Act—it will be able to govern more efficiently if it can rely on responsible public management, not an unreliable corps of "administrative statesmen."

Our orientation is normative as well but with a distinctive difference: its positive dimension. We situate public management within the separate powers as a *distinctive institution*, with the president, Congress, and judiciary, not a "balance wheel" for Articles I, II, and III. Since responsibility, as we note, turns on the character of public servants, we argue that the personnel function constitutes the core of public management. Public management, quite simply, must be a repository of responsible legislative agents. The precept of managerial responsibility sufficiently defines responsibility for purposes of the Constitution—that is, in a republican sense.

We are decidedly not originalists. In our theory, the "energy in the executive" is replaced with the Madisonian values of the precept that pervade the Constitution as written, not as imagined in the framing debate. It further urges that separation-of-powers issues be stressed in modern public management, lest the "man in the field" persist in despising all of the emphasis of the laws that operate on the behavior of managers. Finally, it is individual-level behavior by each and every public manager —not institutionalized behavior—that is central to separation-of-powers research in public management.

This theory of public management, then, has positive implications. Such implications have been widely recognized in the literature on public service motivation. The general finding of this empirical literature is that public officials, when compared to their private sector counterparts, place more value on the social benefits of their work and the integrity of their pursuits (see for example Crewson 1997; Rainey 1982, 1983). James Perry and Lois Wise (1990) argue that public servants draw their motivation from "instrumental" roles in policy formulation and program implementation, "norm-based" feelings of value from serving the public and "loyalty" to government, and a "patriotism of benevolence" that connects them to social programs of personal importance. Such observations are consistent with both the precept and the operation of the mechanism discussed in chapter 5.

In summary, the positive theory of public management in the separation of powers predicts that the mechanism will draw into the bureaucracy precisely the kinds of people who respond to the surveys in the public service motivation literature. That they are in fact found in public service is evidence that the mechanism is in fact operating, albeit to an approximation. Normatively, we submit that reforms must not dilute their dedication to serving the public in our constitutional system. If the personnel function is more explicitly oriented toward the precept, we believe that a more reliable public service will be the result.

The history of public administration and the equilibration of administrative law around its emergent form compel the conclusion that an administrative state is founded on the concepts of responsibility and accountability and the associated requirements of balance, rationality, and judgment. The precept of managerial responsibility defines both the core of public management's constitutional value in the separation-of-powers regime and the primacy of the personnel function as the mechanism that ensures that public management reliably comports with constitutional values. In contrast to the legislative, executive, and judicial branches, constitutional public management is defined by the characteristics of those individuals doing the job. It is that character—expert, dedicated, and respectful of the authority of the people's representatives—that makes public managerial actions constitutional. This conclusion renders the personnel function the centerpiece of the institution of public management. These individuals, behaving as Madison's managers, will ensure responsibility in a republican sense.

This, in concluding, we offer as the solution to the pervasive sense of crisis in public administration. A field obsessed with "performance" and "ethics" and "participation" rather than with its role in constitutional governance will remain vulnerable to existential challenges from the other branches. Legislatures, by imposing administrative procedures and substantive constraints, the courts, by defining the meaning of the separation of powers, and elected executives, by aggrandizing the power of overhead agencies, are well positioned to do for public management what public management will not do for itself. Public administration, as John Millett understands, cannot be a "headless fourth branch" pretending to an autonomy that is above the law. The precept of managerial responsibility must become its head, and the head must draw its power from the willingness of every administrator in the public service to earn legitimacy in the only way open to them under the Constitution's separation of powers.

Notes

1. "The touchstone for legitimacy of public administration within our particular constitutional scheme derives in the main from its role in participating with three specified branches of government to provide for the furtherance of the public health, safety, and welfare" (Wise 1993, 260).

2. For a less incident-driven perspective, see the American Customer Satisfaction Index (ACSI), which tracks trends in customer satisfaction with firms and agencies in the corporate and public sectors. Data for 2003 indicate that the general level of satisfaction with public agencies, at 70.9%, was only slightly less than the level of satisfaction with the private sector, at 73.8%. The ACSI is produced through a partnership of the University of Michigan Business School, the American Society for Quality, and the international consulting firm, CFI Group (www.theacsi.org, accessed 30 January 2004). It measures 7 economic sectors, 39 industries (including e-commerce and e-business), and more than 200 companies and federal and local government agencies.

3. For instructive examples of official investigations into public management issues, see the Columbia Accident Investigation Board's report (CAIB 2003) and the 9/11 Commission's report (9/11 Commission 2004).

4. The word "scientific" in seventeenth- and eighteenth-century usage means the statement and elaboration of practical maxims based on systematic observation, trial, and error. Today we would call such maxims "best" or "smart" practices.

5. The extent to which direct democracy has been institutionalized in the United States varies across time and jurisdictions (Smith and Tolbert 2004). The iconic New England town meeting puts citizens into close contact with administrators, at least at budget time. A strong current of support for greater reliance on direct democracy infuses contemporary public administration, although its proponents seldom make any effort to reconcile their views concerning citizen empowerment with the requirements of administrative law under the separation of powers.

6. This view is most closely associated with William F. Willoughby. Although the idea of a fourth branch of government was influential because of Willoughby's association with the Institute for Governmental Research and the Brookings Institution, it never gained a foothold in the literature of public administration.

7. Donald Smithburg believes the term "responsibility" to be imprecise, noting four dis-

tinct and mutually exclusive usages: moral obligation, responsiveness, accountability, and legitimacy (Smithburg 1951). Roland Pennock believes responsibility to have two primary meanings: accountability and the rational and moral exercise of discretionary power (as noted by Storing 1964). It will become clear as our argument evolves that our concept of responsibility necessarily embraces these several meanings as mutually reinforcing rather than as mutually exclusive. Our definition is, in effect, that of the *Oxford English Dictionary:* "a charge, trust, or duty for which one is responsible." Or, as Storing (1964, 46) puts it, "The question of responsibility is the link between the civil servant's particular business in government and that government's business."

8. Because political activity is interest-based, Madison, argues Lowi (1993, 263), "can be called the father of modern political science as well as the father of the Constitution."

9. Other contemporary scholars emphasize the constitutional and legal foundations of public administration and management. Their contributions are discussed at greater length in chapter 4. A useful source is the symposium on the legitimacy of the administrative state published in issue 3 of the 1993 *Public Administration Review.*

10. An additional argument for employing a rational choice logic is advanced by Aucoin (1990, 126), who argues that the public choice paradigm "emphasizes the role to be played by political authorities as elected representatives in governance. It does not admit to a policy/administration dichotomy that would carve out spheres of responsibility for politicians on the one hand and bureaucrats on the other." This is a considerable advantage over what he calls the managerialist paradigm, which "reasserts the policy/administration dichotomy with a vengeance" (127). The public choice approach, Aucoin argues, "sees politics as pervading management; that is, politics is present in both the formulation and the implementation of policies."

11. Fairlie (1935, 29) notes, however, that Freund "limits his study . . . to powers directly affecting private rights and clearly states that he does not attempt to deal with administrative powers in the management and operation of public services." He quotes Judge Cuthbert W. Pound of the New York Court of Appeals (from an unpublished lecture): "In a narrower sense, and as commonly used today, administrative law implies that branch of modern law under which the executive department of government, acting in a quasi-legislative or quasi-judicial capacity, interferes with the conduct of the individual for the purpose of promoting the well-being of the community" (31).

12. "Modern administrative tribunals have jurisdiction over a wide variety of subject-matters; and there is a sound logic in the refusal of the courts to deal with all on an equal footing" (Dickinson 1927, 155). Dickinson notes administrative adjudication in regulation but also "matters as to which the government is a direct party in interest, i.e., the distribution of pensions or public lands, collection of the revenue, direct governmental performance of public services, and the like" (156).

CHAPTER 2: THAT OLD-TIME RELIGION

1. Kingsley (1945, 89) argues that administrative ideas cannot be abstracted from their political context, "for we shall not then understand them, and their practical application will involve the incorporation of unexamined assumptions into our administrative system."

2. For "a steady and quiet development," see Gaus (1931, 122). The enduring influence of Federalist and anti-Federalist ideas and arguments, and especially of *The Federalist* and also of de Toqueville's *Democracy in America*, is widely acknowledged (see, for example, Rohr 1986, 2002; Van Riper 1987). However, the sustained appreciation and study of public administration originated in the latter decades of the nineteenth century, although the originators are variously identified as either Henry Adams (Karl 1976), Woodrow Wilson (Henry 1987), or Frank Goodnow (Haines and Dimock 1935).

3. According to Van Riper (1997, 218), "The late nineteenth century founders of public administration were collectivities rather than individuals," an observation that holds as well for the first two decades of the twentieth century.

4. White describes the revolt against formalism and abstraction in the 1890s in economics, political science, and law led by Dewey, Holmes, Beard, and Veblen. Dewey and Veblen were strong opponents of Scottish empiricism and of utilitarianism, of Hume, Adam Smith, Bentham, and John Stuart Mill. Historical phenomena had to be dealt with in a historical-cultural manner. Charles Beard, the youngest, quoted Holmes, Pound, Goodnow, and Bentley in his *Economic Interpretation of the Constitution of the United States* (1913).

5. The quotation is from Alexander Pope, *An Essay on Man: Epistle III:* "For forms of government let fools contest, / What e'er is best administer'd is best" (http://eir.library.utoronto.ca/rpo/display/poem1639/html, accessed 17 June 2004), stanza 6, lines 303–304. In the same stanza (lines 305–309), Pope offers further insight for our times: "For modes of faith let graceless zealots fight / His can't be wrong whose life is in the right / In faith and hope the world will disagree / But all mankind's concern is charity / All must be false that thwart this one great end."

6. "Woodrow Wilson largely set the tone for the early study of public administration," says Henry (1987, 39) in a typical homage to the 1887 essay. But, notes Van Riper (1987, 9), "an examination of major political and social science works of the period between 1900 and World War I shows no citation whatever of the essay in any of these volumes." Van Riper adds that, of the textbooks by White (1926), Willoughby (1927), Pfiffner (1935), and Walker (1937), only White cites Wilson's essay. "The 1887 work had no influence whatever on the evolution of either the theory of the practice of public administration in the United States until well after 1950."

7. According to Richard Childs, "ramshackle governments are hard for the people to control." Quoted by Hirschorn (1997, 132).

8. Devised to meet the emergency created by the disastrous hurricane of 1900, commission government promised undivided and able government. A more ambitious version was created in Des Moines, incorporating nonpartisan elections, a merit system, and the initiative, referendum, and recall (Hamilton 1911). Childs, founder (with the Princeton president Woodrow Wilson's support) of the Short Ballot Organization, initially supported the Galveston Plan (Stone, Price, and Stone 1940). Later he indicted commission government and the strong mayor model as incapable of selecting competent people to manage complex departments (Schiesl 1977) and helped conceive the council-manager (later city manager) model, based on three elements: unity of political power in the council, the short ballot, and concentration of administrative authority in an official accountable to the council (Stone, Price, and Stone 1940). The first council-manager government was created in Staunton, Virginia, in 1908. By

1923 some 270 cities were using this model. The number had expanded to over 470 by 1940 (Stone, Price, and Stone 1940).

9. In 1924, the organization was also renamed the International City Management Association.

10. Contemporary notions of "reinventing government" have come full circle on this point. "Running government like a business" may claim to be an antidote to bureaucratic capture by interest groups (though its proponents do not make this claim strongly). Nonetheless, it rescinds the gains to constitutional democracy that come from a professional administration learning from constituent groups as well as legislators. Price (2002), a professor of political science at Duke University and a member of the North Carolina House delegation, states that the congressman has a tripartite role as educator, lawmaker, and ombudsman. Core notions of modern political economy conceive of the legislator's role precisely in this way. Representatives educate the bureaucracy and are ombudsmen for claims from the bureau on behalf of constituents (Fiorina 1977). Administrators process that advice, as well as information from groups that representatives favor and have written into legislation (McCubbins, Noll, and Weingast 1987, 1989).

11. Stone (1975, 83) summarizes the bureau's ideas as including "such innovations as executive leadership and accountability, untangling of administrative and legislative functions, current and capital budgeting including budget hearings, personnel classification, and salary standardization, simplified and integrated administrative structures, centralized purchasing, scientific assessment and tax procedures, full disclosure of public records, informative government reports, and surveys to promote efficiency with better performance."

12. Observe the authors of the Brookings report on Progressive Era reforms: "The movements for the merit system, the direct primary, the popular election of United States Senators, the council-manager plan, and the recall were phases of the effort to keep administration, as well as legislation, in the service of the whole people and to prevent perversions of the democratic process" (U.S. Senate 1937, 10).

13. In 1939 the GRA, in a controversial decision, moved to form the professional association that was eventually to become the American Society for Public Administration (Pugh 1988).

14. John Mabry Mathews, author of what is arguably the first public administration textbook, makes the provocative observation that states are essentially municipal and have more to learn from municipal administration than from national administration (1917).

15. Argues Ford (1900, 185): "Administrative authority in state and municipal government has been so disintegrated that there is no adequate basis for the development of an efficient organ of control."

16. Says B. P. DeWitt of the significance of this development at the state level: "The efficiency movement repairs and adapts the machinery of government which the home rule movement frees, the commission movement simplifies, and the social movement uses in the interest of the people" (1915, quoted in Waldo 1984, 187).

17. "Executives vigorous and safe" is from Hart (1925, 112).

18. According to Pinkett (1965), Gifford Pinchot was the moving force behind creation of the Keep commission (and a member). Roosevelt's and the commission's concerns were not with "parlour theory" about how government should work but with the nuts and bolts of actual

housekeeping (procurement, records management, auditing, personnel administration) and decision making. The emphasis was on administrative responsibility, departmental organization, and decision formulation.

19. An even more ephemeral development had similar precedent-setting influence. To meet the demands of wartime administration, President Wilson created the Central Bureau of Planning and Statistics in 1918 and appointed the Harvard Business School dean Edwin Gay to direct it. Though an ad hoc response to the emergency, "its enduring significance lay in reviving the idea of the Keep and Taft commissions for some kind of central bureau of administration and in providing a haven in which the skills of the academic community were concentrated and its talents demonstrated" (Skowronek 1982, 203). It also emboldened Robert Brookings to continue to press for enactment of an executive budget.

20. In a public statement at its founding, the IGR is described as "an association of citizens for cooperating with public officials in the scientific study of business methods with a view to promoting efficiency in government and advancing the science of administration" (Willoughby 1918, 58).

21. Willoughby helped draft the Budget and Accounting Act, "the greatest reform in governmental practices since the beginning of the republic," according to Harding (quoted in Saunders 1966, 23). The IGR helped staff the first Budget Bureau; its first director, Charles Dawes, had his offices there for a time. Meanwhile, IGR's descriptive-prescriptive publications were having a significant impact in Washington.

22. Also with IGR assistance (in the person of Lewis Meriam), Congress passed the Classification Act in 1923, creating a Personnel Classification Board, which provided the federal government with "a career structure that could prescribe standardized career ladders and foster predictability and similarity of experience among career state officials" (Carpenter 2001, 48).

23. Merriam (1940) estimates the number at 800,000.

24. As noted above, Cleveland, the father of the executive budget movement, chaired the Taft commission and became director of the New York Bureau of Municipal Research. Dawes was the first budget director. Willoughby, a professor of politics at Princeton, became director of the IGR. Charles A. Beard became director of the New York Bureau of Municipal Research Training School in 1915 and of the bureau itself in 1918, whereupon Luther Gulick became head of the Training School. Louis Brownlow became head of ICMA in the 1920s and "was to the city manager profession what Richard Childs had been to the city manager movement— father, inventor, creator, and manipulator of symbols" (Stillman 1974, 49).

25. Goodnow's books on municipal government include *Municipal Home Rule* (1895), *Municipal Problems* (1897), *City Government in the United States* (1904), and *Municipal Government* (1909). Although Dahlberg (1966) argues that the New York Bureau of Municipal Research implemented Goodnow's theory of the separation of politics and administration in a nonpartisan, objective way, these ideas were themes of municipal reform before Goodnow published his 1900 book.

26. In 1928 the Social Science Research Council appointed a Committee on Public Administration (Stone and Stone 1975, 24), whose first chair was Leonard White. By 1935 the chair was Louis Brownlow, director of the Public Administration Clearing House (Gaus 1935). The committee staff was instrumental in creating a research program "to get fixed points of guid-

ance—to add to the store of principles of administration so that, as government faces new problems and expands still further its activities, its regulatory functions, and its economic enterprises, those who must make the administrative decisions may profit by recent and current experience," which must be obtained from practitioners.

27. According to Waldo (1984, 187): "While it is not literally true, as W. E. Mosher remarks, that the phrase 'economy and efficiency' was 'first coined by the bureau movement,' students and reformers of many kinds became quickly and thoroughly enthusiastic about this new approach during the Progressive years."

28. The idea that the emerging practice of administration and management could be usefully assisted by identification of "universal principles" acquired significant, although far from universal, popularity. Identification and reliance on scientific principles were regarded as essential to ensuring the legitimacy of the new field of public administration and management. Their popularity has proven robust. The usefulness of principles and the methods for deriving them—were they syntheses of experience or scientific laws?—were vigorously debated well into the 1940s, providing the foil for the Simon and Dahl critiques of the field. The notion of universalistic principles has enjoyed a renaissance owing to the influence of the "best practices" literature and is the primary format for prescriptive public management in the twenty-first century.

29. The Pendleton merit system "never prescribed a formally fixed or informally legitimized path of education to the bureaucracy as existed in every one of the rationalized states discussed earlier" (Carpenter 2001, 48). The development of education and training for public service is "irrevocably linked" to "the struggle to overcome political patronage, malfeasance, disorder, special privilege, and waste in government" (Stone and Stone 1975, 13). The New York Training School for Public Service had been established in 1911, associated with the ideas of Charles A. Beard, who himself advocated a university-based professional education in public administration. (It merged with the Institute for Public Administration in 1922.) The Society for the Promotion of Training for the Public Service, a forerunner of the American Society for Public Administration, held conferences in 1914, 1915, and 1916, and a journal, *Public Servant*, was begun in February 1916. "University curricula gave increasing attention to government, public issues, and public administration" (Stone and Stone 1975, 29), but more with academic than with professional training. "The developments during the first third of the century both stimulated and discouraged response by the universities" (16). Not until the 1930s did the federal government deliberately search for administrative talent. In the 1930s and 1940s it appeared that a significant advance was in progress in establishing a connection between the newly emerging curriculum in public administration and certain career lines in government" (Waldo 1984, xx).

30. Kettl (2002) regards "traditional" or "classical" public administration as combining Wilsonian and Hamiltonian traditions emphasizing top-down management and control.

31. Henry (2004) regards the politics-administration dichotomy as public administration's first paradigm (1900–1926), followed by the principles of administration (1927–1937).

32. "The first third of the present century . . . was a period during which many of the occupations we now recognize as professions asserted that claim—accounting, business administration, city planning, forestry, engineering, foreign service, journalism, nursing, optometry, public health, social work, teaching, and many others" (Mosher 1975, 3). They were all,

like public administration, pragmatic and problem oriented and were sustained by faith in progress, efficiency, democratic government, and what we now call meritocracy.

33. The Wharton School was founded at the University of Pennsylvania in 1881, business schools at the University of Chicago and the University of California at Berkeley in 1898. By 1911 thirty business schools were in operation (George 1972). Sheldon (1924, 36) says, however, that "our science of management is in the most infantile stage" and "management is in its youth."

34. This was most famously expressed by White (1926, viii): "The study of administration should start from the base of management rather than the foundation of law."

35. The prestige of scientific management was given a significant boost during the Eastern Rate Case hearings by Louis Brandeis's argument, endorsed by Taylor and his followers, that its application would preclude the need for a rate increase by eastern railroads. Taylor's major forum was the American Society for Mechanical Engineers, the locus of sophisticated thinking about management theory and practice.

36. American and British contributors to the growing management literature were particularly self-conscious about methods or intellectual processes. Church (1914, iv, vi) observes that "administration was entering a stage where things could be reasoned about instead of being guessed at. . . . the introduction of reasoning into management as opposed to the old rule-of-thumb school." He identifies three general principles of management: the systematic accumulation and use of experience, the economic control (or regulation) of effort, and the promotion of personal effectiveness (v). Marshall (1921) and Sheldon (1924) reiterate Church's identification of analysis as key to the new management. Sheldon (49) argues that "the management of a generation ago . . . relied on chance or on initiative. . . . It did not pause to analyze, to dissect, to investigate. . . . Modern management is inclined to build upon a surer foundation." According to Person (1926), scientific management codifies and legitimizes standard practices such as functional organization, separation of planning and detail execution, standardization, and coordination. Although as dean of Dartmouth's Tuck School Person organized the first scientific management conference in the United States in 1911, in 1926 he could argue that "consciousness of management as an industrial problem and especially conscious effort to resolve the problem are something new," although "scientific management" had already established certain "standard practices."

Frenchman Henri Fayol's 1916 *Administration industrielle et générale* was ignored in the United States until 1937, but his ideas foreshadowed later developments: there is an optimum degree of centralization or decentralization for each firm; employees do not operate merely as cogs in a machine; a chain of supervision runs from top to the bottom ranks (George 1972). As the most distinguished European management thinker, Fayol views management as a teachable theory concerned with planning, organizing, commanding, coordinating, and controlling.

37. Charles Merriam was a leader in this movement, of which Leonard White was a follower. William Yandell Elliott was a leading critic of scientism, as were Luther Gulick and Charles Beard (Gulick 1926). The movement began to wane after 1930. By the mid-1940s, dissatisfaction with scientism and the state of the profession was acute. Because of scientism, little by little attention had "turned to the inner workings of the political system, to the forces which shaped the end result, and to the manner in which those influences were brought to

bear" (Somit and Tannenhaus 1967, 132), rather than to the ends themselves. Public administration, as discussed further below, was afflicted by the turmoil within its parent discipline.

38. When he wrote *The Process of Government*, Bentley was not a member of APSA. He, along with Wilson, Lowell, and Bryce, was a realist, arguing that the focus of political science should be "the activities which are politics" (quoted in Somit and Tannenhaus 1967, 66). The great task was the study of political groups. He was ignored by political scientists, who persisted in their study of the formal structures and processes of government. "The political science of this [the formative] period tended to be legalistic, descriptive, formalistic, conceptually barren, and largely devoid of . . . empirical data" (69).

39. Of note is Prichard (1892, 19): "Scientific knowledge, skilled labor, systematic organization are all necessary for the conduct of the various municipal departments." The problem is not simply dishonesty. "A scientific organization of departments will, to a very large extent, increase the morality as well as the efficiency of the employee" (22).

40. With strikingly resonant logic, Ford (1900, 182–183) observes (in a review of Goodnow's *Politics and Administration*): "If direct popular supervision of the conduct of government had the importance which the dominant school of reformers attach to it, municipal government should be best administered, since it comes closer to the people than state or national government, and the consequences of maladministration are more direct and immediate in their effect. By like inference, state government should be superior to the national government in quality of administration; but, as a matter of fact, the gradation of satisfactoriness is just the other way."

41. It might have been even faster had not universities been slow in assuming a role in the training of public administrators, a role that did not materialize to a significant extent until the New Deal, which drew scholars to the subject of the new agencies and programs.

42. Kimball's book is primarily descriptive, historical, and prescriptive rather than analytical and critical. Kimball offers a rather doctrinaire defense of the separation of politics from day-to-day administration.

43. Sheldon's appendix to chapter 4 is a systematic comparison of government and business and industry. He believes that business and government were converging on similar principles of management.

44. Goodnow "has been frequently referred to as (and is 'properly called') the 'father of public administration'" (Haines and Dimock 1935, v). Haines and Dimock quote Charles A. Beard in a 1926 luncheon address of APSA: "Mr. Goodnow was the first scholar in the United States to recognize the immense importance of administration in modern society and to sketch the outlines of the field" (vi). "The doctrinal content of public administration was first clearly formulated in this country by Frank J. Goodnow" (Dimock 1933, 259).

45. According to Stillman (1990, 66), "The discovery of administrative law as a unique and important segment of public law was made in the 1880s when Frank J. Goodnow published the first essay on the topic, 'Judicial Remedies against Administrative Actions,' in the first volume of *Political Science Quarterly* (1886). He apologized for his discovery of administrative law by writing 'I am trying to adopt a classification . . . applicable to any nation [which is] generally adopted at present in Europe.'"

46. Haines and Dimock (1935, xii) observe that in *Politics and Administration* Goodnow "showed the inescapable relation between the formulation and the execution of the law" and

"progressed much further toward the present emphasis in administration upon management and actual ways of doing things in contrast with the legal rule relative to the subject."

47. "Although the differentiation of two functions of government is clear, the assignment of such functions to separate authorities is impossible" (Goodnow 1900, 21–22).

48. Key (1942, 146) argues that the notion that politics and administration are compartmentalized is "a perversion of Goodnow's doctrine." "He saw that 'practical political necessity makes impossible the consideration of the function of politics apart from that of administration.'" Dimock (1933, 260) insists that "Goodnow emphasized the discretionary, legislative, and judicial characteristics of administrative officials; in other words, he did not attempt to put law-making and law-enforcement in water-tight compartments." Lepawsky (1949, 44) observes: "Although Goodnow, like Wilson, felt constrained to make the distinction between politics and administration because of the contemporary 'necessity of administrative efficiency,' he also insisted that administration had constantly to be related to politics if government was to work successfully."

49. The discussion of Cleveland is taken from Lynn (2001).

50. Willoughby is now best remembered for his 1927 *Principles of Public Administration*, on behalf of which he provided a dogmatic defense in 1937 with the unqualified assertion that efficient government requires the application of scientific principles achieved through the rigid application of scientific methods of general validity.

51. Later Willoughby (1930) expresses criticism of research bureau work because it did not contribute to the advancement of the science of public administration, i.e., of general principles.

52. Comer's *Legislative Functions of National Administrative Authorities*, published in 1927, is based on his Ph.D. dissertation at Columbia University. An impressive work of scholarship, its citations reveal a growing post-1915 academic literature. Nonetheless, Comer gives due attention to Wilson's 1887 essay and other early work.

53. Gaus (1931, 130) also documents the myriad "extra-legal" organizations, including associations of government professionals, functionally oriented study-advocacy organizations, and new institutions of governmental research. Notably, he speaks of contributions to "the techniques of public management."

54. Waldo (1984, 160) discusses at length "three attempts to deal carefully and critically with the concept of principles": those of L. D. White, Herman Finer, and E. O. Stene. White's "The Meaning of Principles in Public Administration" makes a commonsense case for principles that have empirical justification. But, says Waldo, "White leaves all the important questions unanswered, all the logical distinctions blurred" (162). Finer's "Principles as a Guide to Management" is "an acute treatment" based on causal logic. But, says Waldo, "Finer's analysis of *types* of principles is not complete enough to account for all possibilities" (162). Moreover, Finer is incorrect in saying that normative principles are partly based on causal principles. The opposite may be true: partly impeded by causal principles (163). Stene's "An Approach to a Science of Administration" "represents the furthest extension of two tendencies: the 'principles tradition' in public administration, and the quest for a 'theory of organization'" (165).

55. In an article addressed to city managers two years later, Finer (1935) elaborates: "It is the manager's business to act, and therefore he must combine, interweave, proportion, and

directly apply what he has learned of principles. The principles which he learns in books or from other people are not self-acting. Nor can any principle be applied directly without regard to all the details of the circumstances in which they are to be applied. That is peculiarly the manager's position: to have had the requisite education in principles, and then, by a species of fine tact, to know how much of each and in what peculiar combination of them, he may proceed" (289). The city, insists Finer, "cannot afford to let its manager learn by his and its mistakes. It is cheaper to learn by other people's" (288).

56. Gulick (1933b, 282) easily grasps the significance of basing a definition of principle on a causal relation, noting that many principles have an element of purpose: "'You must do this and you must do that.' . . . We immediately drop into the Ten Commandments when we start stating principles." But he also notes a sharp distinction between choosing the objects (policies) and finding the best means of carrying them out (administration). Finer agrees but says the practical administrator must do both.

57. In the 1939 edition of his textbook, White avoids the use of the term "principles," preferring instead such formulations as "good government requires" (Stene 1940).

58. In Merriam's (1940, 297) view, the administrator's practical rules of thumb refer back to "recognized uniformities of behavior, and also to implicit principles of order, organization, justice, and welfare." In his incisive analysis of various principles for constructing a department, Wallace (1941) decries the possibility of the rote application of abstract principles. For Wallace, context is decisive. He also insists that administration cannot be a true science. In the 1946 edition of his textbook, Pfiffner cites Beard's discussion of the meaning of a science of administration: a body of knowledge and principles for its application. Pfiffner seems to equate principles with "working knowledge," "standard tools and precepts which facilitate management" (8). He finds terms such as "assumptions," "pattern solutions," and "uniformity in the matter of approach" acceptable but has "no disposition to claim that they are principles" (8). He finds congenial the concept of "the generalizing mind" (11).

59. As early as 1922, however, the critical spirit had been manifest in Coker's sharp critique of the "dogmas of administrative reform": economizing through the elimination of duplication and overlap and concentrating power in order to attract able leaders and to locate responsibility. In Coker's view, such principles slighted attention to the need for continuity in work of a technical character; the need to involve unpaid citizens in exercising powers of investigation, advice, and publicity; the need to locate legal responsibility in offices most likely to develop professionalism and pride in performance; and the uselessness of creating positions that are beyond the limits of what an officer can reasonably attend to.

60. The field would not have its own journal until *Public Administration Review* began publishing in 1940.

61. Dimock (1937b, 32) is also critical of Wilson. "Today we cannot accept unqualifiedly the generalization of Woodrow Wilson" concerning administration being "removed from the hurry and strife of politics." "Politics (in the sense of law or policy) runs all the way through administration. Group pressures operate directly and ceaselessly upon every branch and subdivision of public administration."

62. Ten years later, Levitan (1943, 353) offers similar views on Willoughby: The "identification of administration with techniques, most elaborately developed by Willoughby, has been called the 'institutional' approach, perhaps because of its resemblance to the approach of

institutional economics. Whatever the origin of the term, the attention focused on administrative techniques, processes, and procedures has contributed much to the improvement of administration in the modern state," but it is much too narrow to provide a theory of administration, which requires imagination and vision in the service of the philosophy of the state.

63. Herring (1936, 15) notes, anticipating Terry Moe, that "the despised bureaus are in a sense the creations of their critics and . . . while bureaucracy is flayed in general, single bureaus are loyally supported by their congressional sympathizers." As Moe later puts it (1989, 328–329): "A bureaucracy that is structurally unsuited for effective action is precisely the kind of bureaucracy that interest groups and politicians routinely and deliberately create. Most of them, taken singly, would not want it that way. Each actor, if able to design and control a bureaucracy without interference by opposing interests, would create the most effective organization possible and take steps to keep it that way. No one, however, has the power to make these political choices alone. Various actors with various interests have to do it collectively, democratically. And because they are forced to design bureaucracy through a democratic process, their structural choices turn out to be very different indeed from those intended to promote effective organization."

64. Willoughby (1937, 62) lauds the high degree of scientific development of public finance and accounting and asserts that "the most important problem of public administration at the present time is that of devising and installing a system of budgetary procedure adapted to our political systems . . . a problem that scarcely exists in the case of private enterprises."

65. In this vein, Willoughby (1937) distinguishes between "institutional" and "functional" activities, the latter concerned with the specific work of the organization, the former, the "real subject of administration" (44), with which the science of administration is concerned; that is, with maintaining the organization itself, not performed as an end in themselves but as a means to an end. "Institutional activities are of the same general character no matter what the nature of the undertaking. . . . It is one of the prime functions of the science of administration to determine what these principles are and the manner in which they should be applied in meeting varying conditions" (44–45).

66. Pfiffner takes due note of White's 1933 term "the New Management" and finds it apt and expressive.

67. White himself (1933, 145–146) produces a list of devices to consolidate administrative power: enlargement of chief executive office; agencies of general administration reporting to executive; budget systems; administrative fiscal control; contingent funds controlled by the executive; administrative reorganization to permit effective supervision; central personnel, printing, purchasing agencies; and use of overhead agencies, e.g., budget bureaus, to coordinate.

68. Herring (1936) quotes White (1933, 340): "Faced with the steady growth of technological operations in government, to what extent and in what way can citizen participation in administration be preserved? . . . The reconciliation of democratic institutions and a professionalized bureaucracy operating still in the retreating shadow of the spoils system is one of the major perplexities of the future."

69. "Politics should stick to its policy-determining sphere and leave administration to apply its own technical processes free from the blight of political meddling" (Pfiffner 1935, 9). The emergence of the superintendent in school administration is cited as an example of what is

being advocated. But "there is no denial that in a considerable number of instances questions of policy will be closely intermingled with administrative action. . . . The dividing line between policy and administration is much easier to ascertain in a fire department than in a police department, in a recorder's office than in a district attorney's office, and in public works than in poor relief" (10).

70. In the 1946 edition of his book, Pfiffner much more fully develops the politics-administration dichotomy, devising a chart and giving more examples. His examples of the need for a scientific and technical approach at the federal level are the Forest Service and the Public Health Service. The city manager is still featured, and he cites research by Stone, Price, and Stone (1940) that most were nonpartisan administrators. But he is aware of the nuances: "The legislative body did not have to rely upon legislation to control administration, when it could do so merely by controlling the city manager" (23). The British government is cited as an example of a proper separation.

CHAPTER 3: ORTHODOXY AND ITS DISCONTENTS

1. The apogee in fact occurred with the initiation of and the reception accorded to the work of the first Hoover commission by the U.S. Congress (Millett 1949; Emmerich 1950; Sayre 1958; Arnold 1976; Seidman 1998; Kettl 2002).

2. Sayre (1958, 102) lends weight to this view and takes it even further: "Administration was perceived as a self-contained world, with its own separate values, rules, and methods." Svara (2001, 178) notes that Sayre's 1958 article goes well beyond Waldo in enunciating, for the first time as the founding theory of public administration, a dichotomy model emphasizing complete separation of politics and administration. In so doing, Sayre details "the *evolving* discussion of the interaction of politics and administration by asserting instead that this was a new, previously unrecognized concern" (emphasis in original).

3. In the introduction to the 1984 reissue of *The Administrative State* (xliv), Waldo says of the "dogmas of administration": "I do urge that they be seen in historical context, and suggest that thus viewed they are understandable and even in the main were justifiable, appropriate to the historical situation."

4. Waldo (1971, 264) writes that, for two generations, classical ideas "helped the government and people of the United States not only to survive but to achieve important values, many of them democratic values." Such balanced judgments never overcame his early animus toward those ideas, however.

5. Waldo describes *The Administrative State* as "a library project," thus accounting for its "compiled index cards" quality. Further, "it never occurred to me . . . to look very much at the development of institutions and the history of administration" (quoted in Brown and Stillman 1986, 33–34).

6. Waldo (1965a, 17) argues that, whereas the period from World War I to the Depression summarized and synthesized, producing the first textbooks, the post–World War II period "steadily adds without ever summing or subtracting, argues without agreeing or concluding." Yet the former period drew his withering criticism, and Waldo himself was a major influence on the latter period.

7. Waldo (1971, 266) says, however, that "Certainly mid- and late-twentieth-century philo-

sophical movements should be explored and, if possible, used to help us solve our problems. But, so far I am not convinced that, on balance, they solve more problems than they create."

8. Simon (1948, 844) writes a rather scathing review of *The Administrative State*, arguing that Waldo finds more consistency in the early literature than is actually there and that his overall argument is "far too brief, superficial, and confused."

9. Chisholm (1989) provides a detailed and critical analysis of Storing's critique of Simon.

10. Hammond (1990) claims that Gulick recognized before Simon did the rudiments of what would become the theory of bounded rationality. He suggests more generally that Gulick's work was ahead of its time.

11. In a comment on Dahl's article, Simon (1947) argues that applied scientists must concern themselves with all phenomena relevant to the particular set of values involved in the problem and with all potentially relevant values. Thus there cannot be an applied science of public administration, but there can be a field that would properly be described as a field of "political economy" or "social economy" that encompasses (beyond the level of "intelligent amateur") political science, economics, and sociology. Alternatively, or in addition, there can be a pure science of human behavior in organizations based on social psychology, which provides propositions to political economists.

12. In a review of a book advancing principles for organizing industry, Dahl (1947b, 282) observes that "if sheer logical beauty were enough [to validate principles], then we might better return to a study of Fourier and his marvelously contrived *phalanstères*, which had everything in their favor except the possibility of working in a world of living people."

13. Waldo (1952a, 503) patronizingly suggests that Simon might become a major political theorist "if he can resist the temptation to make a career of defense of his first book." That, of course, is the fate that awaited Waldo, who never again produced a work of the originality of *The Administrative State*. For an analysis of the 1952 Simon-Waldo debate, see Harmon (1989).

14. Many additional characterizations of the traditional paradigm, both contemporary and contemporaneous, are cited in Lynn (2001).

15. The phrase is from Waldo (1955). Waldo also writes, "For the better part of a generation, there was hardly a conspicuous dissent in the professional literature from the 'dogmas of centralization,' the 'canons of integration'" (1952b, 87).

16. Lepawsky (1949, 23) documents prevailing perspectives on orthodox tenets: "The POSDCORB idea is . . . widely accepted in American textbooks dealing with administration." He cites Pfiffner's *Public Administration* (1935), Millet's contribution to Morstein Marx's 1959 *Elements of Public Administration*, and White and Smith's textbook (1939, 309). Pfiffner notes exceptions, that rigidity is ill-advised, and he retreats even further in a later edition, but nevertheless advocates a principle of separation. Lepawsky quotes Vieg (1959) as saying that if officials clearly indicate they are agents of policy, then meddling in what they do is unjustified. White is also implicated in propagating the dichotomy. But Lepawsky notes that Gulick (1933a), Herring (1936), and Dimock (1937a) are all arguing that politics and policy are coordinate rather than exclusive. As Gulick (61) puts it, "Governmental institutions cannot be devised to coincide definitely with any scheme of clear-cut division between policy and administration. In the first place, no such division exists in actual affairs. In the second place, it is impossible to make a few clear-cut groupings of actions or work on the basis of the degree of discretion involved." Friedrich (1940) says that the dichotomy is a "misleading distinction."

And Merriam (1940) refers disparagingly to the "high priests of public administration" who "favor an unduly narrow and conflict-free discourse."

17. For example, in *The Administrative State,* Waldo (1984) quotes Cleveland and Buck as follows: "The difference between autocracy and a democracy lies not in its administrative organization, but in the absence or presence of a controlling electorate or representative body outside of the administration with power to determine the will of the membership, and to enforce the will on the administration" (Cleveland and Buck 1920, 15), a nuanced view. But Waldo's ensuing discussion seems cynical toward such professions of faith in democracy, as if they were belied by the "politics-administration formula" that Waldo attributes to prewar thinking.

18. In local government, where the dichotomy might seem to have its strongest claim to relevance, Svara (1999, 679) argues that "the original rationale of the council-manager form is not consistent with the dichotomy."

19. The other two members were Charles Merriam and Luther Gulick. The committee's research staff included many individuals who have made important contributions to the field, including A. E. Buck, Herbert Emmerich, James W. Fesler, James Hart, John D. Millett, and Schuyler C. Wallace.

20. Urwick, coeditor of the special studies for PCAM (1937, 14), saw clearly the trade-off between "scientific management" and democratic self-government, "which places an overriding emphasis on the consent of the governed secured through representative institutions." Urwick believes the Brownlow report to represent scientific management at its best, not in "the details of their recommendations" but in "the intellectual method, the outlook which illuminated their whole enquiry" (Urwick and Brech 1945, 161). Urwick believes centralized, scientifically managed administration to be the protector, the shield of democracy.

21. Contesting the Brownlow committee's doctrines, the Brookings report (U.S. Senate 1937) makes a number of arguments: "No one form of organization . . . is demonstrably better than all others" (8). Moreover, "we are not convinced that any close relationship exists between democracy and purely administrative efficiency. . . . If we are to believe that a particular form of administrative organization will protect us against dictatorship we shall be lulled into a sense of false security and may forget until it is too late the deeper issues involved" (9–10). "The movement for executive centralization of administration in the interest of efficiency has gained much headway; but, along with it, the feeling has grown that such centralization may not be altogether safe unless equal emphasis is given, on the one hand, to the protection of the administration from personal or partisan manipulation and, on the other hand, to the establishment of new devices for insuring popular control" (10). "It is . . . difficult if not impossible to determine whether or not efficiency or inefficiency is to be attributed to organization" (12).

22. As is discussed in the next chapter, James Landis's *The Administrative Process* (1938) addresses independent regulatory functions and argues that they constitute an innovation that enables the extension of government service without upsetting the balance of powers. In general, administration is part of the legislative, not the executive, power.

23. Lepawsky (1949) cites others who address this issue. He quotes Merriam (1945, 61): "Within the circle of larger policy, [the manager] develops smaller areas of policy of his own" (in Lepawsky 1949, 149). Durham (1940) is credited with the term "administrative politics," Key

(1947) of writing of administration as politics, and Kingsley (1945, 87) of calling administration "a branch of politics."

24. But consider this by Friedrich (1940): "We are entirely agreed that technical responsibility is not sufficient to keep a civil service wholesome and zealous, and that political responsibility is needed to produce truly responsible policy in a popular government" (14). He goes on to say, with Gaus, that we are far from this ideal: "Instead of administering according to precedent, the responsible administrator today works according to anticipation" (17). Later, he argues that "at best, responsibility in a democracy will remain fragmentary because of the indistinct voice of the principal whose agents the officials are supposed to be: the heterogeneous masses composing the electorate. But it can be approximated" (Friedrich 1946, 412–413).

25. Regarding discretion, Finer (1941, 339) refers to "the loopholes for administrative discretion or the policy-making power of officials." Such loopholes exist because legislative mandates may not be precise or the statute may be simply misunderstood. Finer endorses officials' "omnipresent sense of duty *to the public*" but says that they cannot be a substitute for subservience to democratic controls. He refers to Rousseau's thought that the people can be unwise but cannot be wrong. He acknowledges the many "drawbacks of political control" but says that they can be remedied and that their consequences are less ominous than granting administrators additional discretion. "The result to be feared is the enhancement of official conceit" (340), he says, and he adamantly insists on devices "to commit and compel the official to change his course" (341).

26. "American democracy, during its independent existence, has been attempting to create an indigenous form of administrative organization, reflecting the complexities of popular control" (Millspaugh 1937, 73).

27. Millspaugh (1937, 73) opposes administrative centralization. "The strong executive type of government . . . tends to produce immediate and superficial results, instead of, and perhaps at the expense of, ultimate and fundamental values." Specifically, "the President's recent proposals for the reorganization of the Federal administration [viz., the Brownlow committee report] call for an especially critical examination."

28. Hyneman's (1939) comments are directed in particular at two books: A. E. Buck's *The Reorganization of State Governments in the United States* (1938) and Porter's *State Administration* (1938).

29. Stene (1940) offers a critique similar in spirit.

30. Merriam (1940, 305–306), a member of the Brownlow committee, identifies the pathologies of bureaucracy: "Arrogance and indifference to the public, lack of sympathy approaching harshness and cruelty, devotion to inflexibility and routine, grumbling at theory and change, procrastination, quibbling and delay; or the opposite of too much great and rash speed without adequate preparation of the public for change."

31. The White quotation is from the *Encyclopaedia of the Social Sciences*. The Wallace quotation is from Wallace (1941, 231–233).

32. In note 24, Levitan (1943) cites the sources for the view he is criticizing: Friedrich, the *Frontiers of Public Administration*, White, the Brownlow report, and Arthur Macmahon.

33. The phrase "collapse and disintegration" is from Waldo (1968).

34. As to the solution, political supremacy, Hyneman (1950, 73) notes that the literature has not advanced beyond where Goodnow and Wilson left it, that administration, though differentiated from politics, was nonetheless to be under "the direction and control of the elected officials of the government."

35. The low point in the search for essentials was undoubtedly the publication of *Theory and Practice of Public Administration: Scope, Objectives, and Methods* (Charlesworth 1968), a mind-numbing collection of essays and discussion transcripts by the field's more senior figures.

36. Kettl has sounded a series of alarums dating back to 1990. The latest is Kettl (2002, 153): "At the dawn of the twenty-first century, neither the theory nor the practice of American public administration proved sufficient for the problems it has to solve." The field, he argues, must be completely transformed.

37. In 1970, the American Society for Public Administration echoed Waldo's warning: "Today's crisis exceeds all historical crises in public administration" (quoted in Ostrom 1973, 12).

38. As neither Wilson nor Weber influenced the New York Bureau of Municipal Research model of administrative organization, the foundation of classical public administration, a more accurate label would have been the Goodnow-Willoughby paradigm.

39. Remaining calm, Mosher (1975) argues that malaise was affecting all academic and educational specialities as each realized its innate inability to handle real problems of the world within its own tradition. The fact that public administration had from its beginning insisted on cross-fertilization among specialties was "its greatest strength and its most vulnerable feature" (6).

40. The same point is made by Levitan (1946, 575). Noting the attacks on democracy founded on the incompetence of legislatures, he says: "If it is accepted in a democracy that the right to decide what the government should or should not do—to determine the course of public policy and action—belongs to the people, then it would appear that only those to whom they have delegated their authority, whom they have chosen to act for them and who are answerable to them, may exercise this function, and these are their elected representatives."

41. Redford (1958, 24–25) quotes Herring: "The concept of public interest is given substance by its identification with the interests of certain groups."

42. "Democratic government," says Redford (1958), "assumes that administration must be subject to control from outside, and integration and hierarchy are devices for insuring this subjection all the way down the line" (79). In other words, exercising authority over workers is not antidemocratic but the opposite. "The primary means of democratic control is through the representative system" (89). He notes Finer's view that Congress should control bureaucracy "to the most minute degree that is technically feasible" but prefers Hyneman's (1950, 85) view that Congress "should not define and describe a governmental undertaking in such detail that administrative officials are rendered incapable of achieving the major objectives toward which the legislation is directed" (89).

43. Overviews that are similar in content and spirit are provided by Davy (1962), Kaufman (1956), and Sayre (1958).

44. Both approaches are sharply contested. Metcalfe and Richards (1993, 115), for example, argue that public choice "largely fails to contribute usefully to our understanding of real-world public management problems." König (1997, 226) argues that legalistic reasoning may be

superior to economic reasoning: "Assessments of effects and successes, analyses of costs and benefits fall short of what legal argumentation is able to perform." The unit of analysis for both Metcalfe and Richards and König is the system as a whole. Metcalfe and Richards prefer a network perspective, however, whereas König (228) argues for "the primacy of politics and democracy as well as the constitutional system of order."

45. Vickers (1983) refers to appreciative judgments, the ability to draw distinctions, to determine that a phenomenon is this rather than that.

CHAPTER 4: RAISING THE BAR

1. The fear in nondelegation is that of the abrogation of legislative authority. Section 16 of article 3 of the New York State Constitution exists for this purpose, providing that no statute "shall be passed which shall provide that any existing law, or any part thereof, shall be made or deemed part of said act, or which shall enact that any existing law, or part thereof, shall be applicable, except by inserting it in such act." In *People ex rel. New York Electric Lines Co. v. Squire*, 107 N.Y. 593, 602 (1888), the court unpacked the intent of that statute as follows: "The object and intent of the constitutional provision was to prevent statute laws relating to one subject from being made applicable to laws passed upon another subject, through ignorance and misapprehension on the part of the legislature, and to require that all acts should contain within themselves such information as should be necessary to enable it, to act upon them intelligently and discreetly. It is obvious that it does not apply to an act purporting to amend existing laws, for in such a case no intelligent legislation could be had at all without a knowledge of the law intended to be amended. It must be presumed that the legislature is informed of the condition of a law which it is called upon to amend. It could never have been contemplated by the framers of the Constitution that any legislator would remain ignorant of the provisions of a law which it was proposed to change, or would require the provisions of such a law to be transcribed into the proposed legislation to enable him to act upon it judiciously and intelligently. Such a construction would lead to innumerable repetitions of laws in the statute books and render them not only bulky and cumbersome, but confused and unintelligible almost beyond conception."

2. What remains is called the "intelligible principle" rule (*Federal Energy Administration v. Algonquin SNG, Inc.*, 426 U.S. 548, 1976). This principle holds that a congressional delegation is constitutionally overbroad—violates the separation of powers—only in cases where standards by which administrative action can be guided are entirely absent. This rule embodies the concern that discerning, in the typical legal proceeding, whether the intent of Congress has been followed is definitionally impossible.

3. President Thomas Jefferson (the antifederalist) and Chief Justice John Marshall (the federalist) fought over a number of issues, including the accountability of judges through impeachment. Writes Weiss (2000, 502–503), "Jacksonianism, with its demand for greater democracy, provided an impetus for the idea of codification. Criticizing the state of the law was no longer just the business of professionals. Laymen regarded the complexity of the law as a manifestation of lawyers' attempts to monopolize and control the law and to exclude ordinary people from legal knowledge."

4. The strength of Taney's language cannot be overstated. He writes, "the Constitution of

the United States delegates no judicial power to Congress. Its powers are confined to legislative duties, and restricted within certain prescribed limits. By the second section of Article VI, the laws of Congress are made the supreme law of the land only when they are made in pursuance of the legislative power specified in the Constitution; and by the Xth amendment the powers not delegated to the United States nor prohibited by it to the States, are reserved to the States respectively or to the people. The reservation to the States respectively can only mean the reservation of the rights of sovereignty which they respectively possessed before the adoption of the Constitution of the United States, and which they had not parted from by that instrument. And any legislation by Congress beyond the limits of the power delegated, would be trespassing upon the rights of the States or the people, and would not be the supreme law of the land, but null and void; and it would be the duty of the courts to declare it so. For whether an act of Congress is within the limits of its delegated power or not is a judicial question, to be decided by the courts, the Constitution having, in express terms, declared that the judicial power shall extend to all cases arising under the Constitution" (*Gordon*, 705).

5. In a vigorous dissenting opinion in *Mistretta v. United States*, 488 U.S. 361, 424–425 (1989), Justice Scalia cites *Williams* as he rebukes the court for permitting the constitutionality of sentencing under guidelines promulgated by the U.S. Sentencing Commission as the use of power under an excessive delegation: "Although the Constitution says that 'the executive Power shall be vested in a President of the United States of America,' Art. II, § 1, it was never thought that the President would have to exercise that power personally. He may generally authorize others to exercise executive powers, with full effect of law, in his place. . . . It is already a leap from the proposition that a person who is not the President may exercise executive powers to the proposition we accepted in *Morrison* [*Morrison v. Olson*, holding constitutional the delegation of investigatory power to an independent counsel] that a person who is neither the President nor subject to the President's control may exercise executive powers. But with respect to the exercise of judicial powers (the business of the Judicial Branch) the platform for such a leap does not even exist. For unlike executive power, judicial and legislative powers have never been thought delegable. A judge may not leave the decision to his law clerk, or to a master."

6. "The Secretary of War is the regular constitutional organ of the President for the administration of the military establishment of the nation; and rules and orders publicly promulgated through him must be received as the acts of the executive, and as such, be binding upon all within the sphere of his legal and constitutional authority. Such regulations cannot be questioned or defied, because they may be thought unwise or mistaken . . . if tolerated [such action] would be a complete disorganization of both the army and navy." *Eliason*, 41 U.S. (16 Peters) 291, 302 (1842).

7. In 1860 President James Buchanan used this executive power to send Cushing to Charleston, S.C., in confidence as a commissioner to the state's secessionist leaders. His dispatch would prove fruitless.

8. The case is *Runkle v. United States*, 122 U.S. 543 (1887).

9. The court held that "title to public office" was exclusively a question of law, while the lower court had rendered its decision in equity. *White*, 171 U.S. 366, 366 (1897).

10. Publication in the *Federal Register* is required. 3 U.S.C., section 301 (2000).

11. Locke (1773, 77): "And because it may be too great a temptation to human frailty, apt to

grasp at power, for the same persons, who have the power of making laws, have also in their hands the power to execute them, whereby they may exempt themselves from obedience to the laws they make, and suit the law, both in its making and execution, to their own private advantage, and thereby come to have a distinct interest from the rest of the community, contrary to the end of society and government." Montesquieu: "When the legislative and executive powers are united in the same person, or in the same body or magistry, there can be then no liberty; because apprehensions may arise, lest the same monarch or senate should enact tyrannical laws, to execute them in a tyrannical manner" (quoted in Frankfurter and Davison 1935, 3). Montesquieu's language is partially quoted by James Madison in *The Federalist, No. 48* (1788). Jefferson (1975, 164): "An *elective despotism* was not the government we fought for; but for one which should not only be founded on free principles, but in which the powers of government should be so divided and balanced among several bodies of magistracy, as that no one could transcend their legal limits, without being effectively checked and restrained by others."

12. In *United States v. Sharpnack*, 355 U.S. 286, 296, n. 12 (1958), the Court notes that Congress responded to *Wayman* with the passage of the Conformity Act of 1872, which states: "That the practice, pleadings, and forms and modes of proceeding in other than equity and admiralty causes in the circuit and district courts of the United States shall conform, as near as may be, to the practice, pleadings, and forms and modes of proceeding existing at the time in like causes in the courts of record of the State within which such circuit or district courts are held, any rule of court to the contrary notwithstanding."

13. 143 U.S. 649 (1892). Though considered dormant, *Field* is distinguished in the line-item veto case, *Clinton v. New York*, 524 U.S. 417 (1998).

14. For example, "Congress cannot delegate any part of its legislative power except under the limitation of a prescribed standard." *United States v. Chicago, M., St. P. & P.R. Co.*, 282 U.S. 311, 324 (1931).

15. *Panama Refining Co. v. Ryan*, 293 U.S. 388 (1935); *A.L.A. Schechter Poultry Corp. v. United States*, 295 U.S. 495 (1935); *Carter v. Carter Coal Co.*, 298 U.S. 238 (1936). The court also relies on the nondelegation doctrine to narrow the scope of a delegation in *Kent v. Dulles*, 357 U.S. 116 (1958).

16. *Fahey v. Mallonee*, 332 U.S. 245 (1947).

17. *Industrial Union Dept. v. American Petroleum Institute*, 448 U.S. 607 (1980); *American Textile Manufacturers Institute v. Donovan*, 452 U.S. 490 (1981); *Mistretta v. United States*, 488 U.S. 361 (1989) (Scalia, J. dissenting).

18. Since the *Loving* case specifically rests on military justice rules in upholding presidential power to determine factors under which courts martial may impose the death penalty, it may not be readily generalizable (Pierre 2002, 107). See also *Whitman v. American Trucking Assns.*, 121 S.Ct. 903 (2001), in which the court notes the presence of an "intelligible principle" limiting executive power—a test established in *J. W. Hampton v. United States*, 276 U.S. 394, 409 (1928)—in upholding section 109(b) of the Clean Air Act. Concurring in *American Trucking*, Justice Thomas suggests that even with such a standard, *some* delegation *might* be unconstitutional.

19. Regulatory statutes like the Interstate Commerce Act give the courts significant trouble in discerning the powers an agency might undertake. Consider Justice Brewer's language in

Interstate Commerce Commission v. Cincinnati, N.O. & T.P. Ry. Co., 167 U.S. 479, 499 (1897): "It is one thing to inquire whether the rates which have been charged and collected are reasonable—that is a judicial act; but an entirely different thing to prescribe rates which shall be charged in the future—that is a legislative act." Wading through one of the most complex statutes in American history, the Court determined that the Interstate Commerce Commission does not possess the "legislative" power to set rates. Such ad hoc judgments represent an uneasy equilibration of the law to the expanding powers of the administrative state, which is the subject of this chapter.

20. Eaton (1880, 392), a Briton whose work inspired the Pendleton Act, says of the period: "Politics have tended more and more to become a trade, or separate occupation. High character and capacity have become disassociated from public life in the popular mind." Woodrow Wilson, a key Progressive, places some of the blame for the problems in American political culture on the waves of industrial-era immigration: "Our own temperate blood, schooled to self-possession and to the measured conduct of self-government, is receiving a constant infusion and yearly experiencing a partial corruption of foreign blood" (quoted in Rohr 1986, 72). Stephen Crane's *Maggie: A Girl of the Streets* (1979 [1893], 28) evokes the paternalistic moralism of the Progressives in the following passage: "She rejoiced at the way in which the poor and virtuous eventually surmounted the wealthy and wicked. The theater made her think. She wondered if the culture and refinement she had seen imitated, perhaps grotesquely, by the heroine on the stage, could be acquired by a girl who lived in a tenement house and worked in a shirt factory."

21. Justice McReynolds and Justice Brandeis were adjacent in seniority in 1924, which would have placed the two side by side in the annual Supreme Court group photograph. McReynolds refused to pose for the photo, which was never taken (Knox 2002).

22. Evgeny Paschukanis published *The General Theory of Law and Marxism* in 1924. He was purged in 1937 and put to death.

23. Indeed Gellhorn reflects that Roscoe Pound's committee, which authored the bill, "would generalize from an episode of naughtiness to say that the trouble with administrative agencies is that *all* of them commit that very same naughtiness *all* of the time. . . . They tended to contemplate their respective navels and then . . . grab some idea from the heavens" (Davis and Gellhorn 1986, 515).

24. The APA, partially through omission, intrinsically creates two categories of both rule making and adjudication. When either rule making or adjudication is conducted on the "record" and after opportunity for a "hearing," it is considered *formal*, and when it is not so conducted, it is *informal*. Formal rule making is covered by sections 553(c), 556, and 557, while formal adjudication falls under sections 554, 556, and 557. Informal rule making, also called "notice-and-comment," is governed in section 553, though informal adjudication is not considered within the APA. In *Citizens to Preserve Overton Park v. Volpe*, 410 U.S. 402 (1971), the Supreme Court held that reviewing courts should make informal adjudication decisions on the basis of the record and, if inadequate, conduct discovery of agency officials or return the case to the agency for the development of such a record. Breyer and others (2002, 660) note that remand is the action chosen by courts in practice.

25. Warning signs of Frankfurter's change of heart on administration led his student, Jaffe (1949, 376) to reminisce, just before *Universal Camera*, about the justice's "respect for 'exper-

tise,' his reluctance even to review the agencies, and his assertion that they as well as the courts must be trusted to observe the law." Jaffe wonders if the reversal of feeling is indicative of Frankfurter's fear that he was "coddling a monster."

26. In *Yao v. Bd. of Regents*, 649 N.W.2d 356, 365 (2002), the Wisconsin Court of Appeals notes that the state legislature had in 1975 changed the law to override the *Universal Camera* decision. The new statute reads, in pertinent part, that "'the court shall . . . set aside agency action . . . if it finds that the agency's action depends on any finding of fact that is not supported by substantial evidence in the record.' Missing from the revised statute is any explicit direction that a court must 'review the whole record,' or that it must determine the existence of 'substantial evidence in view of the entire record,' which were the words in the federal and state enactments that the *Universal Camera* [court] emphasized."

27. The code includes, among others, provisions that prohibit off-the-record technical consultation between agency officials and experts, disqualify an agency official "who presides at the taking of evidence" from initial agency review of a decision, require conformance of evidence rules to those used in "civil, nonjury cases in the United States District Courts," mandate court review of "every final agency action for which there is no other remedy in court," and replace the APA's "substantial evidence" standard with "clearly erroneous" (Pierce 2002, 18).

28. "The fact is that some trial judges admit any evidence that seems reliable, others follow the hearsay rule as they would in a jury case, and still others follow some middle course" (Pierce 2002, 18).

29. The permanent Administrative Conference of the United States was founded in 1968 "to provide suitable arrangements through which Federal agencies, assisted by outside experts, may cooperatively study mutual problems, exchange information, and develop recommendations for action by proper authorities to the end that private rights may be fully protected and regulatory activities and other Federal responsibilities may be carried out expeditiously in the public interest" (5 U.S.C., section 591). Through the years, this committee of between 75 and 101 administrative law and public administration experts would successfully propose the grants of civil penalty authority to agencies, establish procedures for presidential transitions, and encourage alternative dispute resolution in federal agencies. In 1995, P.L. 104–52 abolished the Administrative Conference (109 Stat. 480).

30. An example of the judicialization debate from the left is Zinn's (1968, 115) argument against the so-called "political question" doctrine: "The Court should not assume the political branches (President, Congress) are most competent to determine certain questions, and therefore the Supreme Court should not interfere. It surrenders to the political branches by saying *they* have decided the Vietnam war is okay, and so the Court need not question that, leaving a conscientious objector who challenges the war helpless. That obstinacy of the Court in staying away from 'political' questions has already been breached in the case of legislative apportionment. The principle ought to be extended to other vital issues." What Zinn argues is for courts to weigh in on governmental process matters *generally*.

31. Indeed, interest representation became a key feature of both administrative process, such as through participation in the notice and comment rulemaking process (see Stewart 1975), and the judicial review of administrative action. In *Abbott Laboratories v. Gardner*, 387 U.S. 136, 140–141 (1967), the Supreme Court held, on the basis of the legislative history of the

APA, that evidence existed of "congressional intention that it cover a broad spectrum of administrative actions, and this Court has echoed that theme by noting that the Administrative Procedure Act's 'generous review provisions' must be given a 'hospitable' interpretation." Nonetheless, under section 701(a)(1) of the APA, Congress, through statutory language, can preclude judicial review. The reviewability game came to its apex in *Lujan v. Defenders of Wildlife*, 497 U.S. 871 (1992), where the Supreme Court, in an opinion written by Justice Scalia, holds that affidavits establishing that two members of the interest group used lands "in the vicinity" of lands affected by contested decisions of the Department of the Interior are not sufficient to establish an "injury in fact."

32. P.L. 104–121, section 804(2) provides that "the term 'major rule' means any rule that the Administrator of the Office of Information and Regulatory Affairs of the Office of Management and Budget finds has resulted in or is likely to result in (A) an annual effect on the economy of $100,000,000 or more; (B) a major increase in costs or prices for consumers, individual industries, Federal, State, or local government agencies, or geographic regions; or (C) significant adverse effects on competition, employment, investment, productivity, innovation, or on the ability of United States–based enterprises to compete with foreign-based enterprises in domestic and export markets."

CHAPTER 5: A THEORY OF POLITICALLY RESPONSIVE BUREAUCRATS

1. The delegation problem is similar to the make-or-buy decision of the firm. In their highly influential article, Klein, Crawford, and Alchian (1978) argue that the decision of a firm to internally produce rather than buy a good (say, a part necessary for producing a final product) or to reduce its vulnerability to external markets is affected by the firm's expectation of ex post opportunistic behavior on the contractee's part. If a capital asset needed to produce a part has a high value in alternative uses, the firm will make the part itself rather than buy it. In the legislative delegation context, if the political and policy gains from a bureaucratic decision accrue to the bureau but Congress believes it can appropriate some of those gains for itself, it will not delegate the task.

2. As with delegation itself, this perspective has its origins in the economics of contract. Default rules have an impact on transaction costs and facilitate exchange.

3. Our approach places us in excellent company. In *Managerial Dilemmas*, Miller (1992) uses repeated game theory as well as some of the social choice results on which we rely to uncover some fundamental organizational problems that can be addressed through hierarchy. In a 1996 article in the *Journal of Public Administration Research and Theory*, Hammond and Knott use the results of a spatial model of interinstitutional choice to relate lessons about the separation of powers to public managers. It is in this spirit that we construct this chapter.

4. In this vein, Van Riper (1958, 231) notes a welcome letter from Bryan to Walter Vick, receiver general of customs in 1913: "Now that you have arrived and are acquainting yourself with the situation, can you let me know what positions you have at your disposal with which to reward *deserving Democrats?* Whenever you desire a suggestion from me in regard to a man for any place there call on me" (emphasis in original).

5. Justices Sandra Day O'Connor, William Rehnquist, and Anthony Kennedy joined the dissent, but Scalia's bombast caused O'Connor to detach herself from the first section of the

opinion, wherein Scalia suggests the following: "The new principle that the Court today announces will be enforced by a corps of judges (the Members of this Court included) who overwhelmingly owe their office to its violation. Something must be wrong here, and I suggest it is the Court." He continues, "Today the Court makes its constitutional civil service reform absolute, extending to all decisions regarding government employment. Because the First Amendment has never been thought to require this disposition, which may well have disastrous consequences for our political system, I dissent" (*Rutan* 1990, 93).

6. The Supreme Court's patronage jurisprudence has extensions to the "hollow state" (Milward and Provan 2000). For example, in *O'Hare Truck Service v. City of Northlake*, 512 U.S. 712, 713 (1996), the holdings of *Elrod* and *Branti* are held to further "extend to an instance where government retaliates against a contractor, or a regular provider of services, for the exercise of rights of political association or the expression of political allegiance." Once again, Justice Scalia was irate: "It is profoundly disturbing that the varying political practices across this vast country, from coast to coast, can be transformed overnight by an institution whose conviction of what the Constitution means is so fickle" (the dissent appears in *Board of County Com'rs, Wabaunsee County, Kan. v. Umbehr*, 518 U.S. 668, 668, 1996). In the contracting state, patronage forms something of a classical "default rule" for contract (MacNeil 1974; Williamson 1985). Justice Scalia's argument suggests that knowingly entering a contract with the state implies an understanding of patronage loyalty, which will be the rule applied upon breach.

7. Hargrove and Glidewell (1990) refer to this as an agency "myth"—in the sense of the sociology of institutions (e.g., Meyer and Rowan 1977)—in which the public and authorities "trust" the administrative agencies to do their bidding.

8. This is to say that Congress could develop an elaborate scheme of background checks or even promises of agency employees' first-born children, but they would achieve the same result as in the mechanism that follows. This allows Congress to focus its inquiry and has implications for the treatment of the personnel function (as we discuss subsequently).

9. Whether that allocation is higher or lower than it would otherwise be is indeterminate a priori. A higher allocation may reduce the incentives for accepting largesse from drug manufacturers, a lower allocation may threaten the punishment of downsizing and reduced perquisites.

10. Also noteworthy is the work of Banks and Weingast (1992). They argue that bureaucrats hold an informational advantage over policy-relevant variables, which can be exploited by bureaucrats due to similar information asymmetries. Expertise, not formal authority, gives the bureaucrat the advantage, and Congress wants to defend against strategic behavior based on bureaucratic expertise (see Bendor, Taylor, and Van Gaalen 1987). When the politician's auditing cost is high, the agency can take advantage of the situation (in jargon, extract rents), and this is anticipated by the politician when designing the agency. Auditing costs are a function of the monitoring technology and the ability of interest groups to monitor and report violations to Congress (McCubbins and Schwartz 1984). The bureau is more likely to truthfully reveal information when a cheap monitoring technology can be implemented and when an interest group is sufficiently organized to participate in monitoring. This is the case in, say, business regulation but not in, for example, social welfare policy.

11. "Institutionalized organizations," in the sociology of organizations, are manifestations of norms generated by one failure or another of revelation mechanisms. The "exposé tradition"

of that literature (Perrow 1986) suggests that institutional theory is adept at uncovering evidence of counterproductive norms but not at pointing out how we should change those norms when we see them. Thus our political economy approach is better suited to the principal task of this book.

12. What should be quite clear at this point is that, as Congress, in practice, addresses the monopolistic screening problem in an ad hoc manner, the outcomes it desires become vulnerable to manipulation by the administrative state. This implies that Congress addresses the monopolistic screening problem in a repeated setting, rather than the single-event version discussed above. As policy settings and actors—members of Congress, presidents, agency personnel—change, the revelation mechanism becomes manipulable. Nonetheless, our discussion is sufficient to understand the nature of the congressional agency problem and the role of the personnel function in addressing it.

13. As a delegation mechanism gets to the revelation principle, the reasonableness of assuming budget maximization diminishes. Bendor, Taylor, and Van Gaalen (1987), in this vein, show that a politician can sanction an administrative agency upon discovering untruthful reports of costs, so the optimal incentive schedule maximizes bureaucratic truth-telling.

14. Revealed preference is central to price theory in neoclassical economics. A producer maximizes profit by choosing inputs x and outputs y. Suppose we observe that at some price per product and wage per unit of labor (p', w'), the producer chooses a particular bundle of inputs and outputs (y', x'). Then that bundle (y', x') is revealed as preferred to any other bundle that the producer could have selected but did not.

15. An excellent reference for those interested in a broad yet nuanced introduction to game theory is Binmore (1992).

16. This is related to the famous Arrow (1951) impossibility result in voting mechanisms.

17. As Aristotle explains in the *Politics*, to violate budget balance would be the error of the statesman in treating citizens, who must be heard and whose views must be employed in making governance decisions, either like children—paternalistically acting in their "best interests"—or like slaves, or mere instrumentalities. A violation of efficiency creates a discriminatory state, in which all citizens are not treated equally.

18. The most tenuous assumption is the reliance of the result on the independence of players' beliefs concerning their types. It implies that such beliefs are common knowledge. d'Aspremont and Gérard-Varet (1979, 44) defend this practicality in two ways. First, they consider the similarity of the reasonable assumption in Green, Kohlberg, and Laffont (1976, 384) "that each of the individuals in the society believes that all of the others are drawn independently from a normal population with zero mean." More generally, on the basis of some preliminary empirical evidence, they argue that all agents may agree on some class of individual beliefs satisfying some compatibility condition and ask the central agency to reject any announcement outside this restricted class.

CHAPTER 6: MANAGERIAL RESPONSIBILITY

1. As Wills puts it (1987, 263), Madison's constitution is designed to overcome the "defect of better motives" by providing for "opposite and rival interests" (quoted in Spicer and Terry 1993a, 263).

2. Mayo (1956, 96) argues that "political obligation arises not because a person in office acts in anyone's interest, but because he acts in accordance with rules which are embodied in a certain structure, and because this structure represents the unity of the state which we have called the general will" (quoted in Egger 1965, 328).

3. For overviews of the study of administrative responsibility, see Dotson (1957) and Gilbert (1959).

4. "The solution to the problem of administrative control certainly does not lie solely or even primarily in an extension of external controls" (Levitan 1946, 581). "The extension of external controls will introduce a rigidity fatal to essential resiliency and flexibility, for they will effect either paralysis in administration or dubious honor by their breach" (582).

5. This particular historical development is analogous to the growing awareness during the Articles of Confederation period that effective democracy requires a stronger executive.

6. Says Appleby (1947, 99): "There is nothing so fully democratic as the totality of the political processes in a free society."

7. Of managerial responsibility in general, Fries (1943, 48) argues that "there should be an acute awareness of consequences as influencing the growth and development of a deeper and wider responsibility throughout the specific enterprise involved." This source is identified by Waldo (1952a).

8. The so-called postpositive view was termed the "populist view" by Gilbert (1959, 381). To institutionalize responsibility so as to maximize selected values "would be undemocratically to rigidify administrative organization and activity in the image of certain values mistakenly assumed to be enduringly primary" (Gilbert 1959, 381). The populist school, says Pennock (1952), condemns substantive and procedural constraints on government action as undemocratic, favoring instead multiple avenues of accountability.

9. Rohr is far from the first to view public administration as coping with constitutional defects. As Waldo notes in 1948 (1984), Willoughby (1919b) holds it to be a failure of the framers that responsibility is fairly evenly distributed between the legislative and executive branches.

10. Rohr suggests that congressional staffs may perform a similar function.

11. In Hyneman's (1950) bibliographic note, he says that issues of direction and control are generally discussed under the heading "administrative responsibility." He cites as best sources Graham (1959), Friedrich (1946), Gaus, White, and Dimock (1936), and Levitan (1946).

12. Goodnow (1900) argues that the administrator does not occupy a place but practices a profession, thus precluding the need for detailed judicial intervention in administration.

13. If the preferences of the majority were both the only justification for administrative action and definitive with respect to all aspects of administration, then administration would be reduced to executing the preferences of the median voter. Early public administration scholarship takes pains to point out that such conditions are rarely satisfied. Proactive administration is therefore a necessity.

14. Of responsibility, Van Riper (1958, 549) notes that "our traditional tendency has been to deplore its existence" and that "such an approach is futile unless accompanied by a simultaneous willingness to abolish many of the functions now performed by the federal government."

15. From such axioms investigators may derive theorems and predictions that are submitted to the possibility of disconfirmation; the precept establishes foundations for such investigations.

16. Pennock (1941, 47) duly notes the disadvantages of discretionary delegation: that "it is undemocratic, that it brings sound programs of reform into disrepute by going too far in advance of public opinion, and that it makes it more difficult for affected parties to find out what the law is."

17. This balance has Aristotelian roots: *collective justice* is "one form of partial justice . . . found in the distribution of honors, of material goods, or of anything else that can be divided among those who have a share in the political system," while *individual justice* resembles "a rectifying function in private transactions" (*Ethics*, v. 1130b, 30–34; 1131a, 1).

18. Redford (1969, 111) further notes, "usually, as Herring recognized, policy making will go beyond mere identification and involve some balancing of group interests involved."

19. "Policy," argues Pfiffner (1960, 132), "is, in the administrative situation, the product of three different bodies of thought and knowledge: 'engineering' or means-ends rationality concerned primarily with physical phenomena; behavioral rationality concerned primarily with human behavior; and normative rationality concerned primarily with what ought to be. The good administrator uses all of these models of rationality in making a decision."

20. Dimock (1936b, 46) refers to discretion as "the liberty to decide between alternatives." To be responsible, judgment as between competing values and interests necessarily must be transparently reasonable as well as balanced. A transparently reasonable action, according to Aron (1987), is one for which the relationship between goals and the means for achieving them in the mind of the manager corresponds to the relationship between goals and means for achieving them in reality (or as might be confirmed by independent analysis or perceived by affected communities).

21. "Administrative accountability," notes Morstein Marx (1949, 1134), "at best is secured merely in part by the imposition of legal controls. At worst, when these controls become top heavy and formalistic, they may actually aid and abet the growth of a sharply limited view of responsibility."

CHAPTER 7: PUBLIC MANAGEMENT

1. Gaus is favorably cited as having a nonhierarchical theory of organization.

2. The perspective takes the name of the Minnowbrook Conference Center, operated by Syracuse University, where scholars, including Dwight Waldo, gathered to discuss the plight of the profession.

3. DeLeon (1998, 409) characterizes the Blacksburg Manifesto as founding the legitimacy of public administration on "its guardianship and service to the values of the Constitution and the community of citizens" rather than on "the technical expertise of its practitioners or on top-down control by elected officials." The manifesto is thoroughly criticized by Phillip Cooper and Herbert Kaufmann, who see it as in fundamental conflict with constitutional democracy, which confers power on elected officers and electoral procedures and sanctions (Wamsley and others 1990).

4. At the time of publication, Stone was assistant director in charge of administrative management for the U.S. Bureau of the Budget.

5. Stone talks of how executives use and conserve their time, deal with people, and communicate their ideas.

6. Behn (2001, 196) defines accountability "in practice" as "linear, hierarchical, and uni-directional." "There is an accountability holder and an accountability holdee—an account-ability punisher and an accountability punishee. It is a superior-subordinate relationship. The superior holds the subordinate accountable. The superior punishes the subordinate. The subordinate has no rights or leverage. The subordinate can only cringe in fear." He urges that accountability should avoid such rigidities: "Everyone has some useful feedback to give to everyone else" (191).

7. Bertelli (2005) finds that the pay-banding system implemented for managers in the Internal Revenue Service motivates those employees with the least job involvement but crowds out job involvement among those with the highest levels of that desirable trait.

8. The state of Florida likewise created its Service First program in 2001, which removed civil service protection for over 16,000 employees of the state government (Bowman, Gertz, and Gertz 2003).

References

Aberbach, Joel D., and Bert A. Rockman. 1988. "Mandates or Mandarins? Control and Discretion in the Modern Administrative State." *Public Administration Review* 48:606–612.

Ackerlof, George A. 1982. "Labor Contracts as Partial Gift Exchange." *Quarterly Journal of Economics* 84:488–500.

Adams, Guy B., and Danny L. Balfour. 1998. *Unmasking Administrative Evil.* Thousand Oaks, CA: Sage.

Alchian, Armen A., and Harold Demsetz. 1972. "Production, Information Costs, and Economic Organization." *American Economic Review* 62:777–795.

Allen, William H. 1908. "Instruction in Public Business." *Political Science Quarterly* 23:604–616.

Allison, Graham T. 1983. "Public and Private Management: Are They Fundamentally Alike in All Unimportant Respects?" In James L. Perry and Kenneth L. Kraemer, eds., *Public Management: Public and Private Perspectives*, 72–92. Palo Alto, CA: Mayfield.

Appleby, Paul H. 1947. "Toward Better Public Administration." *Public Administration Review* 7:93–99.

———. 1949. *Policy and Administration.* University: University of Alabama Press.

———. 1952. *Morality and Administration in Democratic Government.* Baton Rouge: Louisiana State University Press.

Arnold, Pari E. 1976. "The First Hoover Commission and the Managerial Presidency." *Journal of Politics* 38:46–70.

Aron, Cindy Sondik. 1987. *Ladies and Gentlemen of the Civil Service: Middle-Class Workers in Victorian America.* New York: Oxford University Press.

Arrow, Kenneth J. 1951. *Social Choice and Individual Values.* New York: Wiley and Sons.

———. 1963. *Social Choice and Individual Values.* 2d ed. New Haven: Yale University Press.

Aucoin, Peter. 1990. "Administrative Reform in Public Management: Paradigms, Principles, Paradoxes, and Pendulums." *Governance* 3:115–137.

Bailey, Michael, and David Braybrooke. 2003. "Robert A. Dahl's Philosophy of Democracy, Exhibited in His Essays." *Annual Review of Political Science* 6:99–118.

Banks, Jeffrey S., and Barry R. Weingast. 1992. "The Political Control of Bureaucracies under Asymmetric Information." *American Journal of Political Science* 36:509–525.

Bardach, Eugene. 1998. *Getting Agencies to Work Together: The Practice and Theory of Managerial Craftsmanship.* Washington, DC: Brookings.

Barnard, Chester I. 1968 [1938]. *The Functions of the Executive.* Cambridge: Harvard University Press.

Baron, David S., and Roger Myerson. 1982. "Regulating a Monopolist with Unknown Costs." *Econometrica* 50:911–930.

Barzelay, Michael (with Babak J. Armajani). 1992. *Breaking through Bureaucracy: A New Vision for Managing in Government.* Berkeley: University of California Press.

Bawn, Kathleen. 1995. "Political Control versus Expertise: Congressional Choices about Administrative Procedures." *American Political Science Review* 89:62–73.

——. 1997. "Choosing Strategies to Control the Bureaucracy: Statutory Constraints, Oversight, and the Committee System." *Journal of Law, Economics, and Organization* 13:101–126.

Beard, Charles A. 1913. *An Economic Interpretation of the Constitution of the United States.* New York: Macmillan.

Beck, James M. 1933. *Our Wonderland of Bureaucracy: A Study of the Growth of Bureaucracy in the Federal Government, and Its Destructive Effect upon the Constitution.* New York: Macmillan.

Behn, Robert D. 1991. *Leadership Counts: Lessons for Public Managers from the Massachusetts Welfare, Training, and Employment Program.* Cambridge: Harvard University Press.

——. 2001. *Rethinking Democratic Accountability.* Washington, DC: Brookings Institution.

Benabou, Roland, and Jean Tirole. 2003. "Intrinsic and Extrinsic Motivation." *Review of Economics Studies* 70:489–520.

Bendix, Reinhard. 1947. "Bureaucracy: The Problem and Its Setting." *American Sociological Review* 12:493–507.

Bendor, Jonathan B. 1985. *Parallel Systems: Redundancy in Government.* Berkeley: University of California Press.

Bendor, Jonathan B., Amihai Glazer, and Thomas H. Hammond. 2001. "Theories of Delegation." *American Review of Political Science* 4:235–269.

Bendor, Jonathan B., Serge Taylor, and Roland Van Gaalen. 1987. "Politicians, Bureaucrats, and Asymmetric Information." *American Journal of Political Science* 31:796–828.

Bentley, Arthur F. 1908. *The Process of Government: A Study of Social Pressures.* Bloomington, IN: Principia.

Bergson, Abram. 1938. "A Reformulation of Certain Aspects of Welfare Economics." *Quarterly Journal of Economics* 52:310–334.

Bernheim, B. Douglas, and Michael D. Whinston. 1986. "Common Agency." *Econometrica* 54:923–942.

Bertelli, Anthony M. 2004. "Strategy and Accountability: Structural Reform Litigation and Public Management." *Public Administration Review* 64:28–42.

——. 2005. "Motivation Crowding and the Federal Bureaucrat." Paper prepared for the annual meeting of the Midwest Political Science Association, Chicago, April 2005.

——. 2005. "Law and Public Administration." In Ewan Ferlie, Laurence E. Lynn Jr., and Christopher Pollitt, eds., *Oxford Handbook of Public Management.* Oxford: Oxford University Press.

Bertelli, Anthony M., and Laurence E. Lynn Jr. 2001. "A Precept of Managerial Responsibility: Securing Collective Justice in Institutional Reform Litigation." *Fordham Urban Law Journal* 29:317–386.

——. 2003. "Managerial Responsibility." *Public Administration Review* 63:259–268.

——. 2005. "Policy Making in the Parallelogram of Forces: Common Agency and Human Services." *Policy Studies Journal* 32:297–315.

——. Forthcoming. "Public Management in the Shadow of the Constitution." *Administration and Society.*

Bingham, Walter Van Dyke. 1939. "Administrative Ability, Its Discovery and Development." Pamphlet 1. Washington, DC: Society for Personnel Administration.

Binmore, Ken. 1992. *Fun and Games.* Lexington, MA: D. C. Heath.

Bowman, James S., Marc G. Gertz, and Sally C. Gertz. 2003. "Civil Service Reform in Florida State Government: Employee Attitudes 1 Year Later." *Review of Public Personnel Administration* 23:286–304.

Brehm, John, and Scott Gates. 1997. *Working, Shirking, and Sabotage: Bureaucratic Response to a Democratic Public.* Ann Arbor: University of Michigan Press.

Breyer, Stephen G., and others. 2002. *Administrative Law and Regulatory Policy.* 5th ed. New York: Aspen Law and Business.

Brown, Brack, and Richard J. Stillman II. 1986. *A Search for Public Administration: The Ideas and Career of Dwight Waldo.* College Station: Texas A&M University Press.

Bruel, Jonathan. 2004. "PARTing Is Such Sweet Sorrow." *The Business of Government* (Journal of IBM Business Consulting Services) Summer: 62–66.

Bryce, James. 1888. *The American Commonwealth.* New York: Macmillan.

Buck, A. E. 1928. *Administrative Consolidation in State Governments.* New York: National Municipal League.

——. 1938. *The Reorganization of State Governments in the United States.* New York: Columbia University Press.

Burgess, John W. 1886. "The American Commonwealth." *Political Science Quarterly* 1:9–35.

CAIB (Columbia Accident Investigation Board). 2003. *Report, Volume I.* Washington, DC: U.S. Government Printing Office.

Caiden, Naomi. 1998. "Public Service Professionalism for Performance Measurement and Evaluation." *Public Budgeting and Finance* 18:35–52.

Caldwell, Lynton K. 1968. "Methodology in the Theory of Public Administration." In James C. Charlesworth, ed., *Theory and Practice of Public Administration: Scope, Objectives, and Methods,* 205–222. Philadelphia: American Academy of Political and Social Science.

Canton, Erik. 2003. "Power of Incentives in Public Organizations When Employees Are Intrinsically Motivated." Paper prepared for the Fifty-Ninth Congress of the International Institute of Public Finance, Prague, August.

Carpenter, Daniel P. 2001. *The Forging of Bureaucratic Autonomy: Reputations, Networks, and Policy Innovation in Executive Agencies, 1862–1928.* Princeton, NJ: Princeton University Press.

Carroll, James D. 1997. "The Warfare on and over American Government in Waldonian Perspective." *Public Administration Review* 57:200–204.

Charlesworth, James C., ed. 1968. *Theory and Practice of Public Administration: Scope, Objectives, and Methods.* Philadelphia: American Academy of Political and Social Science.

Chisholm, Rupert F. 1989. "The Storing Critique Revisited: Simon as Seen in *The Science of Politics.*" *Political Administration Quarterly* 12: 411–436.

Church, A. Hamilton. 1914. *Science and the Practice of Management.* New York: Engineering Magazine.

Cleveland, Frederick A. 1898. *The Growth of Democracy in the United States; or, The Evolution of Popular Cooperation in Government and Its Results.* Chicago: Quadrangle.

———. 1913. *Organized Democracy: An Introduction to the Study of American Politics.* New York: Longmans, Green.

Cleveland, Frederick A., and Arthur Eugene Buck. 1920. *The Budget and Responsible Government.* New York: Macmillan.

Cohen, Daniel. 1998. "S. 981, the Regulatory Improvement Act of 1998: The Most Recent Attempt to Develop a Solution in Search of a Problem." *Administrative Law Review* 50: 699–721.

Coker, Francis W. 1922. "Dogmas of Administrative Reform, as Exemplified in the Recent Reorganization of Ohio." *American Political Science Review* 16:399–411.

Comer, John Preston. 1927. *Legislative Functions of National Administrative Authorities.* New York: Columbia University Press.

Cooper, Phillip J. 2000. *Public Law and Public Administration.* Boston: Wadsworth.

Cox, Gary W., and Mathew D. McCubbins. 1993. *Legislative Leviathan: Party Government in the House.* Berkeley: University of California Press.

Crane, Stephen. 1979 [1893]. *Maggie: A Girl of the Streets.* New York: Norton.

Crenson, Matthew A. 1975. *The Federal Machine: Beginnings of Bureaucracy in Jacksonian America.* Baltimore: Johns Hopkins University Press.

Crewson, P. E. 1997. "Public Service Motivation: Building Empirical Evidence of Incidence and Effect." *Journal of Public Administration Research and Theory* 7:499- 518.

Crozier Michel, and Erhard Friedberg. 1980. *Actors and Systems: The Politics of Collective Action.* Chicago: University of Chicago Press.

Dahl, Robert A. 1947a. "The Science of Public Administration: Three Problems." *Public Administration Review* 7:1–11.

———. 1947b. "Validity of Organizational Theories." *Public Administration Review* 7:281–283.

Dahlberg, Jane. 1966. *The New York Bureau of Municipal Research: Pioneer in Government Administration.* New York: New York University Press.

d'Aspremont, Claude, and Louis-André Gérard-Varet. 1979. "Incentives and Incomplete Information." *Journal of Public Economics* 11:25–45.

Davis, Kenneth Culp. 1969. *Discretionary Justice: A Preliminary View.* Baton Rouge: Louisiana State University Press.

———. 1972. *Administrative Law Text.* 3d ed. St. Paul, MN: West.

———. 1977. *Administrative Law Cases-Text-Problems.* 6th ed. St. Paul, MN: West.

Davis, Kenneth Culp, and Walter Gellhorn. 1986. "Present at the Creation: Regulatory Reform before 1946." *Administrative Law Review* 38:511–533.

Davy, Thomas J. 1962. "Public Administration as a Field of Study in the United States." *International Review of Administrative Sciences* 28:63–78.

Deci, E. L., R. Koestner, and R. M. Ryan. 1999. "A Meta-Analytic Review of Experiments Examining the Effects of Extrinsic Rewards on Intrinsic Motivation." *Psychological Bulletin* 125:627–668.

deLeon, Linda. 1998. "The Spirit of Public Administration." *American Review of Public Administration* 23:407–412.

———. 2005. "Public Management, Democracy, and Politics." In Ewan Ferlie, Laurence E. Lynn Jr., and Christopher Pollitt, eds., *Oxford Handbook of Public Management*. Oxford: Oxford University Press.

deLeon, Linda, and Peter deLeon. 2002. "The Democratic Ethos and Public Management." *Administration and Society* 34:229–250.

deLeon, Linda, and Robert B. Denhardt. 2000. "The Political Theory of Reinvention." *Public Administration Review* 60:89–97.

Dickinson, John. 1927. *Administrative Justice and the Supremacy of Law in the United States*. Cambridge: Harvard University Press.

DiMaggio, Paul J., and Walter W. Powell. 1991. "Introduction." In Walter W. Powell and Paul J. DiMaggio, eds., *The New Institutionalism in Organizational Analysis*, 1–38. Chicago: University of Chicago Press.

Dimock, Marshall E. 1933. "What Is Public Administration?" *Public Management* 15:259–262.

———. 1936a. "The Meaning and Scope of Public Administration." In John M. Gaus, Leonard D. White, and Marshall E. Dimock, eds., *The Frontiers of Public Administration*, 1–12. Chicago: University of Chicago Press.

———. 1936b. "The Role of Discretion in Modern Administration." In John M. Gaus, Leonard D. White, and Marshall E. Dimock, eds., *The Frontiers of Public Administration*, 45–65. Chicago: University of Chicago Press.

———. 1937a. *Modern Politics and Administration: A Study of the Creative State*. New York: American Book Co.

———. 1937b. "The Study of Administration." *American Political Science Review* 31:28–40.

Diver, Colin. 1982. "Engineers and Entrepreneurs: The Dilemma of Public Management." *Journal of Policy Analysis and Management* 1:402–406.

Dotson, Arch. 1957. "Fundamental Approaches to Administrative Responsibility." *Western Political Quarterly* 10:701–727.

Downs, Anthony. 1967. *Inside Bureaucracy*. Washington, DC: Brookings Institution.

Dubnick, Melvin J. 2000. "The Case for Administrative Evil: A Critique." *Public Administration Review* 60:464–474.

Dunleavy, Patrick. 1991. *Democracy, Bureaucracy, and Public Choice*. New York: Harvester Wheatsheaf.

Dunsire, A. 1973. *Administration: The Word and the Science*. New York: John Wiley and Sons.

Durham, G. Homer. 1940. "Politics and Administration in Intergovernmental Relations." *Annals of the American Academy of Political and Social Science* 207:1–6.

Eaton, Dorman. 1880. *The Civil Service in Great Britain*. New York: Harper and Brothers.

Edwards, W. H. 1927, 1928. "The State Reorganization Movement." *Dakota Law Review* 1:1:13–30; 1:2:15–41; 2:1/–67, 103–139.

Egger, Rowland. 1965. "Responsibility in Administration: An Exploratory Essay." In Roscoe C. Martin, ed., *Public Administration and Democracy: Essays in Honor of Paul H. Appleby*, 299–329. Syracuse, NY: Syracuse University Press.

Emmerich, Herbert. 1950. *Essays on Federal Reorganization*. University: University of Alabama Press.

Epstein, David, and Sharyn O'Halloran. 1999. *Delegating Powers: A Transactions-Cost Approach to Policy Making under Separated Powers*. New York: Cambridge University Press.

Fairlie, John A. 1935. "Public Administration and Administrative Law." In Charles G. Haines and Marshall E. Dimock, eds., *Essays on the Law and Practice of Governmental Administration: A Volume in Honor of Frank Johnson Goodnow*, 3–43. Baltimore: Johns Hopkins Press.

Fama, Eugene F. 1980. "Agency Problems and the Theory of the Firm." *Journal of Political Economy* 88:288–307.

Feldman, Daniel L. 1993. "Introduction." *Public Administration Review* 53:237–239.

Feldman, Martha S., and Anne M. Khademian. 2000. "Managing for Inclusion: Balancing Control and Participation." *International Public Management Journal* 3:149–167.

Finer, Herman. 1935. "Principles as a Guide to Management." *Public Management* 17:287–289.

———. 1941. "Administrative Responsibility in Democratic Government." *Public Administrative Review* 1:335–350.

Fiorina, Morris P. 1977. *Congress: Keystone of the Washington Establishment*. New Haven: Yale University Press.

Ford, Henry Jones. 1900. "Politics and Administration." *Annals of the American Academy of Political and Social Science* 11:177–188.

Frankfurter, Felix, and J. Forrester Davison. 1935. *Cases and Materials on Administrative Law*. Chicago: Foundation Press.

Frederickson, H. George. 1971. "Toward a New Public Administration." In Frank Marini, ed., *Toward a New Public Administration: The Minnowbrook Perspective*, 309–331. Scranton, PA: Chandler.

———. 1997. *The Spirit of Public Administration*. San Francisco: Jossey-Bass.

Frederickson, H. George, and Kevin B. Smith. 2003. *The Public Administration Theory Primer*. Boulder, CO: Westview.

Freund, Ernst. 1915. "The Substitution of Rule for Discretion in Public Law." *American Political Science Review* 9:666–676.

Frey, Bruno S., and Reto Jegen. 2001. "Motivation Crowding Theory: A Survey of Empirical Evidence." *Journal of Economic Surveys* 15:589–611.

Friedrich, Carl J. 1935. "Responsible Government under the American Constitution." In Commission of Inquiry on Public Service Personnel, *Problems of the American Public Service*, 3–74. New York: McGraw-Hill.

———. 1940. "Public Policy and the Nature of Administrative Responsibility." In Carl Friedrich and Edward Mason, eds., *Public Policy: A Yearbook of the Graduate School of Public Administration, Harvard University, 1940*, 3–24. Cambridge: Harvard University Press.

———. 1946. *Constitutional Government and Democracy: Theory and Practice in Europe and America*. Boston: Ginn.

Fries, Horace S. 1943. "On Managerial Responsibility." *Advanced Management* 8:45–58.

Fuchs, Ralph F. 1941. "Some Aspects and Implications of the Report of the Attorney General's Committee on Administrative Procedure." *Ohio State University Law Journal* 7:342–357.

Garvey, Gerald. 1995. "False Promises: The NPR in Historical Perspective." In Donald F. Kettl and John J. DiIulio, eds., *Inside the Reinvention Machine: Appraising Governmental Reform*, 87–106. Washington, DC: Brookings Institution.

Gaus, John M. 1923–24. "The New Problem of Administration." *Minnesota Law Review* 8:217–231.

——. 1931. "Notes on Administration: The Present Status of the Study of Public Administration in the United States." *American Political Science Review* 25:120–134.

——. 1935. "The Social Science Research Council's Committee on Public Administration." *American Political Science Review* 29:876–878.

——. 1936. "The Responsibility of Public Administration." In John M. Gaus, Leonard D. White, and Marshall E. Dimock, eds., *The Frontiers of Public Administration*, 26–44. Chicago: University of Chicago Press.

——. 1938. "Review of Luther Gulick and Lyndall Urwick, 'Studies.'" *American Political Science Review* 32:132–134.

——. 1947. *Reflections on Public Administration.* University: University of Alabama Press.

——. 1950. "Trends in the Theory of Public Administration." *Public Administration Review* 10:161–168.

——. 1955. "Public Participation in Federal Programs." In O. B. Conaway Jr., ed., *Democracy in Federal Administration*, 1–20. Washington, DC: U.S. Department of Agriculture Graduate School.

Gaus, John M., Leonard D. White, and Marshall E. Dimock, eds. 1936. *The Frontiers of Public Administration.* Chicago: University of Chicago Press.

Gellhorn, Walter. 1956. *Individual Freedom and Governmental Restraints.* Baton Rouge: Louisiana State University Press.

George, Claude S., Jr. 1972. *The History of Management Thought.* Englewood Cliffs, NJ: Prentice-Hall.

Gerth, H. H., and C. Wright Mills, eds. 1946. *From Max Weber: Essays in Sociology.* Oxford: Oxford University Press.

Gibbard, A. 1973. "Manipulation of Voting Schemes." *Econometrica* 41:587–601.

Gilbert, Charles E. 1959. "The Framework of Administrative Responsibility." *Journal of Politics* 21:373–407.

Gingrich, Newt, and others. 1994. *A Contract with America.* Available at www.federalist.com/histdocs/contract.htm.

Gladden, E. N. 1972. *A History of Public Administration.* Vols. 1 and 2. London: Frank Cass.

Goodin, Robert E. 1996. *The Theory of Institutional Design.* Cambridge: Cambridge University Press.

Goodnow, Frank J. 1895. *Municipal Home Rule: A Study in Administration.* New York: Macmillan.

——. 1897. *Municipal Problems.* New York: Columbia University Press.

——. 1900. *Politics and Administration: A Study in Government.* New York: Macmillan.

——. 1902 [1893]. *Comparative Administrative Law: An Analysis of the Administrative Systems National and Local, of the United States, England, France, and Germany.* New York: G. P. Putnam's Sons.

——. 1904. *City Government in the United States.* New York: Century.

——. 1905. *The Principles of the Administrative Law of the United States.* New York: G. P. Putnam's Sons.

——, ed. 1906. *Selected Cases on American Administrative Law with Particular Reference to the Law of Officers and Extraordinary Legal Remedies.* Chicago: Callaghan.

——. 1909. *Municipal Government.* New York: Century.

———. 1911. *Social Reform and the Constitution.* New York: Macmillan.

Gore, William J. 1956. "Administrative Decision-Making in Federal Offices." *Public Administration Review* 16:281–291.

Graham, George A. 1959. "Essentials of Responsibility." In Fritz Morstein Marx, ed., *Elements of Public Administration*, 2d ed., 437–474. Englewood Cliffs, NJ: Prentice-Hall.

Graves, W. Brooke. 1938. "Criteria for Evaluating the Effectiveness of State Government." *American Political Science Review* 32:508–514.

Green, J., E. Kohlberg, and J. J. Laffont. 1976. "Partial Equilibrium Approach to the Free-Rider Problem." *Journal of Public Economics* 6:375–394.

Gulick, Luther H. 1926. "Municipal Administration." *American Political Science Review* 20: 400–404.

———. 1933a. "Politics, Administration, and the 'New Deal.'" *Annals of the American Academy of Political and Social Science* 169:55–66.

———. 1933b. "Principles of Public Administration." In Clarence E. Ridley and Orin F. Nolting, eds., *City Manager Yearbook, 1933*, 265–288. Chicago: International City Managers' Association.

———. 1937. "Notes on the Theory of Organization." In Luther Gulick and Lyndall Urwick, eds., *Papers on the Science of Administration*, 3–13. New York: Institute of Public Administration.

———. 1990. "Reflections on Public Administration, Past and Present." *Public Administration Review* 50:599–603.

Gulick, Luther, and Lyndall Urwick, eds. 1937. "Studies." In *Papers on the Science of Administration*. New York: Institute of Public Administration.

Haber, Samuel. 1964. *Efficiency and Uplift: Scientific Management in the Progressive Era, 1890–1920.* Chicago. University of Chicago Press.

Haines, Charles G., and Marshall E. Dimock, eds. 1935. *Essays on the Law and Practice of Governmental Administration: A Volume in Honor of Frank Johnson Goodnow.* Baltimore: Johns Hopkins Press.

Hamilton, John J. 1911. *Government by Commission; or, The Dethronement of the City Boss.* New York: Funk and Wagnalls.

Hammond, Thomas H. 1990. "In Defence of Luther Gulick's 'Notes on the Theory of Organization.'" *Public Administration* 68:143–173.

Hammond, Thomas M., and Jack H. Knott. 1996. "Political Institutions, Public Management, and Policy Choice." *Journal of Public Administration Research and Theory* 9:33–85.

Hampshire, Stuart. 2000. *Justice Is Conflict.* Princeton, NJ: Princeton University Press.

Hansen, John Mark. 1985. "The Political Economy of Group Membership." *American Political Science Review* 79:79–96.

Hargrove, Erwin C., and John C. Glidewell. 1990. *Impossible Jobs in Public Management.* Lawrence: University Press of Kansas.

Harmon, Michael M. 1989. "The Simon/Waldo Debate: A Review and Update." *Public Administration Quarterly* 12:437–461.

Hart, James. 1925. *The Ordinance Making Powers of the President of the United States.* Vol. 43, Johns Hopkins University Studies in Historical and Political Science. Baltimore: Johns Hopkins Press.

Hart, Oliver D., and Bengt Hölmstrom. 1987. "The Theory of Contracts." In T. Bewley, ed., *Advances in Economic Theory, Fifth World Congress*, 71–155. New York: Cambridge University Press.

Hector, Louis J. 1960. "Problems of the CAB and the Independent Regulatory Commissions." *Yale Law Journal* 69:931–964.

Henry, Nicholas. 1987. "The Emergence of Public Administration as a Field of Study." In Ralph Clark Chandler, ed., *A Centennial History of the American Administrative State*, 37–85. New York: Free Press.

———. 2004. *Public Administration and Affairs*. 9th ed. Upper Saddle River, NJ: Pearson/Prentice Hall.

Herring, Pendleton. 1936. *Public Administration and the Public Interest*. New York: McGraw-Hill.

Hirschorn, Bernard. 1997. *Democracy Reformed: Richard Spencer Childs and His Fight for Better Government*. Westport, CT: Greenwood.

Hood, Christopher. 1991. "A Public Management for All Seasons." *Public Administration* 69:3–19.

Hood, Christopher, and Michael Jackson. 1991. *Administrative Argument*. Aldershot, UK: Dartmouth.

Horwitz, Morton J. 1992. *The Transformation of American Law, 1870–1960: The Crisis of Legal Orthodoxy*. New York: Oxford University Press.

Howard, S. Kenneth. 1971. "Analysis, Rationality, and Administrative Decision Making." In Frank Marini, ed., *Toward a New Public Administration: The Minnowbrook Perspective*, 285–301. Scranton, PA: Chandler.

Huber, John D., and Nolan McCarty. 2004. "Bureaucratic Capacity, Delegation, and Political Reform." *American Political Science Review* 98:481–494.

Huber, John D., and Charles R. Shipan. 2002. *Deliberate Discretion?* New York: Cambridge University Press.

Huddleston, Mark W., and William W. Boyer. 1996. *The Higher Civil Service in the United States: Quest for Reform*. Pittsburgh: University of Pittsburgh Press.

Huntington, Samuel P. 1953. "The Marasmus of the ICC: The Commission, the Railroads, and the Public Interest." *Yale Law Journal* 61:467–509.

Hurst, James Willard. 1977. *Law and Social Order in the United States*. Ithaca, NY: Cornell University Press.

Hurwicz, Leonid. 1975. "On the Existence of Allocation Systems Whose Manipulative Nash Equilibria Are Pareto Optimal." Unpublished manuscript, University of Minnesota.

Hyneman, Charles S. 1939. "Administrative Reorganization: An Adventure into Science and Theology." *Journal of Politics* 1:62–75.

———. 1945. "Bureaucracy and the Democratic System." *Louisiana Law Review* 6:309–349.

———. 1950. *Bureaucracy in a Democracy*. New York: Harper and Brothers.

Ingraham, Patricia Wallace. 1995. *The Foundation of Merit: Public Service in American Democracy*. Baltimore: Johns Hopkins University Press.

———. 2005. "Striving for Balance: Reforms in Human Resource Management." In E. Ferlie, L. E. Lynn Jr., and C. Pollitt, eds., *Oxford Handbook of Public Management*. Oxford: Oxford University Press.

Ingraham, P. W., S. C. Selden, and D. P. Moynihan. 2000. "People and Performances: Challenges for the Future Public Service." Report of the Wye River Conference. *Public Administration Review* 60:54–60.

Jackson, Robert H. 1940. "The Administrative Process." *Journal of Social Philosophy and Jurisprudence* 5:143–159.

Jaffe, Louis. 1939. "Invective and Investigation in Administrative Law." *Harvard Law Review* 52:1201–1245.

———. 1949. "The Judicial Universe of Mr. Justice Frankfurter." *Harvard Law Review* 62:357–412.

Jefferson, Thomas. 1975 [1801]. "Notes on the State of Virginia." In Merrill D. Peterson, ed., *The Portable Thomas Jefferson*, 23–232. New York: Penguin.

Juran, J. M. 1944. *Bureaucracy: A Challenge to Better Management: A Constructive Analysis of Management Effectiveness in the Federal Government.* New York: Harper and Brothers.

Karl, Barry. 1976. "Public Administration and American History: A Century of Professionalism." *Public Administration Review* 36:489–503.

Kaufman, Herbert. 1956. "Emerging Conflicts in the Doctrines of Public Administration." *American Political Science Review* 50:1057–1073.

Keeling, Desmond. 1972. *Management in Government.* London: Allen and Unwin.

Kellough, J. Edward, and Hoaran Lu. 1993. "The Paradox of Merit Pay in the Public Sector: Persistence of a Problematic Procedure." *Review of Public Personnel Administration* 13:45–64.

Kellough, J. Edward, and Lloyd G. Nigro. 2002. "Pay for Performance in Georgia State Government: Employee Perspectives on Georgia Gain after 5 Years." *Review of Public Personnel Administration* 22:146–166.

Kent, James. 1971 [1826–1830]. *Commentaries on American Law.* New York: Da Capo.

Kettl, Donald F. 1990. "The Perils—and Prospects—of Public Administration." *Public Administration Review* 50:411–419.

———. 1993. "Public Administration: The State of the Field." In Ada W. Finifter, ed., *Political Science: The State of the Discipline II*, 407–428. Washington, DC: American Political Science Association,

———. 2002. *The Transformation of Governance: Public Administration for the Twenty-First Century.* Baltimore: Johns Hopkins University Press.

Kettl, Donald F., and others. 1996. *Civil Service Reform: Building a Government that Works.* Washington, DC: Brookings Institution.

Key, V. O. 1942. "Politics and Administration." In Leonard D. White, ed., *The Future of Government in the United States: Essays in Honor of Charles E. Merriam*, 145–163. Chicago: University of Chicago Press.

———. 1947. *Politics, Parties, and Pressure Groups.* New York: Thomas Y. Crowell.

Kickert, Walter J. M. 1997. "Public Management in the United States and Europe." In Walter J. M. Kickert, ed., *Public Management and Administrative Reform in Western Europe*, 15–38. Cheltenham, UK: Edward Elgar.

Kimball, Everett. 1922. *State and Municipal Government in the United States.* Boston: Ginn.

Kingsley, J. Donald. 1944. *Representative Bureaucracy.* Yellow Springs, OH: Antioch.

———. 1945. "Political Ends and Administrative Means: The Administrative Principles of Hamilton and Jefferson." *Public Administration Review* 5:87–89.

Kintner, Earl W. 1960. "The Current Ordeal of the Administrative Process: In Reply to Mr. Hector." *Yale Law Journal* 69:965–977.

Kirwan, Kent Aiken. 1977. "The Crisis of Identity in the Study of Public Administration: Woodrow Wilson." *Polity* 9:321–343.

Klein, Benjamin, Robert Crawford, and Armen Alchian. 1978. "Vertical Integration, Appropriable Rents, and the Competitive Contracting Process." *Journal of Law and Economics* 21:297–326.

Klingner, Donald E., and John Nalbandian. 2003. *Public Personnel Management: Contexts and Strategies*, 5th ed. Upper Saddle River, NJ: Prentice Hall.

Knott, Jack H., and Gary J. Miller. 1987. *Reforming Bureaucracy: The Politics of Institutional Choice*. Englewood Cliffs, NJ: Prentice Hall.

Knox, John. 2002. *The Forgotten Memoir of John Knox*, edited by Dennis J. Hutchinson and David J. Garrow. Chicago: University of Chicago Press.

König, Klaus. 1997. "Entrepreneurial Management or Executive Administration: The Perspective of Classical Public Administration." In Walter J. M. Kickert, ed., *Public Management and Administrative Reform in Western Europe*, 213–232. Cheltenham, UK: Edward Elgar.

Kooiman, Jan, and Martijn van Vliet. 1993. "Governance and Public Management." In K. Eliassen and J. Kooiman, eds., *Managing Public Organizations: Lessons from Contemporary European Experience*, 58–72. London: Sage.

Kraines, Oscar. 1970. "The President versus Congress: The Keep Commission, 1905–1909: First Comprehensive Presidential Inquiry into Administration." *Western Political Quarterly* 23:5–54.

Krehbiel, Keith. 1998. *Pivotal Politics: A Theory of U.S. Lawmaking*. Chicago: University of Chicago Press.

Kreps, David M. 1997. "Intrinsic Motivation and Extrinsic Incentives." *American Economic Review* 87:359–364.

Kurland, Philip B., and Gerhard Casper. 1975. *Constitutional Law*. Vol. 28, *Landmark Briefs and Arguments of the Supreme Court of the United States*. Arlington, VA: University Publications of America.

Landau, Martin. 1969. "Redundancy, Rationality, and the Problem of Duplication and Overlap." *Public Administration Review* 29:346–358.

Landis, James. 1938. *The Administrative Process*. New Haven: Yale University Press.

Lane, Jan-Erik. 1993. "Economic Organization Theory and Public Management." In K. Eliassen and J. Kooiman, eds., *Managing Public Organizations. Lessons from Contemporary European Experience*, 73–83. London: Sage.

Laski, Harold J. 1923. "The Growth of Administrative Discretion." *Journal of Public Administration* 1:92–100.

Laslett, Peter. 1956. "The Face-to-Face Society," In Peter Laslett, ed., *Philosophy, Politics, and Society: A Collection*, 157–184. New York: Macmillan.

Lazear, Edward P., and Sherwin Rosen. 1981. "Rank-Order Tournaments as Optimum Labor Contracts." *Journal of Political Economy* 89:841–864.

Leiserson, Avery, and Fritz Morstein Marx. 1959. "The Study of Public Administration." In Fritz Morstein Marx, ed., *Elements of Public Administration*, 2d ed., 23–48. Englewood Cliffs, NJ: Prentice Hall.

Lepawsky, Albert. 1949. *Administration: The Art and Science of Organization and Management*. New York: Knopf.

Levitan, David. 1942. "The Neutrality of the Public Service." *Public Administration Review* 2:317–323.

———. 1943. "Political Ends and Administrative Means." *Public Administration Review* 3:353–359.

———. 1946. "The Responsibility of Administrative Officials in a Democratic Society." *Political Science Quarterly* 61:562–598.

Lindblom, Charles E. 1965. *The Intelligence of Democracy*. New York: Free Press.

Lipson, Leslie. 1968 [1939]. *The American Governor, from Figurehead to Leader*. New York: Greenwood.

Locke, John. 1773 [1690]. *An Essay Concerning the True Original Extent and End of Civil Government*. Boston.

Long, Norton E. 1949. "Power and Administration." *Public Administration Review* 9:257–264.

Lowi, Theodore J. 1969. *The End of Liberalism: Ideology, Policy, and the Crisis of Public Authority*. New York: Norton.

———. 1993. "Legitimizing Public Administration: A Disturbed Dissent." *Public Administration Review* 53:262–264.

Lynn, Laurence E., Jr. 1996. *Public Management as Art, Science, and Profession*. Chatham, NJ: Chatham House.

———. 1998. "The New Public Management: How to Transform a Theme into a Legacy." *Public Administration Review* 58:231–237.

———. 1999. "Public Management in North America." *Public Management Review* 1:301–310.

———. 2001. "The Myth of the Bureaucratic Paradigm: What Traditional Public Administration Really Stood For." *Public Administration Review* 61:144–160.

———. 2002. "Democracy's 'Unforgivable Sin.'" *Administration and Society* 34:447–454.

———. 2005. "Public Management: A Concise History of the Field." In Ewan Ferlie, Laurence E. Lynn Jr., and Christopher Pollitt, eds., *Oxford Handbook of Public Management*. Oxford: Oxford University Press.

Maas, Arthur A., and Laurence J. Radway. 1949. "Gauging Administrative Responsibility." *Public Administration Review* 9:182–193.

Macmahon, Arthur W. 1955. "Specialization and the Public Interest." In O. B. Conway Jr., ed., *Democracy in Federal Administration*, 37–54. Washington, DC: U.S. Department of Agriculture Graduate School.

Macmahon, Arthur W., and John M. Millett. 1939. *Federal Administrators: A Biographical Approach to the Problem of Departmental Management*. New York: Columbia University Press.

MacNeil, Ian R. 1974. "The Many Futures of Contracts." *Southern California Law Review* 47:691–816.

Maitland, Frederic W. 1948 [1908]. *The Constitutional History of England*. Cambridge: Cambridge University Press.

Majone, Giandomenico. 1989. *Evidence, Argument, and Persuasion in the Policy Process*. New Haven: Yale University Press.

Marini, Frank, ed. 1971. *Toward a New Public Administration*. Scranton, PA: Chandler.

———. 1993. "Leaders in the Field: Dwight Waldo." *Public Administration Review* 53:409–418.

Marshall, Leon Carroll. 1921. *Business Administration*. Chicago: University of Chicago Press.

Martin, Roscoe C. 1965. "Paul H. Appleby and His Administrative World." In Roscoe C. Martin, ed., *Public Administration and Democracy: Essays in Honor of Paul H. Appleby*. Syracuse, NY: Syracuse University Press.

Mas-Colell, Andreu, Michael D. Whinston, and Jerry R. Green. 1995. *Microeconomic Theory*. New York: Oxford University Press.

Mashaw, Jerry L. 1989. "The Economics of Politics and the Understanding of Public Law." *Chicago-Kent Law Review* 65:123–160.

Maskin, Eric, and J. Riley. 1984. "Optimal Auctions with Risk-Averse Buyers." *Econometrica* 52:1473–1518.

Mathews, John Mabry. 1917. *Principles of American State Administration*. New York: D. Appleton.

———. 1922. "State Administrative Reorganization." *American Political Science Review* 16:387–398.

Mayo, Bernard. 1956. "Is There a Case for the General Will?" In Peter Laslett, ed., *Philosophy, Politics, and Society: A Collection*, 92–97. New York: Macmillan.

McCubbins, Mathew, Roger Noll, and Barry Weingast. 1987. "Administrative Procedures as Instruments of Political Control." *Journal of Law, Economics, and Organization* 3:243–277.

———. 1989. "Structure and Process, Politics and Policy: Administrative Arrangements and the Political Control of Agencies." *Virginia Law Review* 75:431–482.

McCubbins, Mathew, and Thomas Schwartz. 1984. "Congressional Oversight Overlooked: Police Patrols versus Fire Alarms." *American Journal of Political Science* 28:165–179.

McFarland, Carl. 1961. "Landis' Report: The Voice of One Crying in the Wilderness." *Virginia Law Review* 47:373–438.

McNollgast. 1999. "The Political Origins of the Administrative Procedure Act." *Journal of Law, Economics, and Organization* 15:180–217.

Merriam, Charles E. 1940. "Public Administration and Political Theory." *Journal of Social Philosophy* 5:293–308.

———. 1945. *Systematic Politics*. Chicago: University of Chicago Press.

Metcalfe, Les, and Sue Richards. 1993. "Evolving Public Management Cultures." In K. Eliassen and J. Kooiman, eds., *Managing Public Organizations: Lessons from Contemporary European Experience*, 106–124. London: Sage.

Meyer, John W., and Brian Rowan. 1977. "Institutionalized Organizations: Formal Structure as Myth and Ceremony." *American Journal of Sociology* 83:340–363.

Miller, Gary J. 1992. *Managerial Dilemmas: The Political Economy of Hierarchy*. New York: Cambridge University Press.

Millett, John D. 1949. "Post-War Trends in Public Administration in the United States." *Journal of Politics* 11:736–747.

———. 1954. *Management in the Public Service: The Quest for Effective Performance*. New York: McGraw-Hill.

———. 1956. "A Critical Appraisal of the Study of Public Administration." *Administrative Science Quarterly* 1:171–188.

Millspaugh, A. C. 1937. "Democracy and Administrative Organization." In John Mabry Mathews and James Hart, eds., *Essays in Political Science in Honor of Westel Woodbury Willoughby*, 64–73. Baltimore: Johns Hopkins Press.

Milward, H. Brinton, and Keith G. Provan. 2000. "Governing the Hollow State." *Journal of Public Administration Research and Theory* 10:359–379.

Moe, Ronald C., and Robert S. Gilmour. 1995. "Rediscovering Principles of Public Administration: The Neglected Foundation of Public Law." *Public Administration Review* 55:135–146.

Moe, Terry M. 1989. "The Politics of Bureaucratic Structure." In John E. Chubb and Paul E. Peterson, eds., *Can the Government Govern?* 267–329. Washington, DC: Brookings Institution.

Moore, Mark H. 1984. "A Conception of Public Management." In *Teaching Public Management*, 1–12. Boston: Public Policy and Management Program for Case and Course Development, Boston University.

———. 1995. *Creating Public Value: Strategic Management in Government*. Cambridge: Harvard University Press.

Morstein Marx, Fritz, ed. 1940. *Public Management in the New Democracy*. New York: Harper and Brothers.

———. 1945. "The Bureau of the Budget: Its Evolution and Present Role, I." *American Political Science Review* 39:653–684.

———. 1949. "Administrative Ethics and the Rule of Law." *American Political Science Review* 43:1119–1144.

———. 1957. *The Administrative State: An Introduction to Bureaucracy*. Chicago: University of Chicago Press.

———. 1959a. "The Social Function of Public Administration." In Fritz Morstein Marx, ed., *Elements of Public Administration*, 2d ed., 89–109. Englewood Cliffs, NJ: Prentice Hall.

———, ed. 1959b. *Elements of Public Administration*. 2d ed. Englewood Cliffs, NJ: Prentice Hall.

Mosher, Frederick C. 1968. *Democracy and the Public Service*. New York: Oxford University Press.

———. 1975. "Introduction: The American Setting." In Frederick C. Mosher, ed., *American Public Administration: Past, Present, and Future*, 1–10. University: University of Alabama Press.

———. 1992. "Public Administration Old and New: A Letter from Frederick C. Mosher." *Journal of Public Administration Research and Theory* 2:199–202.

Myerson, Roger. 1979. "Incentive Compatibility and the Bargaining Problem." *Econometrica* 47:61–74.

———. 1982. "Optimal Coordination Mechanisms in Generalized Principal-Agent Problems." *Journal of Mathematical Economics* 10:67–81.

Myerson, Roger, and Mark A. Satterthwaite. 1983. "Efficient Mechanisms for Bilateral Trading." *Journal of Economic Theory* 28:265–281.

Nash, Gerald D. 1969. *Perspectives on Administration: The Vistas of History*. Berkeley: Institute of Governmental Studies, University of California.

Nathanson, Nathaniel L. 1963. "Looking Backward, 2000–1963: A Personal View of the Administrative Conference, 1961–62." *Administrative Law Review* 16:33–41.

National Commission on the Public Service. 1989. *Leadership for America: Rebuilding the Public Service.* Lexington, MA: Lexington Books.

Nelson, William E. 1982. *The Roots of American Bureaucracy, 1830–1900.* Cambridge: Harvard University Press.

Nicolaidis, Nicholas G. 1960. *Policy-Decision and Organization Theory.* Publication 11, John W. Donner Memorial Fund. Los Angeles: University of Southern California Bookstore.

9/11 Commission (National Commission on Terrorist Attacks upon the United States). 2004. *The 9/11 Commission Report.* New York: Norton.

Niskanen, William. 1971. *Bureaucracy and Representative Government.* Chicago: Aldine-Atherton.

O'Leary, Rosemary. 1993. *Environmental Change: Federal Courts and the EPA.* Philadelphia: Temple University Press.

Olson, Mancur. 1965. *The Logic of Collective Action: Public Goods and the Theory of Groups.* Cambridge: Harvard University Press.

Osborne, David, and Ted Gaebler. 1992. *Reinventing Government: How the Entrepreneurial Spirit Is Transforming the Public Sector.* Reading, MA: Addison-Wesley.

Ostrom, Vincent. 1973. *The Intellectual Crisis in American Public Administration.* University: University of Alabama Press.

O'Toole, Laurence J. 1984. "American Public Administration and the Idea of Reform." *Administration and Society* 16:141–166.

Overman, E. Sam, and Kathy J. Boyd. 1994. "Best Practice Research and Postbureaucratic Reform." *Journal of Public Administration Research and Theory* 4:67–83.

Patten, Simon N. 1890. "Decay of State and Local Government." *Annals of the American Academy of Political and Social Science* 1:26–42.

PCAM (President's Committee on Administrative Management). 1937. *Report of the Committee with Studies of Administrative Management in the Federal Government.* Washington, DC: U.S. Government Printing Office.

Pennock, J. Roland. 1941. *Administration and the Rule of Law.* New York: Rinehart.

———. 1952. "Responsiveness, Responsibility, and Majority Rule." *American Political Science Review* 46:790–807.

Perrow, Charles. 1986. *Organizations: A Critical Essay.* 3d ed. New York: McGraw-Hill.

Perry, James L. 1986. "Merit Pay in the Public Sector: The Case for a Failure of Theory." *Review of Public Personnel Administration* 7:57–69.

Perry James L., and Lois R. Wise. 1990. "The Motivational Bases of Public Service." *Public Administration Review* 50:367–373.

Person, Harlow Stafford. 1977 [1926]. "Basic Principles of Administration and of Management: The Management Movement." In Henry C. Mecalf, ed., *Scientific Foundations of Business Administration,* 191–203. Easton, PA: Hive.

Peters, B. Guy. 1996. *The Future of Governing: Four Emerging Models.* Lawrence: University Press of Kansas.

———. 1997. "A North American Perspective on Administrative Modernisation in Europe." In Walter J. M. Kickert, ed., *Public Management and Administrative Reform in Western Europe,* 251–266. Cheltenham, UK: Edward Elgar.

Peters, Thomas J., and Robert H. Waterman. 1982. *In Search of Excellence: Lessons from America's Best-Run Companies.* New York: Harper and Row.

Pfeffer, Jeffrey. 1995. "Incentives in Organizations: The Importance of Social Relations." In O. E. Williamson, ed., *Organizational Theory: From Chester Barnard to the Present and Beyond.* Expanded ed., 72–97. New York: Oxford University Press.

Pfiffner, John M. 1935. *Public Administration.* New York: Ronald.

———. 1946. *Public Administration.* Rev. ed. New York: Ronald.

———. 1960. "Administrative Rationality." *Public Administration Review* 20:125–132.

Pierce, Richard J. 2002. *Administrative Law Treatise.* 4th ed. New York: Aspen Law and Business.

Pinkett, Harold T. 1965. "The Keep Commission, 1905–1909: A Rooseveltian Effort for Administrative Reform." *Journal of American History* 52:297–312.

Pollitt, Christopher. 1990. *Managerialism and the Public Services: The Anglo-American Experience.* Oxford, UK: Basil Blackwell.

Pollitt, Christopher, and Geert Bouckaert. 2000. *Public Management Reform: A Comparative Perspective.* Oxford: Oxford University Press.

Porter, Kirk Harold. 1938. *State Administration.* New York: F. S. Crofts.

Pound, Roscoe. 1940. *Administrative Law: Its Growth, Procedures, and Significance.* Pittsburgh: University of Pittsburgh Press.

Price, David. 2002. *The Congressional Experience.* 2d ed. Boulder, CO: Westview.

Price, Don K. 1959. "The Judicial Test." In Fritz Morstein Marx, ed., *Elements of Public Administration,* 475–499. Englewood Cliffs, NJ: Prentice-Hall.

Prichard, F. P. 1892. "The Study of the Science of Municipal Government." *Annals of the American Academy of Political and Social Science* 2:18–25.

Pugh, Darrell L. 1988. *Looking Back, Moving Forward: A Half-Century Celebration of Public Administration and ASPA.* Washington, DC: American Society for Public Administration.

Rabkin, Jeremy. 1987. "Bureaucratic Idealism and Executive Power: A Perspective on *The Federalist*'s View of Public Administration." In Charles F. Kesler, ed., *Saving the Revolution: The Federalist Papers and the American Founding,* 185–202. New York: Free Press.

Rainey, Hal G. 1982. "Reward Preferences among Public and Private Managers: In Search of the Service Ethic." *American Review of Public Administration* 16:288–302.

———. 1983. "Public Agencies and Private Firms: Incentive Structures, Goals, and Individual Roles." *Administration and Society* 15:207–242.

———. 1989. "Products of Simon's Progress: Similarities and Contrasts in Three Major Contributions." *Public Administration Quarterly* 12:392–410.

Redford, Emmette S. 1958. *Ideal and Practice in Public Administration.* Tuscaloosa: University of Alabama Press.

———. 1969. *Democracy in the Administrative State.* New York: Oxford University Press.

Reich, Charles. 1964. "The New Property." *Yale Law Journal* 73:733–787.

Ridley, Clarence E., and Herbert A. Simon. 1938. *Measuring Municipal Activities: A Survey of Suggested Criteria and Reporting Forms for Appraising Administration.* Chicago: International City Managers Association.

Riker, William H. 1995. "The Experience of Creating Institutions: The Framing of the United States Constitution." In Jack Knight and Itai Sened, eds., *Explaining Social Institutions,* 121–144. Ann Arbor: University of Michigan Press.

Roberts, Alasdair. 1995. "The Brownlow-Brookings Feud: The Politics of Dissent within the Academic Community." *Journal of Policy History* 7:311–340.

——. 1997. "Performance-Based Organizations: Assessing the Gore Plan." *Public Administration Review* 57:465–478.

Rohde, David W. 1991. *Parties and Leaders in the Postreform House*. Chicago: University of Chicago Press.

Rohr, John. 1986. *To Run a Constitution: The Legitimacy of the Administrative State*. Lawrence: University Press of Kansas.

——. 1987. "The Administrative State and Constitutional Principle." In Ralph Clark Chandler, ed., *A Centennial History of the American Administrative State*, 113–159. New York: Free Press.

——. 2002. *Civil Servants and Their Constitutions*. Lawrence: University Press of Kansas.

Root, Elihu. 1916. "Public Service by the Bar." *American Bar Association Journal* 2:736–755.

Rosenbloom, David H. 1983. "Public Administrative Theory and the Separation of Powers." *Public Administration Review* 43:219–227.

——. 1994. "The Evolution of the Administrative State and Transformations of Administrative Law." In David H. Rosenbloom and Richard D. Schwartz, eds., *Handbook of Regulation and Administrative Law*, 3–36. New York: Marcel Dekker.

——. 2000. *Building a Legislative-Centered Public Administration*. Tuscaloosa: University of Alabama Press.

——. 2003. *Administrative Law for Public Managers*. Boulder, CO: Westview.

Rosenfarb, Joseph. 1948. *Freedom and the Administrative State*. New York: Harper and Brothers.

Rourke, Frances E. 1987. "Bureaucracy in the American Constitutional Order." *Political Science Quarterly* 102:217–232.

Salamon, Lester M., ed. 2002. *The Tools of Government: A Guide to the New Governance*. New York: Oxford University Press.

Samuelson, Paul. 1947. *Foundations of Economic Analysis*. Cambridge: Harvard University Press.

Satterthwaite, Mark A. 1975. "Strategy-Proofness and Arrow's Conditions: Existence and Correspondence Theorems for Voting Procedures and Social Welfare Functions." *Journal of Economic Theory* 10:187–217.

Saunders, Charles B., Jr. 1966. *The Brookings Institution: A Fifty-Year History*. Washington, DC: Brookings Institution.

Sayre, Wallace S. 1951. "Trends of a Decade in Administrative Values." *Public Administration Review* 11:1–9.

——. 1958. "Premises of Public Administration: Past and Emerging." *Public Administration Review* 18:102–105.

Scalia, Antonin. 1978. "*Vermont Yankee*: The APA, the D.C. Circuit, and the Supreme Court." *Supreme Court Review* 1978:345–409.

——. 1989. "Judicial Deference to Administrative Interpretations of Law." *Duke Law Journal* 1989: 511–521.

Scheingold, Stuart A. 1972. *The Politics of Rights: Lawyers, Public Policy, and Political Change*. New Haven: Yale University Press.

Schiesl, Martin. 1977. *The Politics of Efficiency: Municipal Administration and Reform in America, 1800–1920*. Berkeley: University of California Press.

Seidman, Harold. 1998. *Politics, Position, and Power: The Dynamics of Federal Organization*. 5th ed. New York: Oxford University Press.

Selznick, Philip. 1943. "An Approach to a Theory of Bureaucracy." *American Sociological Review* 8:47–54.

Shapiro, Martin. 1981. *Courts: A Comparative and Political Analysis.* Chicago: University of Chicago Press.

———. 2002. "Judicial Delegation Doctrines: The US, Britain, and France." *West European Politics* 25:173–199.

Sheldon, Oliver. 1924. *The Philosophy of Management.* London: Sir Isaac Pitman and Sons.

Shepherd, George B. 1996. "Fierce Compromise: The Administrative Procedure Act Emerges from New Deal Politics." *Northwestern University Law Review* 90:1557–1683.

Shepsle, Kenneth A. 1992. "Congress Is a 'They' Not an 'It': Legislative Intent as an Oxymoron." *International Review of Law and Economics* 12:239–256.

Shipan, Charles R. 2004. "Regulatory Regimes, Agency Actions, and the Conditional Nature of Congressional Influence." *American Political Science Review* 98:467–480.

Siffin, William J. 1956. "The New Public Administration—Its Study in the United States." *Public Administration* 34:365–376.

Simon, Herbert A. 1946. "The Proverbs of Administration." *Public Administration Review* 6:53–67.

———. 1947. "A Comment on 'The Science of Administration.'" *Public Administration Review* 7:200–203.

———. 1948. "Review" of Dwight Waldo, *The Administrative State. Journal of Politics* 10:843–845.

———. 1952. "'Development of Theory of Democratic Administration': Replies and Comments." *American Political Science Review* 46:494–496.

———. 1976 [1947]. *Administrative Behavior: A Study of Decision-Making Processes in Administrative Organization.* 3d ed. New York: Free Press.

———. 1995. "Guest Editorial." *Public Administration Review* 55:404–405.

Simon, Herbert A., Donald W. Smithburg, and Victor A. Thompson. 1950. *Public Administration.* New York: Knopf.

Simon, Herbert A., Victor A. Thompson, and Donald W. Smithburg. 1991. *Public Administration.* New Brunswick, NJ: Transaction.

Simon, Herbert A., and others. 1941. *Determining Work Loads for Professional Staff in a Public Welfare Agency.* Berkeley: Bureau of Public Administration, University of California.

Skowronek, Stephen. 1982. *Building a New American State: The Expansion of National Administrative Capacities, 1877–1920.* New York: Cambridge University Press.

Smith, Daniel A., and Caroline Tolbert. 2004. *Educated by Initiative: The Effects of Direct Democracy on Citizens and Political Organizations in the American States.* Ann Arbor: University of Michigan Press.

Smithburg, Donald W. 1951. "Political Theory and Public Administration." *Journal of Politics* 13:59–69.

Somit, Albert, and Joseph Tannenhaus. 1967. *The Development of American Political Science: From Burgess to Behavioralism.* Boston: Allyn and Bacon.

Spicer, Michael W., and Larry D. Terry. 1993a. "Advancing the Dialogue: Legitimacy, the Founders, and the Contractarian Argument." *Public Administration Review* 53:263–267.

———. 1993b. "Legitimacy, History, and Logic: Public Administration and the Constitution." *Public Administration Review* 53:239–246.

Spiro, J. Herbert. 1969. *Responsibility in Government: Theory and Practice*. New York: Van Nostrand Reinhold.

Stein, Harold, ed. 1952. *Public Administration and Policy Development: A Case Book*. New York: Harcourt and Brace.

Stene, Edwin O. 1940. "An Approach to a Science of Administration." *American Political Science Review* 34:1124–1137.

Stewart, Richard B. 1975. "The Reformation of American Administrative Law." *Harvard Law Review* 88:1667–1813.

Stillman, Richard J., II. 1974. *The Rise of the City Manager: A Public Professional in Local Government*. Albuquerque: University of New Mexico Press.

———. 1990. *Preface to Public Administration: A Search for Themes and Direction*. New York: St. Martin's.

Stokes, Kenneth M. 1992. "Practical Reason and Systems Practice." Available at www.iuj.ac.jp/faculty/kmstokes/mono/monogr17.html. (Excerpted from Kenneth M. Stokes, *Critique of Economic Reason*. Monograph 6. Tokyo: International University of Japan.)

Stone, Alice B., and Donald C. Stone. 1975. "Early Development of Education in Public Administration." In Frederick C. Mosher, ed., *American Public Administration: Past, Present and Future*, 11–48. University: University of Alabama Press.

Stone, Donald C. 1945. "Notes on the Governmental Executive: His Role and His Methods." *Public Administration Review* 5:210–225.

———. 1975. "Birth of ASPA—A Collective Effort in Institution Building." *Public Administration Review* 35:83–93.

Stone, Harlan Fisk. 1936. "The Common Law in the United States." *Harvard Law Review* 50:4–26.

Stone, Harold, Don K. Price, and Kathryn H. Stone. 1940. *City Manager Government in the United States: A Review after Twenty-Five Years*. Chicago: Public Administration Service.

Storing, Herbert J. 1962. "The Science of Administration: Herbert A. Simon." In Herbert J. Storing, ed., *Essays on the Scientific Study of Politics*, 63–150. New York: Holt, Rinehart and Winston.

———. 1964. "The Crucial Link: Public Administration, Responsibility, and the Public Interest." *Public Administration Review* 24:39–46.

———. 1965. "Leonard D. White and the Study of Public Administration." *Public Administration Review* 25:38–51.

Svara, James H. 1999. "Complementarity of Politics and Administration: As a Legitimate Alternative to the Dichotomy Model." *Administration and Society* 30:676–705.

———. 2001. "The Myth of the Dichotomy: Complementarity of Politics and Administration in the Past and Future of Public Administration." *Public Administration Review* 61:176–183.

Taylor, Mark C. 2004. "What Derrida Really Meant." *New York Times*, October 14, p. A29.

Thach, Charles C. 1935. "The Inadequacies of the Rule of Law." In Charles G. Haines and Marshall E. Dimock, eds., *Essays on the Law and Practice of Governmental Administration: A Volume in Honor of Frank Johnson Goodnow*, 269–286. Baltimore: Johns Hopkins Press.

Tolbert, P. S., and L. G. Zucker. 1983. "Institutional Sources of Change in the Formal Structure of Organizations: The Diffusion of Civil Service Reform, 1880–1935." *Administrative Science Quarterly* 28:22–39.

Truman, David B. 1971. *The Governmental Process: Political Interests and Public Opinion*. 2d ed. New York: Knopf.

Urwick, Lyndall. 1937. "Organization as a Technical Problem." In Luther Gulick and Lyndall Urwick, eds., *Papers on the Science of Administration*, 47–88. New York: Institute of Public Administration.

Urwick, L., and E. F. Brech. 1945. *Thirteen Pioneers*. Vol 1, *The Making of Scientific Management*. London: Management Publications Trust.

U.S. General Accounting Office. 2002. *Exposure Draft: A Model of Strategic Human Capital Management*. GAO-02-373SP. Washington, DC.

U.S. Senate, Select Committee to Investigate the Executive Agencies of the Government. 1937. *Investigation of Executive Agencies of the Government*. Washington, DC: U.S. Government Printing Office.

Van Riper, Paul P. 1958. *History of the United States Civil Service*. Evanston, IL: Row, Peterson.

———. 1987. "The American Administrative State: Wilson and the Founders." In Ralph Clarke, ed., *A Centennial History of the American Administrative State*, 3–36. New York: Free Press.

———. 1990. *The Wilson Influence on Public Administration: From Theory to Practice*. Washington, DC: American Society for Public Administration.

———. 1997. "Some Anomalies in the Deep History of U.S. Public Administration." *Public Administration Review* 57:218–222.

Vickers, Sir Geoffrey. 1983. *The Art of Judgment: A Study of Policymaking*. New York: Harper and Row.

Vieg, John A. 1959. "The Growth of Public Administration." In Fritz Morstein Marx, ed., *Elements of Public Administration*, 2d ed., 3–22. Englewood Cliffs, NJ: Prentice-Hall.

Waldo, Dwight. 1948. *The Administrative State: A Study of the Political Theory of Public Administration*. New York: Ronald.

———. 1952a. "'Development of Theory of Democratic Administration': Replies and Comments." *American Political Science Review*, 46:501–503.

———. 1952b. "Development of Theory of Democratic Administration." *American Political Science Review*, 46:81–103.

———. 1955. *The Study of Public Administration*. Garden City, NY: Doubleday.

———. 1961. "Organization Theory: An Elephantine Problem." *Public Administration Review* 21:210–225.

———. 1965a. "The Administrative State Revisited." *Public Administration Review* 25:1:5–30.

———. 1965b. "Public Administration and Culture." In Roscoe C. Martin, ed., *Public Administration and Democracy: Essays in Honor of Paul H. Appleby*, 39–61. Syracuse, NY: Syracuse University Press.

———. 1968. "Scope of the Theory of Public Administration." In James C. Charlesworth, ed., *Theory and Practice of Public Administration: Scope, Objectives, and Methods*, 1–26. Philadelphia: American Academy of Political and Social Science.

———. 1971. "Some Thoughts on Alternatives, Dilemmas, and Paradoxes in a Time of Turbulence." In Dwight Waldo, ed., *Public Administration in a Time of Turbulence*, 257–285. New York: Chandler.

———. 1984. *The Administrative State: A Study of the Political Theory of Public Administration*. 2d ed. New York: Holmes and Meier.

Walker, Harvey. 1930. "Theory and Practice in State Administrative Organization." *National Municipal Review* 19:249–254.

———. 1934. *Law Making in the United States.* New York: Ronald.

———. 1937. *Public Administration in the United States.* New York: Farrar and Rinehart.

Wallace, Schuyler C. 1941. *Federal Departmentalization: A Critique of Theories of Organization.* New York: Columbia University Press.

Wamsley, Gary L., and others. 1990. *Refounding Public Administration.* Newbury Park, CA: Sage.

Wamsley, Gary L., and James F. Wolf, eds. 1996. *Refounding Democratic Public Administration: Modern Paradoxes, Postmodern Challenges.* Thousand Oaks, CA: Sage.

Warren, Kenneth F. 1993. "We Have Debated ad Nauseam the Legitimacy of the Administrative State—But Why?" *Public Administration Review* 53:249–254.

Weingast, Barry, and W. Marshall. 1988. "The Industrial Organization of Congress; or, Why Legislatures, Like Firms, Are Not Organized as Markets." *Journal of Political Economy* 96:132–163.

Weiss, Gunther A. 2000. "The Enchantment of Codification in the Common-Law World." *Yale Journal of International Law* 25:435–532.

Weko, Thomas J. 1995. *The Politicizing Presidency: The White House Personnel Office, 1948–1994.* Lawrence: University Press of Kansas.

Wengert, Egbert S. 1942. "The Study of Public Administration." *American Political Science Review* 36:313–322.

West, William F. 1985. *Administrative Rulemaking: Politics and Processes.* Westport, CT: Greenwood.

White, Leonard D. 1926. *Introduction to the Study of Public Administration.* New York: Macmillan.

———. 1927. *The City Manager.* Chicago: University of Chicago Press.

———. 1933. *Trends in Public Administration.* New York: McGraw-Hill.

———. 1935. *Introduction to the Study of Public Administration.* Rev. ed. New York: Macmillan.

———. 1936. "The Meaning of Principles in Public Administration." In John M. Gaus, Leonard D. White, and Marshall E. Dimock, eds., *The Frontiers of Public Administration,* 13–25. Chicago: University of Chicago Press.

———. 1939. *Introduction to the Study of Public Administration.* Rev. ed. New York: Macmillan.

———. 1942. *The Future of Government: Essays in Honor of Charles E. Merriam.* Chicago: University of Chicago Press.

———. 1954. *The Jacksonians: A Study in Administrative History, 1829–1861.* New York: Macmillan.

———. 1955. *Introduction to the Study of Public Administration.* 4th ed. New York: Macmillan.

White, Leonard D., and T. V. Smith. 1939. *Politics and Public Service: A Discussion of the Civic Art in America.* New York: Harper and Brothers.

White, Morton G. 1949. *Social Thought in America: The Revolt against Formalism.* New York: Viking.

Whitford, Andrew B. 2004. "Incentives and Tournaments in Public Organizations." Paper prepared for the annual meeting of the Midwest Political Science Association, Chicago, April.

Wiebe, Robert H. 1967. *The Search for Order.* New York: Hill and Wang.

Williamson, Oliver. 1985. *The Economic Institutions of Capitalism: Firms, Markets, and Relational Contracting.* New York: Free Press.

Willoughby, W. F. 1918. "The Institute for Government Research." *American Political Science Review* 12:49–62.

———. 1919a. "Democratization of Institutions for Public Service." In Frederick A. Cleveland and Joseph Schafer, eds., *Democracy in Reconstruction,* 146–161. Boston: Houghton Mifflin.

———. 1919b. *An Introduction to the Study of the Government of Modern States.* New York: Century.

———. 1927. *Principles of Public Administration.* Baltimore: Johns Hopkins University Press.

———. 1930. "Appendix III: A General Survey of Research in Public Administration." *American Political Science Review* 24:39–51.

———. 1937. "The Science of Public Administration." In John Mabry Mathews and James Hart, eds., *Essays in Political Science in Honor of Westel Woodbury Willoughby,* 39–63. Baltimore: Johns Hopkins University Press.

Wills, Garry, ed. 1987. *The Federalist Papers by Alexander Hamilton, James Madison, and John Jay.* New York: Bantam.

Wilson, Woodrow. 1885. *Congressional Government: A Study in American Politics.* Boston: Houghton Mifflin.

———. 1887. "The Study of Administration." *Political Science Quarterly* 2:197–222.

Wise, Charles R. 1993. "Public Administration Is Constitutional and Legitimate." *Public Administration Review* 53:257–261.

Yates, Douglas. 1982. *Bureaucratic Democracy: The Search for Democracy and Efficiency in American Government.* Cambridge: Harvard University Press.

Zinn, Howard. 1968. *Disobedience and Democracy: Nine Fallacies of Law and Order.* New York: Vintage.

Index